The
MARILYN
SYNDROME

Breaking Your Love Addiction Before It Breaks You

ELIZABETH MACAVOY, PH.D.,
& SUSAN ISRAELSON

A division of Shapolsky Publishers, Inc.

The Marilyn Syndrome

S.P.I. BOOKS

A division of Shapolsky Publishers, Inc.

Copyright © 1992 by Elizabeth Macavoy, Ph.D.,
and Susan Israelson

For any additional information, contact:

S.P.I. BOOKS/Shapolsky Publishers, Inc.
136 West 22nd Street
New York, NY 10011
(212) 633-2022
FAX (212) 633-2123

Previously published as *Lovesick: The Marilyn Syndrome*
in 1991 by Donald I. Fine, Inc., New York

ISBN: 1-56171-160-8

10 9 8 7 6 5 4 3 2 1

Printed and bound in the United States of America

Contents

Part I
RECOGNITION
THE ANATOMY OF LOVESICKNESS

Part II
RECOVERY
1. CLEANING UP YOUR ACT

2. STARTING OVER: A REPROGRAM GUIDE

Introduction

Right now we are witnessing a breakthrough in psychology that has come in the last ten years. It is a result of research findings in the field of family therapy, which measured the impact of alcoholism on the lives of all the family members. Prior to this, the parent or parents had been treated for their illness, the children ignored. These studies showed that the adult children of alcoholics paid the price for the sins of their fathers or mothers. The rejection and neglect they suffered as children poisoned their adult lives.

These discoveries have given birth to a revolutionary new psychology that is drastically changing the traditional ways of understanding and treating the adult children of all dysfunctional families. People who've been suffering from the inability to form healthy relationships with loving partners, addicted instead to rejecting partners and self-destructive relationships, are no longer being neglected, shelved or ignored. For the first time they're being treated for an emotional illness that comes as a result of their "dysfunctional" upbringing and lack of "unconditional love"—the new terms of this new psychology.

As a clinical psychologist in private practice, I had specialized in the treatment of addictions. After reading Stanton Peele's pioneering book, *Love and Addiction*, I began to treat people who were addicted to destructive love relationships as I would if they were addicted to drugs and alcohol.

Five years ago, the publication of Robin Norwood's book, *Women Who Love Too Much*, gave me further commitment and inspiration. Norwood's book had tremendous impact. It made millions of women who were suffering from the pain of being addicted to unavailable men aware for the first time in their lives that this was an illness—they loved too much. The extraordinary success of the book created an equally extraordinary demand. Since women now knew they had an illness, they wanted to get better.

They came to me for help, book in hand. I began to run several Women Who Love Too Much support groups while continuing my private practice.

Susan Israelson, the coauthor of this book, originally came to my group for help. She was a writer who by her own admission had loved too many, too much. She'd just left a man whom she'd been living with for four years because she realized that the relationship was killing her—things had started to go very wrong in her body and she was so depressed that she didn't care. After a separation of three months, her ex was getting married to a woman he'd just met. Susan was insane with jealousy, obsessed with the other woman. Why was he marrying her and not Susan? She couldn't stand the thought of them together. The pain was overwhelming. She'd failed in every relationship she'd ever had. She thought she was a loser, there was nowhere left to run, her life was over.

She wanted to get better. I wanted to help.

Over four years we shared the stages—the ups and downs, the fears and joys, the slips and victories as I guided her out of her "hell" into recovery. Then we translated what was happening to paper.

Between every line is guts and honesty. Is this what we really mean? Did we say it right? Are you sure? We pushed each other to our own limits. We knew that only our total commitment to the truth—no matter how hard it was to handle—could help others. Nothing less would work.

The first day we talked about writing this book, Susan, thinking as usual in questions, said to me, "Why is it that all the major loves of my life never loved me back and anytime someone loved me, first I clicked off, then got rid of them? You know something funny? I don't think I love too much, I don't know how to love at all! I must be sick in the head. Lovesick. That's what it is, I'm lovesick."

We began to call the illness lovesickness.

Susan's dysfunctional upbringing and the lack of unconditional love as a child had robbed her of the ability to love herself, to accept love from others or to love in a healthy way as an adult. She was addicted to rejecting partners who couldn't love her back in every area of her life. For her, rejection equaled love. Needy, lonely, desperate to fill that empty space inside her, she'd been trying to find love all her life to escape the pain, inadvertently causing more. She'd trapped herself in vicious cycles trying to get love from people who could only reject her—then became addicted to the pain. The illness was progressive. Each time her hopes were high, a new love was going to save her. Each time those hopes were dashed, it was harder to pick up the pieces. Susan *was* sick over love—lovesick.

This book is intended to define lovesickness, its causes and symptoms and to serve as the first self-help recovery book for anyone who suffers from the pain of fruitless lovequests, the agony of terrible relationships and the anguish of self-hate. The high recovery rate achieved by Susan and the other group members has served as a motivating force.

Recovery from lovesickness takes place in stages. We have structured this book to parallel the process.

About the group.

When I started my first support group, one of my great surprises was that the women who sought me out were some of the most attractive, professionally successful, talented and capable women I had ever met. They were all college educated—doctors, nurses, dentists, teachers, artists, art historians, art directors, writers, actresses, film makers, journalists, accountants, entrepreneurs, producers, executives, secretaries. Their ages ranged from twenty to sixty-five.

The common denominator among them all was that regardless of how accomplished they were, they didn't believe in themselves, were in extreme pain, hated themselves. Whether they were single, married, living with someone, dating, they were all involved in self-destructive love relationships, dying to find love but only finding rejection. They all came from dysfunctional families. The common cause in the group was a commitment to recovery, to doing the work, to getting better, to changing their lives for the better, no matter how hard it was, no matter how much work it took. Working with the group has been one of the most rewarding and challenging experiences of my life. I would like to thank every member of the group for letting me share the gift of their recovery; for their contribution.

The quotes used in the book come from group members whose names have been changed.

Although this book has been written for an audience of women, who tend more to join support groups and look for help, I have been treating more and more lovesick male patients who are unable to form loving relationships, who can choose only unavailable, unattainable or rejecting female love partners. The fact is that lovesickness has no gender; it applies to men as well.

—Elizabeth Swiecicka Macavoy

Foreword

When I walked into group that first Wednesday night at seven (actually seven-fifteen, I was always running late) I was dying. My mind, my spirit, my body, on separate tracks anyway, had run amok. I had no job and no prospects; an unpublished novel along with the world's largest pile of rejection slips in one drawer, an unproduced screenplay and the world's second largest pile of rejection slips in another drawer; the world's longest list of tragic romances in my head. I was still obsessing over the man I'd lived with for four years in spite of the fact that he never slept with me and had just gotten married to someone else. I was running on empty, trapped in a snake pit of addictions, wondering why "such a nice girl" was losing the ball game, always finishing last.

After all the years of losing, I'd finally lost it.

That was four years and a different life ago, the amount of time it takes to go to college, the amount of time it's taken for me to totally change absolutely everything, and I mean *everything* in my life. (When I started recovery, a lifelong devotee to instant gratification, I thought that if I took an aspirin, I would wake up one morning and be perfect; my headache, in this case my lovesickness, would be gone. Just like that. So much for that theory; aspirin, of course, is truly great—but not that great.)

In the beginning I felt like I was setting out in a tiny, leaky boat to see if the world was flat or round while everyone else was taking the Concorde around the world. Recovery has been like that, a series of discoveries . . . recognitions that happened in group. Then I had to do the homework to convert theory into practice.

The first time I went to group, I cautiously listened to everyone's war stories of unrequited loves, obsessions and addictions to bad guys. The first recognition was that I wasn't alone in the world with a unique problem that my friend used to call moviestar sickness, a nonspecific illness with lots of pain and suffering. Everyone in group had similar problems to mine. We were all Women Who Loved Too Much. Elizabeth said that loving too much was an acquired emotional illness because we came from dysfunctional families and did not get unconditional love.

"I don't understand. What's a dysfunctional family? What's unconditional love?"

"A dysfunctional family is one in which one or both parents are alcoholics, workaholics, divorced or otherwise disabled mentally or physically. Unconditional love means that they love you just for being born, just the way you are."

"Thank you." Fine, I had my answer. I let the unconditional love stuff go because it didn't apply, but I got that I came from a dysfunctional family. My father had been a workaholic-and-a-half. A thunderbolt exploded in my head. After six shrinks, three groups, Est and Arica, I'd finally hit a home run! I felt like Odysseus coming home.

During the second group Elizabeth used Marilyn Monroe as an example. She said that Marilyn, no matter how beautiful, sexy and successful she was, would look at herself in the mirror and see an ugly failure because she had low self-esteem. While I'd written my novel, I'd had a picture of Marilyn, the shot of her skirt billowing up in "The Seven Year Itch," on my desk as an inspiration. I'd thought of her as a kindred soul, felt connected, but I didn't know why. Thunderbolt number two struck. Marilyn had the same problems as I did. We both hated ourselves. The whole group had moviestar sickness; we started to call it the Marilyn Syndrome, because we discovered that Marilyn was just like us. Group became the Greek chorus in my life, the reality check, the backbone of my recovery.

Then came owning, 'fessing up to my cross-addictions, recognizing that I was an 'aholic. It wasn't a question of what I was addicted to; rather—what *wasn't* I addicted to? The answer was coffee because I had such trouble sleeping, and shopping because Mother did enough for both of us. (I'd been a chain smoker but had miraculously stopped smoking five years ago thanks to Lucy M.) Going on the wagon with everything cold turkey was hell on wheels. Was life worth living without sex and drugs and rock and roll? In the beginning I wasn't so sure. I would give it all up, hit the mats, slip back. Little by little I kicked them all, till I can honestly report that I'm a clean machine. Yes, I'm a born-again girl scout, deserve a merit badge, five gold stars, and a round of the Hallelujah Chorus. And they said it couldn't be done!

When I finally broke through denial and discovered that my relationship with my family was lovesick, that this was the source of my lovesickness, I was devastated. I did what I was supposed to do, cut the cords, separated, then foundered on the rocks, lonely, depressed between Scylla and Charybdis, it was their fault . . . I blamed them, it was my fault . . . I blamed myself. I was guilty, I was rocking the family boat, I was going to be their ruination. A rough trip was had by all, months of high seas, hurricane winds, stormy weather. Then I got it. It wasn't their fault. It wasn't my fault, either. It was nobody's fault. Lovesickness was part of my heritage, just like curly black hair. That was the turning point. It gave me the power to take my power back. It was my life, I could choose to live it anyway I wanted to. I could change; take responsibility for myself for a change. I could grow up at last, be a grown-up. They didn't have to change. (My family stood by me through the storm. Thanks, Fritzi, for being there. Thanks, Peter, Susie.)

The next discovery brought me to my knees. If I was sure about anything, I was smart. I had great grades in school, a B.A. from a fine college. The biggest blow to my self-esteem, what there was of it, was discovering that the voice in my mind, every thought, belief, perception, inclination, evaluation, decision and judgment from the time I woke up in the morning (preferably late) until I went to sleep at night was wrong, had always been off. Not just a little, either. Totally. One hundred and eighty degrees wrong. If I believed someone was good they were bad. If I thought something was black it was white. I, Einstein, the great genius, would have to start over and unlearn, or learn, depending on how I looked at it, everything.

It was at this stage of the game that thanks to central casting (her phrase) Lili Townsend, the original Minister of Fun, my amiga, goddess-sister appeared on cue, as if by magic. She indeed brought magic and fun, two sorely missing elements to what had been a very dull party; her philosophy, "If it's not fun don't do it and if you *must* do it make it fun." Lili became my metaphysical fitness trainer. We began to do, create visualizations together, ceremonies that were able to get me out of my head (where I spent most of my time) into another space. It was during the visualizations I discovered my star, the universe, the lost continent of my spirit, unfroze my heart, connected with my *self*, with Great Spirit.

During this period I had two bad-news relationships, from the first hot sparks till the last dying embers fizzled out. The good news was that with group's support I got out faster. That wasn't good enough. I took drastic action and went cold turkey on men. I had to have a love affair with myself before I could be with another man in yet another lovesick relationship.

Falling in love with myself, like any new relationship, has had its ups and downs, victories, slips, hits and misses. It has meant changing my priorities from him first, to me first, not all that easy as it turns out. It was possible only with a lot of help from my friends, support, understanding and love from my buddies, my network and group. We spent hours and hours on the phone every day discussing, dissecting, questioning, problem solving; what would a healthy person do? There is no way I could have done it without them. No way. Thank you Margie, Lisa, Liz, for saving my life.

What about a *him*? How am I doing now? If I'm such a big mouth have I learned how to have a love relationship? Am I having a relationship? In these four years I've had seven relationships. I don't count those first two disasters although the group referred to them as learning experiences. Since I've emerged from the isolation booth, I've bitten the bullet, accepted the lovesick challenge, I date only nice guys and restrain myself from blowing them out of the water. It's a toss up which was worse in the beginning, that or taking a walk when I was attracted to someone and the sparklers went off or I learned that someone I thought was a nice guy wasn't.

Lately I've discovered that I can be with someone nice, enjoy his company, have fun, tell the truth, appreciate his good qualities, accept his imperfections, not try and change him, let him be. The opposite is also true. I can't, won't ever go back, be with a Mr. Wrong again. Never. Ever. Not a chance. No way. I haven't got time for the pain. Nothing is worth that pain, nothing. I've worked too hard on me to give it up, lose it or me for a him.

Speaking of work, working on this book with Elzbieta (her name is Polish) has been quite an experience. We come from two different worlds, planets, intergalactic opposites, New York and Poland, Libra and Aries, dark and light, size 10, size 4, in breaks she browsed at book stores, I exercised. Perhaps my greatest discovery has been learning about relating, having a relationship, from working, working on it, working it out with Elzbieta, my partner. No one is perfect. Honesty is the only policy. Criticism doesn't kill. You can get nice and angry and still be nice. There's no such thing as just black or just white. We found a middle ground.

Recovery is a full time job. Work in progress. It's been getting easier. I see big time progress. First there were hours, then days, weeks, now months that I've been obsession free. There are many times now, when I feel happy and recognize that I'm feeling happy, even when I'm alone. I wished myself Happy New Decade this past New Year's and meant it. I'm going to have a happy new decade, I'm having a happy new life, the time of my life. This nice girl is winning the ball game.

—Susan Israelson

The authors would like to thank the following publishers and authors for their permission to reprint:

Excerpts from GODDESS by Anthony Summers reprinted with permission of Macmillan Publishing Company, Victor Gollanez Ltd, and Curtis Brown Ltd. Copyright © 1985 by Anthony Summers.

Excerpts from JOE AND MARILYN copyright ©1986 by Roger Kahn, published by arrangement with William Morrow & Co.

Excerpts from MARILYN by Gloria Steinem. Text copyright © 1986 by East Toledo Productions, Inc. Reprinted by permission of Henry Holt and Company, Inc.

Excerpts from MARILYN MONROE CONFIDENTIAL by Lena Pepitone and William Stadiem and Maurice Hakim, copyright © 1979 by Lena Pepitone, William Stadiem and Maurice C. Hakim. Published by Simon and Schuster, reprinted with permission of Lena Pepitone, William Stadiem and Maurice C. Hakim.

Excerpts from MARILYN by Norman Mailer copyright © 1973 by Norman Mailer and Alskog, Inc. Reprinted by permission of Grosset & Dunlap.

Excerpts from the book MY STORY copyright © 1974 by Milton H. Greene. From the book "My Story" by Marilyn Monroe. Originally published by Stein & Day, Inc., reprinted with permission of Scarborough House/Publishers and Milton H. Greene Studios A.B.I.

Excerpts from THE UNABRIDGED MARILYN: Her life from A to Z by Randall Riese and Neal Hitchens. Copyright © 1987 by RGA Publishing Group. Reprinted by permission of Contemporary Books, Inc., Chicago.

Excerpts from MARILYN MONROE: A LIFE OF THE ACTRESS copyright © by Carl E. Rollyson, Jr. is reprinted by permission of UMI Research Press, Ann Arbor, MI.

Excerpts from LEGEND, THE LIFE AND DEATH OF MARILYN MONROE by Fred Lawrence Guiles, copyright © 1984 by Fred Lawrence Guiles. Originally published by Stein & Day, Inc., reprinted with permission of Scarborough House/Publishers and the author.

Last year, a patient of mine whom we'll call Mary Jane begged to come into my group. She was involved in a relationship with a bad guy whom she couldn't leave no matter how hard she tried. It was better than being alone and vulnerable to sleeping around with men in this time of Aids. She admitted that she'd been with hundreds of men and drank too much. She was over her head in debt from her compulsive shopping expeditions.

Mary Jane had just read twenty-five of the newest and latest books on addiction. She felt that there was a conspiracy among all authors. It was a set up. They all identified her as a sick person with problems but they left her high and dry, since none of them could tell her how to get better.

This book is dedicated to everyone suffering from lovesickness who wants to get over it.

It takes a great deal of hard work and courage but recovery is possible.

Part I

RECOGNITION

THE ANATOMY OF LOVESICKNESS

A Few Questions First

Have you been trying to get married all your life but the right person never seems to come along no matter how hard you look?

Are you stuck in a bad relationship that makes you miserable but you just can't seem to get out of it?

Do you seem to be attracted only to bad partners while the good ones don't turn you on?

Are you the only one you know who's alone and desperately lonely while everyone else is getting married and having kids?

Does everyone ask you how come you've got so many things going for you but you don't seem to have any self-confidence?

Do you look in the mirror every day with horror no matter how many people tell you how attractive you are?

Do you overdo and binge out either on alcohol, substances, food, sex, shopping, or all of them while other people can manage on only one drink, eat three normal meals a day, have one puff, or three credit cards with no balance?

If you've said yes to most or all of these questions you're suffering from an emotional illness we call lovesickness.

If you've said yes to most or all of these questions, this book is for you.

"You need a friend"

This book is written as a friend talking to you. Someone you can trust, who's been there before, who can guide you through the rough patches, congratulate you on your victories, help you handle your slips.

It will anticipate your reactions and feelings, tell you what to expect, what to do or not to do, what you're going to feel and how to deal with it as you go on the road from recognition to recovery.

3

You can change if you want to. You can break your lovesick molds.

All you have to do is follow this book's advice, stay open to new possibilities, decide to make your recovery the number one priority in your life, then do the work.

Recovery is about taking baby steps, day by day by day.

You can win.

You can get over lovesickness.

You can recover.

Yes, you can!

A LEGEND OF OUR TIME

Once upon a time a beautiful little girl was born to parents out of wedlock. Her father abandoned her at birth. Her mother, mentally ill, could not bring up her daughter, so she was passed on to her sister, who, in turn, put her niece into a foster home, then an orphanage. The little girl grew up to be the most beautiful and desired woman in the land, her hand sought by all the princes.

No matter how famous or successful she became, she didn't believe it. She'd been rejected so often as a little girl that she spent all of her time trying to make people love her. Desperately unhappy, always slightly depressed, she began to drink and take pills to dull the pain. She married three times to men who didn't approve of her. When those relationships failed, she couldn't let go. A succession of suitors followed but she had poor judgment, rejecting worthy admirers and pursuing men who used her, men who were unavailable, married or incapable of loving. She took all the responsibility for not being able to make these impossible relationships work. Caught in a vicious cycle, terrified of being alone, insanely jealous, anxiety ridden, chronically depressed, she became addicted to alcohol, pills and sex. When she looked in the mirror she hated herself, thought she was ugly, a failure, unlovable.

She had twelve or thirteen abortions, more than twenty operations, made seven attempts at suicide. She died at thirty-six.

Her name was Marilyn Monroe.

She was lovesick.

"Fasten your seat belts, this may be a bumpy ride"

What you're about to read could be very upsetting. This information is new, something you may have buried so deeply and for such a long time that when you unearth it, you'll feel as if you have a raw wound. You may deny it. You may not want to face it. You may feel like running away from it. You may get nauseous or depressed. You may have an anxiety attack or feel like crying. You may get angry. You may get the message, think you understand it all, then mysteriously lose it.

The patterns described here are extreme. Whether you have traces of lovesickness or a severe case, please don't panic, overidentify with the worst scenarios, feel like more of a victim or beat yourself up for being the way you are, lovesick. Just read it slowly, take as much as you can handle, at your own pace. It works best if used as a work book. Follow all the suggestions, utilize all the tools, do the exercises, the visualizations, the affirmations. It works if you do the work.

The first step of recovery is to recognize how you got that way, what being lovesick means, patterns, symptoms and syndromes, great escapes. From recognition comes your ability to change, break old patterns, molds, addictions and start over.

Any change that you make has to be for the better.

Lovesickness is a learned pattern. It can also be unlearned.

You can recover from lovesickness.

CHAPTER 1

The Causes

HOW IT ALL BEGAN

I spent my entire childhood being jealous of my cousin, Chris. According to Mother he was perfect, a saint and she would have been happy to trade him for me anytime. I remember her complaining to me for hours every day, "Why aren't you like your cousin, Chris?" His clothes were never dirty, his toys were always organized in neat piles or lined up on a shelf, never broken or smashed, his books were perfect, no ink spots, torn out pages or erasures. I always thought that he should have been her child, not me . . . maybe then she would be happy and stop rejecting me every day of my life.

—BESS

You come from a lovesick family. Your parents could not give you *unconditional* love for whatever *their* reasons. You did not experience, "I love you the way you are" but rather, "There's something wrong with you the way you are," "I'll love you when you're like your sister," "I'll love you when you obey me, when you do it my way."

By the time you were five you got the message, there *was* something wrong with you. You were no good, bad, tainted, unlovable. By the time you were five you'd learned to hate yourself, you'd become lovesick.

As a lovesick adult, you recreate what you believe, that you're unlovable, dooming yourself to relationships with rejecting, unavailable or unattainable partners who can't love you back. You're unable to form healthy relationships whether with a love partner, a friend or a business associate. Instead you substitute obsession, rejection and pain for love.

Along the way you've also become cross-addicted to sex, food, drugs, pills, alcohol, shopping, work, abusing them to escape from

6

your ongoing despair. As a result of being brought up lovesick, you never learned to love yourself for who you were but grew up hating yourself for who you were not.

WHAT IS UNCONDITIONAL LOVE?

My father was not around much when we were growing up. He worked so hard that even on those rare moments when he was home, he was too tired to play with us. Mother became both parents. She was so critical that it seemed as if she were around too much. She was always complaining. Nothing I ever did was good enough, right. Everything had to be her way or it was wrong. I remember trying to make my bed "the right way." She'd come in to inspect and rip it up, do it her way.

"You look fat in that dress, dear. You should go on a diet." "Your hair looks terrible. Can't you do something with it?" "How will you ever get a man if your bedroom is so messy?" Negatives. That's all I ever heard. All my life.

—ALICE

Unconditional love is a healthy parent's essential message to their child. "I love you just because you were born, because you're my child. You're perfect just the way you are."

Unconditional love is constant and unwavering. It comes from parents who are healthy, who love themselves, so that they can allow their children to be whomever and whatever they want to be, no matter how different.

Unconditional love from a parent creates self-love in the child.

WHAT IS A LOVESICK FAMILY?

A lovesick family is one in which parents are unable to provide their children with *unconditional* love, proper nurturing, are unable to meet their child's emotional needs. Lovesick parents come from lovesick families themselves. As children they never experienced *unconditional* love. When they became parents they had no role model to follow of how to love themselves, their spouses or their children in a healthy way. They couldn't give you what they didn't have to give, what they never experienced themselves. Damaged, unhappy, insecure and out of touch with their own feelings, they didn't know how to be a loving, accepting mother or father, how to give *unconditional* love. Therefore they could not allow their children to develop their own individuality; they were threatened by any deviation from their own behavioral patterns.

As lovesick parents, they raised you the only way they knew how, which was lovesick. This was not a conscious choice, but rather a conditioned response, unconsciously transmitted from one generation to another. A multigenerational cycle. Lovesick parents create lovesick children who, as adults, have lovesick marriages and then create lovesick children.

Lovesickness is multigenerational: passed on from one generation to another, inherited by one generation from another.

OTHER WAYS TO TELL A LOVESICK FAMILY

No, I never knew my father. My mother once told me he died in an accident when I was quite young. In fact, he left my mother when he heard from her that I was on the way . . . My mother had a nervous breakdown and had to be sent to the hospital for a rest when I was only five years old. That's what caused me to spend my childhood in and out of foster homes . . .

My mother's best girlfriend at this time, Aunt Grace, was my legal guardian, and I was living in her home . . . One day she packed my clothes and took me with her in her car. We drove and drove without her saying a word.

When we came to a three-story red-brick building . . . I saw this sign . . . LOS ANGELES ORPHANS' HOME.

I began to cry. "Please, please don't make me go inside. I'm not an orphan, my mother's not dead"

I may have been only nine years old . . . The whole world around me just crumbled . . .

When a little girl feels lost and lonely and that nobody wants her, it's something she can never forget as long as she lives.

—MARILYN MONROE

A lovesick family can further be defined as one in which one or both parents are: alcoholic; drug users; mentally or physically ill; mentally or physically absent; compulsive in such behavior as eating, working, cleaning, gambling, spending, exercising; physically abusive to the other parent or to the child; inappropriate in their sexual behavior to the child, ranging from seductiveness to incest; promiscuous in their sexual behavior outside the marriage.

Other lovesick attitudes and behaviors are: constant arguing; chronic unresolved tension; extreme rigidity about money, sex or religion; competitiveness with each other and/or the children; playing favorites; unaddressed sibling rivalry; an overdisciplined family with rigid rules; a too permissive family with no structure; a smothering family whose ties were too close to allow bonding outside the original family unit; an overdominating parent together with an overly submissive one; cultural matriarchy—the mother plays the role of father and mother; the early death of a parent; remarriage to a rejecting parent; divorce in all of its variations; parents whose lives become threatened or deteriorate in some fashion by the very act of parenting.

"No, this isn't about me!"

You may deny what you just read. You don't come from a lovesick family. Your family was perfect. You feel sorry for anyone who comes from a lovesick family. Too bad for them. The truth is that the more you deny that there's anything wrong with your family, the higher the probability that you come from a lovesick family.

LET'S PRETEND:
PLAYING BY DYSFUNCTIONAL RULES

Lovesick families run by dysfunctional rules: Touching, hugging, embracing, holding, kissing, the physical manifestations of love, of closeness are nonexistent. Physical closeness, tenderness, warmth are inhibited. There is repetitive insistence on giving hugs and kisses when it isn't genuine. Intimacy is nonexistent.

> Nobody ever called me their daughter. No one ever held me. No one kissed me. Nobody. And I was afraid to call anyone "Mom" or "Dad." I knew I didn't have any . . .
>
> —MARILYN MONROE

Lovesick parents are unreliable or unpredictable in their behavior, not there when they are needed.

Family problems are not addressed or resolved. If a problem occurs it is camouflaged rather than dealt with. Family members cannot freely express their perceptions, feelings, thoughts, desires and fantasies. Open communication is either out of the question, or worse, punishable. Promises are broken. Secrets are kept from each other or are betrayed. Problems are denied. Guilt is inflicted. Mistakes are not forgiven, but rather used, held onto. Cruelty, fear, ridicule, disgrace, humiliation, shame, negativity, sarcasm, inconsistency and silence become the bylaws as they numb, then destroy, any possibility of healthy relating.

The more dysfunctional rules are practiced in your lovesick family, the more lovesick you become.

For some lovesick parents, raising a child becomes a game of control and domination. The children have to do what the parents want them to do, to be, think, act, and feel like. In other families, the children are neglected or ignored, no matter how hard they try to please, to win approval, attention or love.

Whether a child is controlled or neglected, playing by dysfunctional rules causes lovesickness.

THE FANTASY BOND AND THE BLACK MAGIC COMPLEX

I always thought of my mother as my best friend. One day I went to visit her in California. I was looking forward to seeing her; she'd been away for three months. In the first three minutes of my arrival she screamed at me. My fingernail polish didn't match my toenail polish. I couldn't believe my ears. Something happened. Something snapped. A veil lifted. I finally heard what she was saying. Everything that came out of her mouth was a criticism. Worse, I realized that it had been that way all my life. Getting that my mother was hypercritical, destructive and controlling was the greatest shock of my life. I'd thought that she was perfect and I was the one all messed up.

—FRANCINE

As a child, your parents were the god and goddess of your very small universe. It was inconceivable to you that they could not love you the way you were. You couldn't handle it, didn't understand it. In order to survive you had to block out wrongdoing on your parents' part and take the blame yourself. You developed an ego defense mechanism called the *fantasy bond* making the lovesick switch, "There's absolutely nothing wrong with *my* parents . . . something is wrong with *me*." They were perfect, loving parents—something was wrong with *you*, that's why they couldn't love *you*, *you* didn't deserve love, *you* were unlovable.

You denied it. Then you reversed it, taking the responsibility, the blame, for provoking them. They weren't bad, *you* were. By the time you were five this had become your essential belief system, you were no good, and all you deserved was rejection. The more lovesick your family was, the greater your denial that there was anything wrong with your parents, the more responsibility you took for things being wrong.

We call this paradoxical thinking the Black Magic Complex. It's a distorted sense of reality based on the childhood belief system that you had superhuman power to cause things to go wrong. If your parents were screaming at each other, it was your fault. If your parents abused you, they became the best parents who ever lived. If your parents were drinking, you denied that they were alcoholics and blamed yourself for their unhappiness. If your father controlled you ruthlessly, you worshipped him, blamed yourself.

As an adult, the Black Magic Complex continues to operate in every area of your life. If your husband is unfaithful to you or flirts with another woman at a party, you deny that he's a womanizer. It's your fault, you're not attractive enough. You go to bed with a man who comes on like gangbusters. He doesn't call you back. You deny that he was a bad guy or that it was a one-night stand. Instead you suffer. You didn't say the right thing. You weren't interesting enough. You didn't wear the right dress. You didn't look good enough. You were bad in bed.

Denial, the fantasy bond and the Black Magic Complex distort the way you experience life.

The fantasy bond and the Black Magic Complex cause lovesickness.

THE GREAT DIVIDE: HIDE AND SEEK

"You're no good the way you are."

"I can't love you if you're different from me."

By the time you were five you got the message. As a child from a lovesick family, you became afraid to be you, since each time you tried to be yourself you were punished for it. As a result you had to figure out another way to be. Another you. In order to survive, you surrendered your you unconditionally. First you buried, smothered, squashed, hid, learned how to deny your own feelings, thoughts, desires and needs.

"I can't be who I am. It's not safe. It's not good. No one loves me the way I am. Each time I try I get into trouble. Better hide who I am so I won't get hurt. If I don't have any feelings then I can't get in trouble for them."

This accomplished, you tried to figure out what *they* wanted. You sought their approval. You tried to do anything and everything you could think of to please them. That way you could insulate yourself from criticism, from being wrong.

You've been playing hide and seek ever since. The inner self, call it the soul, the mind's eye, the ego, the spiritual center, the higher self, the true self, your *you*, as we call it, became inhibited and repressed.

The other, *lovesick* self, as we call it, took over. The development of this self at the expense of the other was the beginning of all your troubles. The lovesick self, which now controls you, is externally oriented, constantly looking for approval from the outside, desperately seeking love from everyone, people-pleasing, needy, insecure, full of self-hatred and self-denial. This self feels empty and unlovable.

By the time a child from a lovesick family is five years old, she's disabled from the unconditional surrender of the real self and the creation of this lovesick self. **Hiding your self causes lovesickness.**

YOU'VE LOST THAT LOVING FEELING

> It dawned on me that other people—other women—were different than me. They could feel things—I couldn't.
>
> —MARILYN MONROE

Ask you how do you feel? You're stumped. You don't know for sure. You haven't known how you felt since you buried your feelings. As a lovesick child, it wasn't safe to feel and express what you felt, "I don't like doing my homework when all the other kids are out playing," "I don't feel good about wearing this dress, I don't like this color it makes me look ugly." You heard, "You have to wear this dress, I bought it for you. I don't want to be ashamed of you, why are you always causing problems and fighting with me?"

As a lovesick child by the time you were five you had buried, squashed all your feelings: feeling good, feeling happy, feeling love, feeling hate, feeling angry, feeling anything that would make you vulnerable to disapproval, criticism, rejection.

As a lovesick adult you can't feel a feeling. You don't feel love for yourself or worthy of receiving love. You've surrendered your you . . . the ability to feel almost anything except an occasional eruption of anger, fear, anxiety. Instead you feel numb most of the time. You can expect only the worst. Once you lost that loving feeling for yourself and buried your feelings for everything else, you became lovesick.

Burying your you, squashing your feelings, creates the black hole and causes lovesickness.

THE BLACK HOLE

What am I? What can I do? I am nothing. Nothing. I am empty!

—MARILYN MONROE

As a lovesick child the only way to survive was to deny your own feelings, thoughts and desires. You buried them deep inside. From that time on you've experienced a void, a bottomless pit, a black hole. Nothing's there. Nobody's home.

As a lovesick adult the black hole terrifies you. You spend your life trying to fill it up with anything and everything. You'll try almost anything to escape from the pain, to numb it for a minute, an hour, a day, a week. Anything. Whatever works. Whatever you can find. Then you become addicted to it. You need it. You have to have it. You can't live without it. Anything is better than that empty feeling.

I always felt that I was a misfit. Something was wrong with me. Perhaps because I was premature. He or they or whoever was in charge had left out a part. My inside. The only people who noticed were the men in my life. However, sooner or later every one of them would say, "What's the matter with you? Don't you believe in yourself? Don't you have an identity of your own? You can't live off mine, anymore. I don't want to be with a woman who doesn't know who she is. I'm looking for a partner, not a parasite." After the inevitable breakup I'd gain thirty pounds, trying to fill the black hole with food. That didn't work either. I'd be too fat to attract another man.

—S.I.

As a lovesick adult, out of touch with your feelings, you give others godlike power over you. Obsession with a *him* is the ultimate escape. You fantasize about the man on the white horse who's going to sweep you into his arms and rescue you from your loneliness, from your emptiness, from yourself, so you can live happily ever after. You can spend twenty-five hours a day filling yourself up by thinking about a him, imaginary or real. He can save your life, liberate you from the black hole. You try to become him, take on *his* hobbies, sports, restaurant preferences, interests, tastes, identity. Your friend calls you up on the telephone and asks you how you are: "John's doing fine. His new project is so interesting. He's getting a raise. I just bought him a Swatch. I had to go to five stores before I found the right one. I hope he likes it. What do you think? Do you think he'd rather have a Swatch or a Casio?"

The more empty you feel, the more desperate you become, the greater your need to run away from yourself, the bigger the dive into others and other escapes. Drugs. Food. Alcohol. Sex. Shopping. Working. Together. Separately. Anything to stop the black hole from swallowing you up alive.

The search is fruitless, a vicious cycle. You're unable to identify your own feelings, dependent on others for a feeling transfusion. You feel numb, dead inside, alone, lonely. You spend your life running away from yourself . . . running in circles, trying to fill a bottomless pit with someone else's you at the cost of your own. You feel empty, godless, spiritually bankrupt; life is in your hands and you've botched it.

The black hole causes lovesickness.

HATING YOURSELF:
MIRROR, MIRROR ON THE WALL,
WHO'S THE UGLIEST OF THEM ALL?

When I look in the mirror all I can see are my faults. It's a well-worn litany that I've gone through daily as long as I can remember. "I'm fat." "Why wasn't I born with straight hair." "My thighs are too big." Now

I've added, "I'm beginning to get wrinkles." "I wonder if I should get liposuction." "If I had enough money for a facelift I would really look great. When someone compliments me on my appearance, or tells me I'm beautiful, I think they must be crazy.

—KAREN

Your parents did not provide you with the gift of love—*unconditional* love. You weren't acknowledged, encouraged, approved of or recognized. The words and the feelings weren't there: "You're wonderful . . . *the way you are.*" "I love you . . . *the way you are.*" "You're beautiful . . . *the way you are.*"

Instead negative opinions and criticisms became embedded in your consciousness as the accurate reflection of who you were.

"You're wrong." "You're bad." "You can't do anything right." "You'd be great if only you were . . ." "You're not worth paying attention to." "Who could love you the way you are?"

By the time you were five years old you'd become a prisoner of your negative conditioning as well as a victim of the dysfunctional rules set up in your family. The pattern of self-hatred set in.

As a lovesick adult, your loving feelings for your you are buried, so hating yourself has become your way of thinking, of being, of feeling, your only identity. No matter what you look like, you feel ugly. No matter what your accomplishments, you feel unsatisfied. The only feelings you feel good about are bad. The only feelings you feel comfortable with are negatives. The only feelings you can recreate are putdowns. You're unlovable, there's something wrong with you, you don't deserve to be loved.

"I'm too fat." "I'm too skinny." "I'm ugly." "I didn't do it right." "I didn't do enough." "I said the wrong thing." "I should have known better." "If only I were blonde." "If only I were brunette." If only you were better, in every way, then your life would work.

Self-hatred destroys, undermines you in every area of your life: you don't believe in yourself, expect only the worst to happen, dramatize your faults and shortcomings, never feel worthwhile, hate your body and the way you look, find fault with and criticize yourself for any little imperfection, and ignore any compliments because they don't fit your negative belief system. Every day is a battle that you have to lose in order to win. To feel good you have to feel bad.

Self-hatred causes lovesickness.

"Don't beat yourself up!"

Please don't hate yourself more because you've just read about how much you hate yourself. That's the easy way out. That's what you always do. Instead, begin to observe how often you criticize yourself during the day, but don't beat yourself up for that.

THE LOVESICK BLUEPRINT

As a lovesick adult you're stuck in a vicious cycle recreating being rejected in the name of love. For you rejection equals love. You can only choose rejecting partners, bonding with them through rejection, the same way you're bonded to your parents. You can only be attracted to people who reject you; the more they reject you, the more you love them, the stronger the fantasy, the obsession, the fantasy bond, the same way it was with your parents.

Rejection is love. The more unavailable, unattainable, rejecting, the more love, the higher the pedestal, the stronger your obsession. This has become the blueprint of your lovesick life, for all your relationships since you were five.

The lovesick blueprint: rejection = love.

THE LOVESICK EQUATION

You did not get unconditional love as a child from your parents and that made you feel unable to feel love, unable to accept love, unable to love yourself, unable to love anyone except someone who rejected you: lovesick!

Your lovesick relationship with your lovesick parents
+ their inability to give you unconditional love
+ your fantasy bond connection to them
+ the Black Magic Complex
+ the lovesick blueprint
+ the black hole
+ your addiction to rejection, to pain
+ your inability to love yourself
= LOVESICKNESS

WHAT IS LOVESICKNESS?

Lovesickness is an emotional illness. It's an acquired pattern of self-destructive behavior and belief systems; the condition of denying who you are and living by who you are not; the substitution of second-guessing for feelings; the denial of your inner self and needs, replacing them with an external value system; the trap of living life and relating to others, not from the position of who you are and what you want, but what you think the other person wants or thinks you should be. It's reverse thinking, a belief system that you can win love by being who you are not and lose love by being who you are.

Lovesickness robs you of a proper relationship model for your adult life, as the need to get approval from a rejecting parent becomes replaced by the need to get approval from a rejecting partner.

"It's a normal reaction to get upset or anxious."

You may feel afraid, angry or overwhelmed. You may still be denying what you've read. Remember that this may be the first time you've thought about these problems. Please don't worry. It's okay to feel the way you feel, whatever you feel. Don't quit. Keep going. Becoming aware of the causes of lovesickness is the first major step in your recovery. You have to go through this in order to come out the other side, and you will. Recovery from lovesickness is possible. It takes baby steps day by day by day. You can get over lovesickness.

CHAPTER 2

The Great Escapes

BLOWING YOUR COVER

This chapter is going to blow your cover. You've been so down, so unhappy for such a long time that you've become addicted to almost anything, everything to fill up the black hole, to cover up your feeling of emptiness, of being unlovable. The next step in the process of recovery is to recognize your great escapes, as we call them. The trouble with these great escapes is that they backfire, trap you, add to your problems and create more self-hate, more pain. This is when the going gets tough especially if you've been kidding yourself: "No. I'm not an alcoholic or a compulsive overeater or a pothead or a workaholic or stuck in another of a series of rotten relationships."

SEX AND DRUGS AND ROCK AND ROLL

As Romanoff recalls it,

> Marilyn drank champagne, and some vodka, and would take sleeping pills . . . I remember Marilyn telling me one of her problems was that she'd taken pills so long, they didn't work for her the way they did for other people. So she'd begin about nine in the evening, and build up that lethal combination of booze and pills . . .
> Marilyn's psychiatrist, Dr. Greenson, wrote to a colleague, "Above all, I try to help her not to be so lonely, and therefore to escape into drugs or get involved with very destructive people, who will engage in some sort of sado-masochistic relationship with her . . ."

Ongoing anxieties, overwhelming fears, loneliness, failure and insecurities were your constant companions as you grew up, haunting you for as long as you can remember. Because you hated yourself, because you felt a black hole inside, because you felt so empty, you began to seek relief in any form, any anesthetic or way out, escape or cover up, anything that worked. When it wore off, you went back for more. Needy, constantly in pain, you began to overuse, abuse it. As the vicious cycle of need and escape set in, you became addicted.

As a lovesick child, chocolate may have been your first experienced escape. By the time you reached puberty, you added new escapes. You became boy crazy. Then came alcohol. Drugs. Pills. Sex. Individually or together.

As a lovesick adult your primary escape is to have a relationship with a rejecting, unattainable or unavailable partner, a "him." That way you can avoid your emptiness, fill up the black hole by getting lost in someone else, exchanging your existence for theirs, your tormented reality for your partner's. You get high on the challenge, the drama, the excitement, the thrills, the adrenalin rushes, the rejection. Then you get addicted.

But you're also cross-addicted. You'll try anything. Whatever works. Whatever's available. Then get obsessed by it, fixated on getting it, on escaping. You may simultaneously be: a sexaholic, an overeater, an alcoholic, a substance abuser, a pothead, a workaholic, a pill freak, a compulsive shopper. You can never say no to anything—desperately seeking instant gratification.

You've become trapped in vicious cycles, trying to escape from the black hole and your old pain by creating new pain. Each time you escape, you come down from your high, crash and feel lower, more anxious than before because you have a hangover, the "why did I do that" blues. You get ever-diminishing results from ever-increasing efforts.

BOY CRAZY

As a teenager I was the only one who never had a boyfriend, while everyone had steadies. When I was fifteen I got a wild crush on my best friend's boyfriend, Jeff. I was crazy about him. I thought only about Jeff for two whole years. I used to follow him around like a puppy dog, hungry for any bone he would throw me, anything he would say to me. My friend didn't like him that much and finally left Jeff for someone else. That fall I went to college. Jeff was the first one to come and visit me there. I don't know what it was, but as soon as he told me that he was in love with me, I couldn't stand him anymore. I wondered how I could have wasted my time for so many years on such a jerk.

—S.I.

By the time you entered your teenage years, the lovesick blueprint was already imprinted: rejection equals love. With your first love, that big crush, you *unconsciously* transferred the old pattern of being rejected by your lovesick parents to the opposite sex. You chose an unavailable, rejecting or unattainable partner without realizing it: someone who couldn't love you who thus recreated the same feelings you'd experienced as a child. You were unlovable, no good, bad, wrong. The more he rejected you the more you wanted him. The more unavailable he was, the more you wanted him, the more obsessed you became with getting him. You could fantasize about him twenty-five hours a day, fill the black hole and forget about yourself.

"If only he would notice me, I could be happy." "If he called me up and asked me out for a date my problems would be over."

Getting a "him" became your great escape from your lovesick self. You began to worship, obsess over him. Landing him, like the quest for the holy grail, was a lost crusade from the start, doomed to failure although you believed it was going to save you. You picked a "him" who's life centered exclusively around sports, someone too old, too young, or involved with someone else. You followed him around, called him if you dared, hung up on him if you didn't, became a walking glossary of knowledge about him, dreamt about him, began to live for him.

When the inevitable happened and your superhuman efforts to get him to love you, notice you, even to say, "Hi", failed, you became depressed and sank to the lower depths of despair. The end of the world had come. What was wrong with you? Why didn't he love you? You were the only girl on the block who didn't have a boyfriend. You were alone with your fantasies and no one to go out with. Depressed, unhappy, obsessed, you waited by the telephone for the call that never came, cried your eyes out, slept during the day, couldn't sleep at night. You went on an eating binge, smoked or snorted, drank, cut school, failed a course or two, were unable to study. You possibly considered suicide, overpowered by pain so terrible you couldn't stand it, so upsetting that you couldn't cope with it. You were dying to be loved, but were trapped by the lovesick blueprint: rejection equals love. You couldn't get love from someone who couldn't love you, someone unavailable, unattainable or rejecting. Your first loves were unrequited; they had to be—you were lovesick.

At the same time, you rejected any advances coming from available partners. Too fat. Much too ugly. Bor-r-r-ing. Too nice. Too short. There was always something wrong with a him who liked or loved you. You became further victimized by peer pressure for you were the only one who never had the "right" boyfriend. If you settled for a substandard him whom you felt was the only one you could get, you beat yourself up for not doing better.

As you suffered through your teenage years, the lovesick patterns became set: anyone who you wanted didn't want you: anyone who wanted you, you didn't want.

MR. WRONG IS MR. RIGHT

That summer of 1948 a young widow named Mary D'Aubrey, living with her mother on Harper Avenue in Hollywood, blundered into a bedroom to find her brother Fred in bed with his new girlfriend. "Hi! Can I have some juice?" was Marilyn's cheery greeting. Fred Karger was then thirty-two, ten years older than Marilyn, and shakily married to another woman. He was director of music at Columbia Pictures and an accomplished composer best remembered today for the theme of From Here to Eternity.

Marilyn had found a family and for the first time she was dizzily in love . . . Marilyn later told Ben Hecht, . . . "When he said, I love you to me, it was better than a thousand critics calling me a great star . . ."

When Marilyn wept he would tell her, "You cry too easily. That's because your mind isn't developed. Compared to your figure it's embryonic."

As a lovesick adult, scarred by past conditioning, haunted by the ghost of your original wounded relationship, you've continued your addiction to relationships with unavailable, unattainable or rejecting partners.

If you think he's Mr. Right—you can be sure he's Mr. Wrong.

If you're attracted to him he has to be:

Married. Married but not admitting it. Separated but not divorced. Newly divorced. Just separated. Breaking up. On the rebound. Living with someone else. Engaged. Hopelessly in love with someone else. Seeing someone else. Involved with a serious girlfriend. A womanizer.

A gigolo. An ineligible or perennial bachelor. A workaholic. A mysogynist. An alcoholic. A substance abuser. A user. A social climber. A drug dealer. A compulsive gambler. A bisexual. A homosexual. Emotionally wounded. An out-of-towner. Just visiting.

THE GROUCHO MARX CLUB

Lovesick people work off a double standard. You fall like a ton of bricks for Mr. Wrong but you reject, destroy or submarine any Mr. Right who threatens you and your basic lovesick belief that you're unlovable, don't deserve love. When you have so much energy invested in hating yourself, there's no way you can accept love from others. We call this belonging to the Groucho Marx Club from Groucho's famous line, "I wouldn't belong to a country club that would have me for a member."

You reject nice people, Mr. Rights, good guys. You're allergic to them. They don't turn you on, not the way the bad guys do. Instead they bore you, bring out the worst in you, irritate and annoy you. You get angry at them just for being alive. You don't give them a chance, can hardly make it through a date. You get very creative, find a million ways out, a jillion things wrong with them, a billion excuses to get rid of them: "I'm not attracted to him sexually." "He doesn't know how to dress." "He's never going to get anywhere in life." "He's rich but so vulgar." "He has no taste, what a tacky apartment." "He's not smart enough." "He's not from a nice enough family."

You see only negatives or create them, become possessed by externals, things that you'd forgive or not even notice, if only he had the good sense to reject you. If he makes the tragic mistake of being nice to you, or horror of horrors, falls in love and wants to be there for you emotionally as well as sexually, you want to destroy him. You make him pay for his stupidity by insulting him, picking fights and getting argumentative. You get creative in masterminding the big switch: changing his love and admiration to scorn and hatred, so that he'll leave you and you don't have to take the responsibility for leaving him.

Johnny Hyde, an important agent thirty years her senior, felt much more for Marilyn than she did for him. It was Hyde who helped her get the small but crucial role in John Huston's Asphalt Jungle, who praised her talents to every important producer in Hollywood, and who made sure that she was seen at all the right parties.

"Kindness is the strangest thing to find in a lover—or in anybody," she wrote about Hyde. "No man had ever looked on me with such kindness . . . He knew all the pain and all the desperate things in me. When he put his arms around me and said he loved me I knew it was true. Nobody had ever loved me like that. I wished with all my heart that I could love him back . . . You might as well try to make yourself fly as to make yourself love.

—MARILYN MONROE

He says he'll call you at seven and when he does you get angry. You call him names to yourself, "What a wimp! How can he be so predictable? I can't stand him. He's already called me twice today, making up excuses, he misses me, ugh!" You get bitchy and make him sorry he called.

You'd rather die than go to bed with him. You get amazingly inventive in coming up with excuses, variations on the old I-have-a-headache theme, "Sorry I just got my period . . . it must have been something I ate . . . I'm waiting for the lab report from the gynecologist."

Of course if Mr. Wrong asks you to pay your fare to his cold water shack in Wyoming so you can camp out for two weeks and rough it, you can't wait to go. It doesn't matter that you're a city girl, terrified of snakes. True love conquers all.

I pursued Billy for months, so in love with him that I couldn't see straight, but he was always elusive, which made me even hotter. He left me for a few weeks, said he needed some time away. I went crazy with anxiety. What if he didn't come back? What if he met someone else? He called me up when he returned, asked me to meet him at our favorite bar and proposed. I felt like a light switch in my head clicked off. I looked at him disgusted and wondered how I could ever have loved him. I told him I never wanted to see him again.

—ALEXANDRA

Mr. Wrong is Mr. Right + The Groucho Marx Club = Lovesickness

The combination of Mr. Wrong is Mr. Right and your charter membership in the Groucho Marx Club sabotages then destroys any possibility of having a normal relationship, of getting love.

THE ANATOMY OF A LOVESICK RELATIONSHIP

Stage 1: Fatal Attraction

When (Arthur) Miller met Marilyn he was married, with two children, to a willowy brunette a year younger than himself . . . According to Cameron Mitchell . . . he was walking to lunch with Marilyn one day when she suddenly stopped short. A few yards away, leaning against the wall of a sound stage, were two men—(Elia) Kazan and Miller. Miller, a gangling giant of a man, had caught her eye, and she asked Mitchell who he was. Mitchell made perfunctory introductions . . .

Marilyn and Miller met again later the same week, at a party . . . Marilyn turned up afterward at 4:00 A.M. wanting to talk. According to Natasha Lytess, "I'd seldom seen her so contented . . . she took off her shoe and wiggled her big toe. 'I met a man, Natasha,' she said. 'It was Bam! You see my toe? This toe? He sat and held my toe. I mean I sat on the davenport, and he sat on it too, and he held my toe. It was like running into a tree! You know, like a cool drink when you've got a fever.'"

Natasha Lytess recalled that "immediately after the first meeting with Miller, I could tell Marilyn was in love with him."

The first time you see or meet him, that obscure object of desire, you're drawn to "him" with such intensity that you can barely breathe, a moth to the candle, a chemical reaction, an overpowering attraction, a fatal attraction. It feels like sparks flying, electricity, hotter than the Fourth of July. Your adrenalin starts to flow, your blood rushes, you start to shake, tremble. You feel like a marshmallow, a jellyfish, weak in the knees, giddy. He's irresistible. This is it. He's the one, the answer to your prayers. If you can't have him you'll die. Wedding bells begin to chime.

When you first spot Mr. Wrong, the first few seconds are pregnant with the past. Something about the way he looks or acts, the way he dresses or holds himself, a gesture, his smile, his eyes or lips. Something triggers your memory. Unconsciously you've found someone who resembles your lovesick parent in body, mind or spirit. Your radar is unerring. On a subconscious level you've found a partner with perfect potential, someone who will reject you.

The hotter the attraction, the closer the resemblence to your rejecting parent, the greater the potential rejection, the more you'll be hurt. But you're blind to the impending tragedy and your need to self-destruct. Your personal doomsday machine arrives and you put out the welcome mat. In a split second you've fallen in love at first sight with a man you can never have or who would never want you.

The very reason that you're attracted is the reason it will never work—you've found another him who can't give you what you want. You pick him out of a crowd with unerring precision. He's the one who gives you a rough time, but you're deaf, dumb and blind to the warning signals. Rather than turn you off, they add fuel to your fire. Three of your girlfriends tell you, "That guy's a bastard, stay away from him." You believe you're Wonder Woman, you can make him change. He says, "I'm a bad guy, don't get involved with me." You think how nice, so honest. He comes on at a party, tells you you're the greatest, asks for your phone number, tells you he'll call you on Tuesday. You're so excited that you barely notice that he's buzzed around every woman in the room. He calls you Tuesday, two weeks later. You've been frantic waiting by the telephone, but think, with all that competition, how lucky he called at all.

Stage 2: The Impossible Dream

Now that you've found him you pursue him, focusing all of your energy on a cold, distant partner while your own hot, totally unrealistic, great expectations run wild. This is it. You're going to marry this one. You call him the next day, promise him a home-cooked meal, some business or social contacts, ask him to a dinner party, an art opening, whatever you think will work to get him. You think of nothing else but how to win him over, to make him fall for you. Strategies more clever than Napoleon's enter your mind. You confer with your friends, ask everyone's advice on how to hook the fish, never mind that he's a shark. Everything you do, think about or plan centers around him. You shower attention and love on him with such fervor and zeal that you neglect everything and everyone else around you, especially yourself. You cease to exist. You've become an extension of him. *You* get lost in *him*.

You start a relationship with him. Then you take charge. He's got some flaws, a few bad habits, he needs some improvements, alterations, a little direction, a lot of care. There'll be some changes made.

Stage 3: Control Tower, Control Freak

You're attracted only to the neediest cases; then you relate by controlling. He's not alright the way he is, poor thing, he needs your help so that he can get better. He needs direction, so that he can change and become perfect. How has he been surviving all these years without you? How lucky he is you found him; just in the nick of time, it's not too late. He can become the perfect long- or short-term project with you in the driver's seat.

From your control tower, you direct two different flight patterns.

Playing Doctor, The Caretaker, Mending Broken Wings

Playing doctor, mending broken wings and caretaking lets you run away from yourself and temporarily exorcise that black hole inside. You fill up your time by arranging your partner's day and life. You substitute giving for loving, try to make yourself indispensable through your enthusiastic overassistance. You do unto others so you don't have to do for yourself. What insurance. Think of what you can get in return: undying gratitude, endless paybacks, he'll love you forever.

Something wrong? You can play nurse and mend him. He's just separating from his wife and he's one of the walking wounded. What an oppportunity. A goldmine. Hours of work. You can be his maid, cook, executive shopper and personal secretary. You build him a new nest. You find him a place to live, a mover, a locksmith, a shrink, a divorce lawyer and the three latest self-help books on how to get through a divorce. When he moves into his new apartment you unpack for him, stock up his refrigerator, send his clothes to the cleaners and buy him a vacuum cleaner. With every chore and errand your hopes are high, he's going to see that you're perfect, wonderful, loving and giving that you'll earn his Good Housekeeping Seal of Approval or better yet a degree, that MRS you've been waiting for. You can take care of him better than that horrible wife he talks about incessantly. You bill and coo. Your future is clear, two lovebirds together. But you picked the wrong bird. The moment his broken wing is fixed he flies the coop. He doesn't need you anymore and finds a better nest. You have a crash landing but there's no one there to pick up the pieces. After all the things you did for him.

The Cecil B. DeMille Syndrome

When I first met Harold I thought he was a nice guy but what lousy taste. I couldn't believe his house. Neo-bachelor, tacky, the worst. No, I take that back, the way he dressed was the worst. Short socks, the kind that showed his calves when he crossed his legs and those shoes— someone told him they were good for walking but they looked ortho- pedic. I had to help him become stylish.

—LINDA

Your lovesick parents controlled you. You carry on this control tradition unconsciously. You become the Cecil B. DeMille of others' lives, the ultimate control freak. You'd rather do everything yourself because you don't believe that he's capable of doing it the right way, your way. You can't delegate responsibility: you tell someone to do something, then do it for him; take charge and organize social events, shopping expeditions, trips, weekends, reservations—producing, di- recting and controlling it all. You don't understand give and take or fifty–fifty. Your life depends on having things the way you want them and you're *very* rigid about it. You want it *your* way.

While the ability to organize can put you in good stead at work, it prohibits you from having a healthy relationship, for only someone needy can put up with being controlled, mothered or smothered. You pay a price for footing the bills. Your beautiful Pygmalion gets ugly, turns on you and leaves you for a better offer, or makes you suffer in direct ratio to the amount of your giving. You've chosen a rejecting partner to shower with gifts, hoping that he will thank you with love. But Thanksgiving never comes. You end up suffering, in pain once again, wondering why.

Stage 4: Paradise Lost, The End of the Affair

Little by little Mr. Right turns into Mr. Wrong. Dr. Jekyll becomes Mr. Hyde. He starts acting up, doing things his way, balking at your control. He criticizes you, forgets to call when he promised, disap- pears for a few days. Gone is the hot sex, the passion that's there only when and if he wants it. At first you don't believe that anything's gone wrong, that this wonderful, perfect relationship is on the rocks. You wonder what's the matter with you. You redouble your efforts to do things for him.

Your relationship becomes a macabre game you keep playing to lose. You play phone tag, chasing him all over town, imagining the worst. Jealousy and paranoia drive away your sanity. He's doing it with some- one else, he has another girlfriend. You follow him on the street or drive by where he says he's going to be to see if his car is really parked there. It's not. You call him at the office ten times a day to make sure he's there. He avoids you, is curt or hangs up. You try to please him by throwing a dinner party. He flirts with all your girlfriends, propositions your best friend. He stops making love to you altogether. You're afraid to ask him why.

The inevitable has happened, your paradise lost. You've fallen for someone who keeps changing the rules, who keeps you in constant fear of abandonment or emotionally off-balance, a rejecting, unattainable or unavailable man, recreating the way it was at home, the relationship you had with your lovesick parents. Your great expectations sour. You change. Billing and cooing becomes bitching and bickering. You become sarcastic and don't believe anything he says. You try desperately to suppress those feelings, because you're running on fear. "Better be nice, otherwise he'll leave me." You're afraid to tell him anything's wrong or that you're unhappy, miserable and depressed. If you tell the truth he might leave you.

You stay with this painful charade of a relationship, prolonging it as long as possible, because you're addicted to the rejection, no matter how bad it is, how much it hurts. You call up your friends and complain, desperate, bitter. They give you advice: "Leave him, he's lousy, no good." You think they're crazy. You get to a point when no one wants to be around the two of you anymore because you're so hostile to each other. Even though you try to control your jealousy, it keeps popping up at the wrong times. Of course he doesn't provoke it, it's your imagination that he's flirting with everyone else and ignoring you. You suggest a marriage counselor, a sex therapist or a shrink. You drag him there. After a few sessions the therapist tells you to leave him. "What does the therapist know?"

You start to feel sick. Your tooth acts up. You get a back attack, develop a fibroid or an ulcer. You're so depressed you can barely get out of bed. You're under a black cloud. Finally, when you can't take it anymore, you don't want to live anymore, you try to leave him whether you're married, living with him or just dating, after one night . . . four months . . . fifteen years. But you're stuck. Your demons come out to haunt you: "isn't a relationship, no matter how bad, better than being alone?" You waffle, you waltz, you worry, you leave, come back, change your mind, again and again. Finally, somehow or other, by default or rejection comes the bitter end. No matter what happened it's your fault because you were no good, bad, unlovable. You hold on to the good memories, block out the bad, make the worst relationship you ever had into the greatest. Life is pain and love is pain. It hurts to be alone. It hurts to be in a relationship. Love means not getting love, and you never do. How can you? Then one day, you see another him across a crowded room and start all over again.

Fatal attraction + Mr. Right is Mr. Wrong + the Groucho Marx Club + The Impossible dream = A vicious cycle

YOUR OTHER GREAT ESCAPES

Sex and the Single (or Married) Girl, One Night Stands

Long after the divorce from DiMaggio, Marilyn became an easy mark for anyone who could get close to her. She told one journalist in a New York bar that she was afraid that she had "gotten hooked on sex." Indeed, in her later years she went from one night stand to one night stand.

You confuse sex and physical attraction with love. When you're lonely, feel the need to be loved or just plain needy; you escape into sex. You go out on the trail for a sex fix, like an alcoholic on a bender or a foodaholic on a binge. The heat is on and so is the chase, a bar, a cocktail party, an art gallery opening, the street. You spot him. Those good old sparks fly. Your stomach turns over. You've found a partner. Someone who'll play the game with you. You come on to each other, both high on lust. It feels so hot that neither one of you can stand it. You take him home or go home with him.

Aided by alcohol, drugs and false pretense, the seduction continues. You protest, you're not that kind of girl. The struggle on the couch gets more intense. You have a few moments of real doubt. You shouldn't be that easy. You should wait. This isn't right. You smoke another joint or have another drink. You allow him to talk you out of it. He wants you *so* much. You want him *so* much. The trail of your clothes leads off into the sunset, to the bedroom. Wild sex, passion unfettered by feelings, 99 and 44/100% pure lust. The sex is tinged with the illicit, with guilt—two lost souls using each other's bodies. A perfectionist, you want to be the best and practice has made perfect. Your performance wins an academy award. Best lover of the night. The miracle has happened, you're finally connected with another human being. You're filled up. Happy. High. Rescued for a few minutes from being alone, you feel self-confident, secure, in love. All the feelings that have eluded you in every day life emerge for an all-too-brief time. Lust plus body contact plus a "him" equals love.

You come. The Big "O". For a few seconds, perhaps the only time all day you feel good or he comes and you fake it. Then you come down. Either way, you have nothing to say to each other afterwards. You both feel awkward. You want to hug him and he wants to be left alone. He picks up his strewn clothes and leaves, promising to call you the next day. The game is over but you won't play by the rules. You become obsessed with your partner. You wait for his phone call, praying for a second date, another chance at happiness. He doesn't call. Your life stops. Anxieties fly around the room on broomsticks. "I met the perfect man and now I've ruined it." "If I'd just kissed him instead of going all the way, he would have called me."

Little by little it dawns on you, he's not going to call. Stuck in guilt and remorse you light up a joint, pour yourself a drink and go out in search of love, one more time.

Fantasy Trips

As a lovesick teenager you began living in fantasyland to escape. You developed crushes or became infatuated with your Science teacher, Marlon Brando, Mick Jagger or the Pauls—Newman or McCartney— then began to obsess about them.

As a lovesick adult you live in your own dream world, replacing normal relating with fantasy obsessions. You devote all your time and energy to dreaming, hoping and plotting that somehow, someway, somewhere and against all odds, you'll be able to turn a wisp of thin air into the real thing. The more remote your fantasy, the stronger your obsession. You obsess about the CEO of your company who doesn't know you exist, a man who smiled at you once on line at the supermarket, Sam Shepard, Don Johnson, Mel Gibson, Kevin Costner, Kurt Russell, Tom Cruise or Alec Baldwin. The artist who's work you complimented at the gallery opening said, "Thank you," then walked away. You turn that "thank you" into a fantasy: he was crazy about you, only had eyes for you, saw no one else in the room. Then you take it further: you're going to get married, have beautiful children and live happily ever after.

You make Sam Spade look like an amateur. You've been on more stakeouts than Dirty Harry. You could have found Jimmy Hoffa if you'd had a crush on him. The obsessed can do anything when obsessed. You meet him at a Halloween party. He's dressed as a pirate. You're a cat. He smiles and says, "Hi sexy!" You say to yourself, "Oh my God, it's him, Mr. Right. My last chance at happiness." You have to leave the party before you can give him your telephone number. Now what do you do? You remember that his name is James. The rest is a little hazy. He works at a sports magazine, or was it in the sports department of a television or radio station? He said something about playing softball in the park. Why didn't you pay more attention? James. Jim. Jimmy. You'll call him Jimmy, it sounds more intimate. You have to find Jimmy. The average person would be baffled and give up but not you! You launch "Operation Jimmy." You phone every sports magazine, local and network television and radio station in town, only to find out that there are fifty Jimmies that fit your description. You plan the great stakeout. You'll casually bump into him while he's playing softball.

Three weeks go by, your feet hurt from canvassing 150 softball diamonds and you've become a sports media expert, but no Jimmy. You reluctantly phase out of the active stage of Operation Jimmy but under no circumstances will you give up the obsession. It could drag on for years or until a fresher fantasy captures your imagination.

Meanwhile you can't give a real man or relationship a chance, for how could he possibly compete with your daydreams? You neglect yourself, your own needs and your work, by fantasy-love possessed.

Never Too Thin

You're never too thin. You suffer from eating disorders, struggle with obesity, anorexia, bulimia and a fat/thin life yo-yo. You have a well-established starve/binge routine. The mirror is a horrible reminder of your fatness and the scale your worst enemy. Your whole day is ruined if you gain a pound, if you can stand weighing yourself. You've been on every diet in the world for as long as you can remember. You got addicted to diet pills. Five hundred calories a day and placenta injections worked until you fainted. You lose the weight, then gain it back, because when you look at yourself in the mirror, even if you're thin, you see the fat person you hate.

It was one of those perfect July days. I walked down the beach looking at everyone else having a good time but me: couples holding hands, kissing, families with little children, laughing. I was the only one in the world alone. I wondered how could I feel so empty, so depressed on such a gorgeous day. All of a sudden I thought about those Oreos stashed away in the cupboard. Wasn't there some ice cream left over, too? I sprinted to the house, devoured the Oreos in three minutes, polished off the ice cream in two. I raced downtown to the supermarket and bought

Reese's peanut butter cups, two Drake's chocolate covered cakes, a pint of Ben and Jerry's New York Super Chunk Fudge, a pint of Rocky Road and a box of Entenmann's chocolate chip cookies. I ate until my stomach hurt, till I couldn't eat anymore. I didn't taste anything, I hadn't been hungry.

—S.I.

Your eating binges always make you feel the same way, high and guilty. You know that you'll feel miserable later, but for those instants, you're out of control, helpless and incapable of stopping—stuffing, chewing, swallowing as fast as you can. You don't taste, you consume, pig-out. Instant relief from your upset, until the next morning when you have a food hangover. You've eaten so much that you hate yourself, every waking moment. You won't leave the house because you're too fat. No one will love you because you're too fat. Your closet has clothes in three sizes: fat, fatter and fattest. You won't look in a mirror for fear of seeing that ugly, horrible person. Who is the fat lady? It's you.

Liquor Is Quicker

Her birthday had been on a Friday . . . The Greensons gave her a champagne glass with her name engraved inside. "Now," Marilyn said, "I'll know who I am when I'm drinking."

You may be the adult child of an alcoholic where drinking is in your veins or just like to drink. Either way you don't acknowledge your addiction. You're not an alcoholic, not you. You rationalize by thinking that you only do social drinking and real alcoholics hit the sauce alone. (You, of course, don't do anything alone.) You have a few drinks at lunch, a few more at cocktail hour, one or two at dinner and a bottle of wine. You barhop or hang out and have a couple more. Just so you can talk to people, so you're not alone, so you can find a sex partner. You tell yourself that you can stop whenever you want—that you don't need booze—but as with everything else in your life, once you start, you can't stop. You rely on alcohol to enhance your mood, give you a lift, smother your lonely thoughts or feelings. Everything becomes so funny. Everyone is so interesting. You're funny and interesting. It's so much easier to start a conversation, to pick someone up, to seduce them when you're high. Your inhibitions fly away. So does your bothersome morality. How can anything be wrong with drinking when it makes you feel so right?

Make it go away. My frustration. My loneliness. That's how I always felt as I walked into a bar alone. After a few drinks I began to feel that skyrocket high, all along saying to myself that I shouldn't be doing it again. I was giving in to my impulse. Ashamed, I'd have another drink to get numb. Then I became a predator. I'd start to search for someone to sleep with, pick up a stranger, take him home and do it. After it was over and I was sober I felt disgusted with myself, with him. I couldn't wait for him to leave.

—MARY JANE

The mornings after. Those why-did-I-do-it, how-could-I-have-done-it ones. That's when you pay with big-time guilt and remorse. You beat yourself up to the tune of the throbs in your head. I'm never going to drink again. Your resolution lasts till cocktail hour, until the second drink and you feel funny, interesting and seductive again.

Up In Smoke

Marijuana. You've been smoking it as long as you can remember. You pride yourself on the fact that you're not a pot head. You're not addicted, not you. No way, José. You don't do it during the day. You can stop any time you want. You don't need it. It just makes life more pleasant. Mellows you out. Thank god it changes your behavior. You feel on top of the world. Confident. Courageous. You'll do almost anything when you're stoned. You get the urge to call . . . "the callies." Why not call the people you shouldn't call? You have an infinite amount of bad-news phone numbers so why not try them all? Better still, smoke another joint, go to a party and pick someone up. It's soo easy when you don't have any of those bothersome inhibitions. Everyone knows how good sex is when you're stoned. So sensual. So hot. Sooner or later you get the munchies. Your diet goes out the window. You eat everything in sight. The old Chinese mustard in your fridge on the stale wheat thin is not enough, so you find the only deli open twenty-four hours and binge out.

Your life becomes a blur of lost evenings. Your memory does not serve you well. You feel hazy the next morning. "Did I really say that? Did I really do that?" You can't exactly pin down where you were, what you were doing and with whom. You hope you didn't say or do anything stupid. You don't remember sex as great as it must have been. Then you get on the scale and to your horror you've gained five pounds. You can't remember anything night after night after night. You're a head and that's behind.

Pop, Pop and Away

I'm so proud of myself. I only took four sleeping pills last night.

—MARILYN MONROE

Uppers. Downers. Greenies. Speed. Dexies. Diet pills. Sleeping pills. Ludes. Codeine. Xanex. Valium. Ecstasy. There isn't a pill you haven't popped in your whole life, then become addicted to. Perish the thought of a day without two aspirin; you read somewhere that it's good for you. You even O. D. on vitamins—what's a mere 100 grams of Vitamin C when you can take 1000? It's insurance, just in case you were exposed to a cold, to anything. You pop whatever's new and improved, whatever's the latest, whatever you can get from your doctor, your friend who knows a doctor, your friend who has an extra prescription or an extra pill and if you can't get them from your doctor you change doctors. Your medicine cabinet closely resembles a pharmacy, an arsenal of prescription bottles lined up, side by side. You know enough about the properties of each pill to get a degree in pharmacology. You know which prescriptions are one-time only, which are those upsetting new triplicate laws, what's refillable. Unfortunately so does your druggist because you've tried every story on him: a robbery in your apartment, an unfortunate flood, your bag stolen at the airport, your doctor is on vacation, your dog ate your prescription. When you're out of pills you're down and out.

You go up and down depending on what time of day, what pill you pop. You enter the Valium of the dolls and chill out or fly on them. You have interludes of ludes: so great for sex. You pop dexies to get through exams, do laxatives, diet pills and diuretics to lose weight; Xanex to smooth out the rough corners; "E" for a real truth shot. To tell the truth, you can't go to the bathroom, work, go out on a date, relax, sleep or function without the help of pills. You've been swallowed alive by your pills.

Can't Buy Me Love

"You're ugly." "You're fat." "You don't have a date for Saturday night." "You're not going to get a raise." During the day, those voices start gnawing at you. You'll do anything to stop them. You escape in a cab or your car and head right to Bloomingdale's, Saks or the mall— anywhere as long as they take credit cards. You enter with your hopes high. It's your chance to change your image. A golden opportunity to create a new, different, better, improved you. You start looking around. Who are you going to become today? What new you? Shall it be Leopard Lady? Sexy? Irresistible? The bad girl? Doris Day? Preppy? The girl next door? Which one will work the best?

You start feverishly gathering up every animal-printed thing in sight, triumphant at every find. You get even more creative at the cash register, the moment of truth. You hope that your math is wrong, that you have a little credit left on your American Express card. If it comes up bad you'll use another card. If all else fails you'll give them a check. You finesse your way through the purchase. You try to look honest. Sincere. You don't want them to think bad things about you. You don't want them to think that you can't get credit, or don't pay your bills on time or at all.

You prepare yourself in case the dreaded line comes: "I'm sorry, ma'am, but I can't get authorization for your card." "Oh my goodness, my husband must have put his trip to Europe on the wrong card." Or, "That's funny, I paid that bill last week. You can't trust the mail anymore. I'll have to use my Visa." You walk out of the store high, acting and feeling as if you're the heiress to the Rockefeller fortune. The more shopping bags the better, status ones. You cherish them all, the crisp black and red of the Saks bag, the reassurance of Bloomies Big Brown Bag, the old-money green of the Ralph Lauren bag. You've bought a new you.

You wear it that night, but under the brand new outfit is the same old you with the same old problems. You still feel insecure, nothing has changed, you've failed again and those bills—how are you ever going to pay them? The day's price tag costs you more than money.

Married to the Job

You whistle while you work. You thrive on your job and the constant adrenalin rushes you get from the aggravation, the nonstop pressure from juggling all those balls. The phone never stops ringing with people asking your advice or telling you what they need. You feel so important. You're the only one who can do it all. Come in early, stay late and come back for more. You feel so valuable. It's so good for your ego. See how much you accomplish every day? A workload that would kill anybody else, but you can get it done. You can do anything. With hardly enough time to go to the bathroom and gobble down lunch, the escape is perfect, there's no time for you or your problems.

When you're away from work you're unable to relax, that unfinished piece of business haunts you. You can't sleep at night revved up on your own nervous energy. You think about tomorrow: the campaign you have to present; the new line you have to show the salesmen coming in from out of town; the speech you have to write or rewrite; how you're going to handle your boss; your secretary is going on vacation, did she do everything she had to, will the temp know what to do?

Of course you're not a workaholic. You have a social life, more or less, except that no one seems to like to be around you. You're either too tired, too strung out or too edgy. Everyone complains that you don't return phone calls, that you break dates. You're boring company because you're wiped out from your day and can talk only about work because you don't know about anything else, you haven't had the time to keep up. You try to make plans for weekends only, but something always comes up, workwise. "I'm so sorry but would you mind if I meet you at ten instead of eight? If ten's too late, how about next week sometime?" If you go away, you feel guilty the whole time, preoccupied, worrying about Monday. You can't wait till Monday comes. You miss work. All that excitement is a hard act to follow. Relaxing can be detrimental to your health; so is working. Is there life after work? Of course not. You've traded in living for working, your job *is* your life. You're married to your job.

Phone Mate/Phone Hate, Call Waiting and the Callies

"Do you know who I've always depended on?" Marilyn had asked reporter W. J. Weatherby, "Not strangers, not friends. The telephone! That's my best friend. I love calling friends, especially late at night when I can't sleep. I have this dream we all get up and go out to a drugstore."

Call it addiction, a terminal case of the callies or advanced telephonitis, but you can't live without your phone; the extension cord, your umbilical cord, your lifeline, plugs you in and connects you to people and what's happening out there in the real world. Your phone plus call waiting, call forwarding, your answering machine and your remote dial-in code. A mere machine has infinite power to make or break your day. It runs and ruins your life. It's a schizophrenic devil, the best friend you ever had and your worst enemy. You have a love/hate relationship with it. When it's good, it keeps you from being lonely and allows you to escape. You can talk to five continents, or five friends, stay in touch, network, gossip. You can check in, keep up, make plans, find out the weather, the movie times or just the right time.

When it turns on you it becomes a highly sophisticated, electronic instrument of torture. Call waiting. You experience the sound of the phone not ringing. He doesn't call you when he should. You call him when you shouldn't, along with everyone else. Many are called but few call back. You call, then hang up, just to hear "his voice" one more time. If someone calls you and hangs up, you get hung up on who hung up.

He tells you that he's going to call you at six. At five you begin to worry if he will or won't. At ten of six, your anxiety has mounted. What if he forgot? Will he call you? You pace nervously, paralyzed, incapable of doing anything except waiting. You agonize over the urge to call him. By six-ten, if the phone hasn't rung, you're sure that you'll never hear from him again. You know he's forgotten. Something's gone wrong. He doesn't want to see you ever again. Anguished, fixated on getting the call, your life stops. The voices in your head go to war: "Call him. Don't call him. You shouldn't call him. Call him. Should I call him? Why isn't he calling me?" You know deep down inside somewhere, that if he really wants to get in touch with you he'll call you, but by six-thirty you can't stand it anymore. Possessed by demons, you call him. Nothing else matters, including the consequences.

If anything goes wrong with your beautiful new phone that you chose because it was so slick, sexy, black, red and hot or your new, improved remote call-in toll-saver answering machine that you've more or less figured out how to work, you go crazy. You have a full-fledged anxiety attack, 9-point-5 on the Richter Scale. Your call to the telephone company is an impassioned plea, "You've got to help me. My phone is broken and you've got to fix it instantly. I can't get through the day without it." This is not far from the truth; your life *is* in jeopardy. You take your Panasonic back to the store in a state of sheer panic: "You've got to help me, something's wrong. Please fix it. Now. Today. While I'm standing here—I'll pay anything!"

You do. The phone bills that you pay late each month because you can't afford them are staggering. Your habit costs thousands of dollars each year. Call waiting is Heartbreak Hotel. The telephone, your best friend is your worst enemy.

"Courage Camille!"

What you've just read may make you may feel cornered, stripped, panicky, anxious, frightened, fearful, depressed, down, nervous or all of the above. You're going to feel as if you just painted yourself into a corner and there's no way out. Please don't panic. In order to break these lovesick patterns you have to get conscious of them first. You have to see where you've been and where you are in order to change, to recover. And you will. You're going to live through this. There's light at the end of this tunnel. There's a way out. This is the way out. Please don't escape. Stay with it!

CHAPTER 3

Symptoms and Syndromes

"Your Daily News is Daily Blues!"

You're beginning to understand lovesickness, its primary causes, your escape routes. There are lovesick behavioral patterns as well, traps, the problems that come up just getting through the day, every day, all the little disturbances, the upsets. They sting like the beach flies of a sticky August day. And you've most likely believed until now that you were the only one who was infested. Everyone else is normal, you're the only one who's been bitten, stung, messed up. You aren't the only one. The bad news is that these are the symptoms and syndromes of lovesickness. The good news is that you can get over them.

IDENTITY CRISIS

"Who am I? What do I feel? What should I think? What should I do? S.O.S. I'm drowning, I'm sinking, I'm lost without you. Please save me. I'll give you a big reward."

Who are you? Why are you? Who can you get to fill you up? What can you do to run away from yourself? How can you escape from you? What should you think? What should you believe? You don't know. You've lost your you. As you've become more and more depressed, hopeless, desperate, spiritless, disconnected from the world outside, from God, from yourself within, from love, your world has become blacker, bleaker, smaller. You've become a tragic heroine, your life a Greek tragedy because you have a tragic flaw: there is no you, nobody's home, you're an empty shell. You're trapped in the black hole, a hopeless little princess with a kingdom the size of a shrinking pea, waiting, hopes waning, that some day your prince will come and save you before you die from loneliness, because there is no you, you're empty inside and nothing can ever fill you up, there is no God and you're out of spirit, spiritually bankrupt.

You run on empty on the highway of life limping along from gas station to gas station hoping against hope that one of them has super-soul, so you can fill yourself up with somebody else's you. You feel numb, dead inside. You don't know who you are, what you feel, where you begin, end. You aren't okay the way you are, so you've become an attention junkie desperately seeking love and approval by being who you're not. You try to become anybody else, to please everyone, anyone, the world.

THE GREAT DEPRESSION

I was never used to being happy so that wasn't something I ever took for granted. You see, I was brought up differently from the average American child because the average child is brought up expecting to be happy.

—MARILYN MONROE

Marilyn called Dr. Greenson's son and daughter at home. She sounded heavily drugged, said she was unhappy, and they hurried over.

"She was in bed naked, with just a sheet over her," Danny Greenson remembers . . . "This woman was desperate. She couldn't sleep—it was the middle of the afternoon—and she said how terrible she felt about herself, how worthless she felt. She talked about being a waif, that she was ugly, that people were only nice to her for what they could get from her. She said she had no one, that nobody loved her. She mentioned not having children. It was a whole litany of depressive thoughts. She said it wasn't worth living any more."

You've been down and out in Beverly Hills, Houston, New York or wherever you live. You've been depressed all your life and probably don't even realize it, your companions negative emotions: despair, anguish, unhappiness, hopelessness, pessimism. Most likely you've been unaware of these feelings as constants because you've swept them under the rug by using different escapes to cover them up. But the constant unhappiness is always there, a minor key, a pervasive blue note because the foundation of your life is built on marshy ground, a belief system that something is wrong with you, you're no good the way you are.

By now you have a history. You keep saying to yourself it's always something. It is. You're stuck in recreating vicious cycles where you lose, get rejected and can never find the only thing you're looking for: love. You don't understand why you're always unhappy, so naturally you blame it on yourself. You feel doomed like Sisyphus to push a heavy rock up a mountain every day of your life that comes down every night. Your life is hopeless. You're stuck in mire and there's no way out. You're barely able to leave your house. Everything seems threatening, overwhelming, too hard to handle. Anything new puts you into a tailspin, how are you going to cope? You want to sleep away your life or you have insomnia every night from a pile of worries, stacked sky high. You have little or no energy. You cry. It feels so normal to be unhappy that you take it for granted. Life is pain. Pain is life. Color it black.

ALONE MEANS LONELY

"How can you be so lonely?"
  "Have you ever been in a house with forty rooms? Well, multiply my loneliness by forty."

—MARILYN MONROE

You'd rather do anything than spend time with the person you dislike the most, you. You're your own worst company. Being alone means facing the black hole where your demons reside. You know how awful you are so why should you bother to keep company with a loser. It's a waste of time. All you can do is divert your thoughts and energy to others. Being alone makes you feel so bad. There's no one to do anything for, take care of, pamper. You'll go to any desperate extreme rather than be alone, overstay your welcome at places, at work and in relationships. You're the last one to leave a party, you'll close down a bar or a restaurant and you'll burn the midnight oil at work. You're compulsive about filling up your calendar with things to do, places to be, people to meet, every second, so you don't have to be alone. It doesn't matter what you're doing as long as it's something; or who you're with, as long as it's someone.

If you're stuck at home alone you become incapacitated. There's a lot of things you want to do but you're frozen. You can't read your new book, watch the video you rented, listen to your new tape. The last thing in the world you could do would be to make dinner-for-one.

I was alone last night and I panicked. I went through my phone book and called everyone I knew. No one was home. I was the only person alone in the United States of America. Desperate, I finally got someone I barely knew on the phone and asked her what she was doing.

"I'm enjoying being alone."

"What do you mean?"

"Oh, I'm doing things that I never get a chance to do."

"What things?"

"Cleaning out my pocketbook. Doing a little laundry. Reading a book. You must know what I'm talking about."

I didn't.

—MELANIE

You get on the phone and start calling everybody. After you've left twelve desperate messages on the machines of everyone who's out having a good time but you, you sit in a chair virtually catatonic and obsess over the fact that you're the only loser in town, the only one who's unhappy, not married, not in a relationship or home alone on Friday night. The phone is silent. You're forgotten. You might as well go to sleep or go on an eating, alcohol, drug or sex binge—anything to fill the black hole and stop the loneliness. Anything.

CHAMELEON

When her courtship with Miller began, Marilyn began to read the books he recommended, practiced cooking, adopted his friends and his country life-style . . . Before their marriage in the summer of 1956, Marilyn spent a great deal of time learning about Judaism. Miller himself was not religious but she wanted to be part of his family's tradition. "I'll cook noodles like your mother," she told him on their wedding day. On the back of a wedding photograph, she wrote: "Hope, Hope, Hope."

You lost your you in the black hole as a child. As a lovesick adult you have no concept of who you are or what being you feels like. Like a chameleon, you take on the surrounding emotional climate adjusting your responses to your perceptions of what you think will win approval, what you think might be the right thing to do or say. You say and do things you don't want to say or do. You overextend yourself as you seek the crumbs of others' validation. Caught in this lovesick pattern of taking on the moods and opinions of others as a true representation of who you are, you become a yo-yo, totally controlled by others, acting rather than feeling, your own feelings numbed, frozen in pain and panic. God forbid you make a mistake! What if you can't figure out what they want? Or say the wrong thing?

He asks you out to dinner and politely inquires what your favorite food is. "Oh, I don't know. Anything. I don't care. I like everything. It doesn't matter to me. Whatever you like. I'm agreeable. You tell me." You end up eating what you hate but were afraid to tell him, the only food you're allergic to, get headaches from, Chinese.

You never get what you want because you're afraid to ask because second-guessing replaces feelings and life. You spend all your energy becoming who you are not. You fade into the woodwork. You give away your power, refuse to acknowledge you have any, wonder why you have a power failure. You give your vote away and wonder why you've lost the election.

The trouble with being a chameleon is that without someone to color your life and merge with, you cease to exist.

SHOPPING FOR LOVE

Marilyn could not forget Karger. At Christmas 1948 she went to a fashionable jeweler, and bought Karger a $500 watch on the installment plan. She was broke at the time, and would spend two years paying it off.

Buying love is the only way you know how to relate. Being needed by others equals being loved. You spend your life figuring out not what you need, but what other people want, losing yourself in the process of shopping for your partner's love. You've become the world's greatest expert, the Sherlock Holmes of needs detecting, Santa Claus, 365 days a year. You're the perfect gift-giver, give the best compliments in the house, help out with anything. You go to four different markets looking for the perfect bread, organic vegetables and salad, the freshest chicken, the wine to go with them, then you cook a gourmet dinner. Of course, you clean up afterwards.

The price of shopping for love is high. You pay dearly, with self-neglect, the inability to recognize or meet your own needs. All you have to offer is what you can buy or do for someone else. Inevitably, you've spent all your time and money on a partner who can't appreciate it and leaves you once he gets a better offer. He moves on and you get stuck with the bill.

THE POLLYANNA SYNDROME

You're nice to a fault. You learned to be nice as a lovesick child hoping that this would earn love from your parents. We call this the Pollyanna Syndrome because as an adult you're a people pleaser, so anxious to be liked and loved that you're the nicest person anyone has ever met, a Pollyanna smiling bravely and sweetly through all adversity. You say and do nice things for others. You're the one who can never do enough, would give anyone the shirt off your back, never assert yourself or venture your own opinion, especially if it's going to rock the boat. You don't dare have a dissenting opinion. If someone criticizes you, your back goes up like a cat's. You panic, become defensive, cower, lie down.

You're afraid of your real feelings, terrified of expressing them, fearful of being rejected, of not pleasing people so you whitewash your own feelings and needs; never get angry. However, if someone crosses you in whom you have no investment in pleasing, like a cab driver who takes a turn down the wrong street, suddenly you let him have it with your misdirected wrath.

The Pollyanna Syndrome is a defense mechanism, a disappearing act: if I'm nice to them they'll love me. The trouble with being a Pollyanna is that nice-to-a-fault girls finish last.

HONESTY IS YOUR WORST POLICY

You're out of touch with your own feelings, unable to tell the truth. As a chameleon you substitute people-pleasing guesswork for the truth. As a Pollyanna, even if you think you know how you feel, you're afraid to say it, because it might hurt someone or be taken the wrong way. Since honesty is your worst policy, you become the Queen of White Lies. Of course you tell them in the name of being nice, fearful of the repercussions of truth telling: "You look great!" (They don't.) "You don't look fat." (They do.) "You're not imposing on me at all." (They are.) "Of course I want to see you again." (You don't.) "Please call me." (You don't want to see them.) "I'll call you." (You don't.)

You end up by hurting people. You make a date that you don't intend to keep with someone you don't like because you can't say no. (Lie one.) You break it at the last moment with some kind of excuse. (Lie two.) He calls you again. Rather than tell him that you can't stand him, he's a creep, you ask him to call you back another time. (Lie three.) When he does you put him off again and again and again. (Lies four through six.)

You're caught up in a network of white lies. Honesty is anxiety provoking. You never express your feelings, censor anything that smacks of controversy, avoid saying anything that might make you look bad.

To tell the truth you can't tell the truth.

THE SEVEN VEILS, INDECENT EXPOSURE

You wear seven veils, afraid of exposure. There's nothing underneath. You hide under them. If someone discovers who you really are, or worse your big secret, that there's nobody home—it will be all over. Curtains. As a lovesick adult, you veil who you are, what you think, what you feel, what you want, your vulnerabilities as well as your strengths, your you. If someone wants to know or starts to probe you panic, fearful of exposure.

You choose partners who don't care what's underneath your seven veils, who can't see through them. Should you accidently become involved with a person who wants to peek, you're threatened by their honesty, fearful of their direct questions: "Tell me all about yourself. I want to know everything about you." Normal questions for anyone else, for a lovesick person it's an invasion of privacy. You don't want to tell your secrets. He won't like you if he discovers who you really are. You become defensive and run away or blow him off, terrified of being exposed as a fraud. The problem with your seven veils is that no one can love someone who's not there.

GOOD, BETTER, BEST ... PERFECT

She [Marilyn] was often late for appointments because she completely redid her make-up, and even had her hair shampooed and reset several times, in her nervousness that she looked exactly right.

Marilyn gave a dinner party for friends. Miller recalled that, "She did nothing else for two days. I never saw anyone so worried about a simple meal. Actually the whole thing was overdone, too formal, too meticulous, too manicured. She worked herself into a frazzle about the whole affair."

As a lovesick child you didn't get love for who you were, so you tried to become perfect. As a lovesick adult you're driven to perfection, your no-fault insurance against being wrong or rejected. No matter what you do, how hard you try, the perfectionist demons inside you are never satisfied. There's always something wrong. You could have done the job better, or faster. You become victimized by your own impossible standards and judge yourself without mercy.

You're afraid to experiment. You can't allow yourself that margin of error. You're terrified of making a mistake. It means that you're not perfect. You protect yourself against it with "preventive perfectionism." You won't let anyone in your apartment if you didn't clean it. You won't go to a party if you don't have the right dress. You won't go out on a date because you gained two pounds the day before. You're late for your dinner date because you did your hair over for the fifth time. You beat yourself up; never let yourself rest. Something's always wrong. Your "you didn't do it right" demons go to work: "I'm wearing the wrong earrings." "I put too much salt in the salad dressing." "I put on too much makeup." "I'm not making enough money."

Perfectionism is self-tyranny, a trap. It disables you, prevents you from winning and enjoying life because nothing you ever do is ever good enough.

INDECISIONS, INDECISIONS

On the day of the Grauman appearance, hairdresser Gladys Whitten, whom Marilyn called "Gladness," received a panic-stricken call from Marilyn. "I need your help," said the voice from miles across the city, "please come Gladness, and bring your mom." It sounded like a real crisis, until Marilyn explained: "I can't decide which dress to wear."

The combination of being a perfectionist and a people pleaser turns your decision making process into a Greek tragedy, every time. Making even a small decision on your own becomes a huge problem. It takes over, terrifying, then immobilizing you.

Should I wear a red dress or a yellow? A simple decision is cause for panic, putting you in a state of anxiety. Which one makes you look better? Which one makes you look thinner? Which one will give you a better chance at success? The decision takes on titanic proportions. Your life depends on it. Choosing between the two becomes a struggle. You get emotionally disabled by the decision-making process. At this point, you're under a state of siege with maximal stress. You call up the whole world trying to get an answer. You become possessed by the decision. Red or yellow. Yellow or red. When and if you finally decide to wear yellow, you worry some more, afraid that you've made the wrong decision, you should have worn red. You change your mind and your dress for the third time. By this time you're a nervous wreck. There's no way you can figure out what to do. The minutes are ticking away. You've broken out into a cold sweat. If only God could come down and decide for you and take you out of your misery. You finally decide, "All right, I know it's the wrong decision but I'll wear the red." As soon as you leave your house you start beating yourself up for not wearing the yellow. You're late for where you were going. Your date is blind with fury, so angry that he doesn't care what you're wearing since you made him wait forty-five minutes.

Indecision sabotages you. The tiny daily decisions, an apple or an orange, chocolate or vanilla, which movie to go to, what clothes to take on a trip, take on a life of their own as you change them from a choice of pleasure into instruments of torture. By the time you make a decision, you're exhausted, everyone around you is angry at you and you've succeeded in creating another in an ongoing series of no-win situations.

SPACE INVADERS:
JEALOUSY IS CRAWLING ALL OVER ME
PARANOIA WILL DESTROY YA

Monroe, however, outdid her own legendary insecurity. She convinced herself that fellow actress Cyd Charisse wanted to have blonde hair like herself. Assured that Charisse's hair would be light brown, Marilyn replied knowingly, "Her unconscious wants it blonde." Just to be on the safe side, the studio darkened the hair of even the fifty-year-old actress playing the part of a housekeeper. Scriptwriter Bernstein was ordered to remove any and all lines suggesting that Marilyn's screen husband, Dean Martin, could be attracted to any other woman.

Nobody's home, which throws you at the mercy of three space invaders, jealousy, her first cousin, paranoia, and competition. You constantly compare yourself to everyone else, come out second best and suffer, or imagine that she is going to steal him away. Almost everyone else is better than you. Smarter. Brighter. Prettier. Thinner. More successful. More capable. More athletic. Longer legged. Bigger breasted. The list is endless. You're dying to be what you're not and hate who you are. If you're blonde you're jealous of brunettes. If dark you're jealous of blondes. You deny your own good qualities, don't believe anyone who tries to compliment you and envy the entire universe.

Paranoia, jealousy and competition are your escorts to any social event, especially parties. You're positive that the enemy, another woman who could become "the other woman" or "his new love," could be anywhere. She could steal your man. He's going to flirt with her. You become so anxious that you create what you're most afraid of. Your beast in the jungle, jealousy, takes over. Your mood changes, you become fixated on his every move. You don't act or relate normally to anyone, looking over their shoulder, filled with fear. Mr. Wrong, your companion of choice, provides you with a good reason to be jealous. He ignores you and flirts with everyone. You see him talking to *her*. The space invaders attack: He's going to like her better than me. She's prettier. She's got a better body. She's got better legs. She's better dressed. He's going to leave me for her.

You watch him like a hawk. Is he going to take her card, give her his? He's smiling that come-on smile. You've lost him to her. You go crazy, feel insane, over the edge. Your whole evening is ruined. You try to repress your rage, but you can't. You throw your arms around him to make sure that she knows that you own him. Then you give her your best dirty, if-looks-could-kill look and wait until you leave the party to decimate her: "Who was that older, pearshaped woman you were talking to?" "Poor thing I don't know what I'd do if I had her piano legs."

You drown in a sea of jealousy and a whirlpool of paranoia since you have no life raft, no you to come to your rescue.

CLOUDED VISION, GODS OF MERE MORTALS, PEDESTALS

She chose Joe DiMaggio . . . What better way to gain the love and support she craved than to become the wife of this quiet man whom sportswriters called the "Last Hero"? What could be a better bulwark against her own depressions and insomnia than this handsome stoic who seemed to have no moods?

"I had thought I was going to marry a loud, sporty fellow," Marilyn wrote about their first date. "Instead I found myself smiling at a reserved gentleman in a gray suit . . . I would have guessed he was either a steel magnate or a congressman." . . . The marriage itself lasted barely nine months . . . Once in possession of Marilyn, he resented her career, disliked the invasion of his own privacy that their marriage brought about, and was angered by both Hollywood's sex-movie use of her body and by any immodest clothes in daily life. Even a low-necked dress could set him off, and Marilyn took to wearing Peter Pan collars and dresses that were her usual skintight style, but exposed little bare skin . . .

Marilyn later wrote, "Many of the things that seem normal or even desirable to me are very annoying to him."

Soon Marilyn's marriage degenerated . . . There is some evidence that his anger led him to treat her with violence.

You made the fantasy bond switch as a lovesick child. As a lovesick adult you've turned everything around, upside down, and reversed it ever since. Mr. Right is Mr. Wrong, a good-looking user, your best friend. Your vision is as distorted as a carnival mirror. You can't see straight. Your judgment is off. One-hundred-eighty degrees. You misjudge people, confuse friends and foes, create gods of mere mortals, giving them the ultimate power over your life. All that matters is that they like you, never mind who they are. If they don't like you, fire you, yell at you, criticize you, don't call you, you're devastated. Someone everyone else sees as a wimp becomes the greatest person you ever met. You're surrounded by the losers of the world, who prey upon you as you kill yourself to be nice to them.

You meet a man, or a woman. What you see and think about them is based solely on how they look because you can't see inside because your vision is clouded. You make character judgments based on what they're wearing, their appearance, exteriors. You rely on their looks, clothes, accessories, hairstyles or jobs to give you clues and insights into their personalities.

You fall in love with him because he has a beautiful profile and elegant clothes. The reality is that he's only got one suit and a reputation as a social climber. You deny the reality. Reverse it. Even when he uses you—asks you to buy him another suit, to introduce him to all your friends—you still think he's perfect. When he leaves you for someone richer, who has more contacts, can buy him better suits, has a town house and a country house rather than just an apartment, it's your fault. You've done something wrong. Not only have you made that original bad judgment, you stick to it no matter what. Then you get stuck.

Lost in the stars, you can make only bad calls about people and situations that you're involved with. You're truly shocked when the truth comes to light and always Hurt with a capital H. You're more in touch with your dream of what could be than with the reality of what is. Every day you board the fantasy express, blind to what's really happening and the inevitable aftermath, another disappointment.

VICTIM

When you never succeeded in your quest for the Holy Grail, getting love from parents who didn't love themselves and couldn't love you, you became used to failure, to losing, to being a victim. As a lovesick adult you've become addicted to losing, to failing and failure no matter how talented and smart you are, or how hard you work. It's not okay for you to win. You can't allow it, just the same way you can't accept love, because it feels wrong. If you start to win you sabotage it; if someone loves you, you sabotage the relationship. You're stuck in this life pattern, a love and life victim. You allow yourself to be taken advantage of in everyday life situations and exploited at work, continuing the same lovesick pattern of denying yourself and fulfilling the demands of others with the hopes that this will win their approval and love. You can never do enough, at work, at play, at home, in bed.

Since you can't say no to anything you end up by taking on more than you can handle: The boss asks you if you can stay late to type an extra two hundred pages. You say yes although you have other plans, your own work to do and couldn't possibly finish before three o'clock in the morning.

Your girlfriend asks you if she can throw a little party at your house. You end up by supplying food and liquor for a hundred people, none of whom you know. You're ashamed to ask her for help or money, she never offers.

You can't say no to bad deals, surround yourself with people who take advantage of you, users who you don't even like, work for bosses who exploit you. You're attracted to them, can smell them a mile away. You play it out over and over again, because that's the only way you know how to play: playing to lose.

You try harder and harder to keep your life together with worse and worse results. Since you've surrounded yourself with the wrong people, you're exploited, taken for granted. No one thanks you. You feel hurt, upset and frustrated all the time, but there's no escape because whatever's gone wrong is your fault. As time goes by you accept constant failure and being a loser as your natural position in life, no matter how great your capabilities and, talents, victimized by your bad judgment, fear of telling the truth, the need to please and get love from someone who can't give it to you.

SORRY, IT'S MY FAULT

That old Black Magic Complex has you in its spell. You take more than the lion's share of guilt and blame in every area of your life. You're incapable of acknowledging the good things in your life, ignoring them, but if something goes wrong it's your fault. If you go to the islands for a week's vacation and it rains two days out of seven, it's your fault, you should have picked a different island. If your boyfriend is in a bad mood and screams at you, it's your fault, you put him in the bad mood. If a business project falls through, an account is lost, a deal queered in spite of the fact that there are a hundred other people involved, it's your fault. You should have tried harder. He doesn't call you back after a date, it's your fault. A golden opportunity to beat yourself up. You were too stupid or too ugly or too fat or too thin or you didn't wear the right clothes or you didn't do something right.

You hear those voices, "You can't do anything right; it's your fault." You beat yourself up day in and day out, year in and year out and can only be around people who reinforce this position. You're a loser. You can't win. Life is a bitch and then you die and it's your fault.

"This is rough going, but please stay with it."

You may be in overwhelm by now. We've been talking only about your negative patterns, which for you is like bringing coals to Newcastle. Please bear with us. The doomsday machine is not here. You're going to get to a better place. In order for you to see the light we have to expose the dark side of your conditioned patterns. These patterns have trapped you in self-abuse long enough. But as we've mentioned before, the only way to get rid of them is to see them for what they are and understand what they've been doing to you. This process is painful. Unfortunately there's some more to go. Please go at your own pace.

Before you can go into the recovery phase and break those patterns, we have to finish the recognition process. Please acknowledge yourself; this is pretty rough going and you've made it through so far.

Remember that any change you make is going to be for the better. You're already taking the first steps to recovery by sticking with this.

RUSSIAN ROULETTE

The question remains whether her pregnancies were tubular or hysterical. Greene claims she once had a fearful abortion that made it impossible for her to be pregnant . . . What may be the best explanation from a friend who knew Marilyn well, is that she had had many abortions, perhaps so many as twelve! And in cheap places—for a number of these abortions came in the years she was modeling or a bit player on seven-year contracts—thus her gynecological insides were unspeakably scarred, and her propensity for tubular pregnancies was increased . . .

"She never wore a diaphragm?"

"She hated them," said the woman friend . . .

Now, with Miller, faithful to Miller, she will have an operation and then another to make a child possible, and will claim to have other pregnancies—what stays constant is the depth of depression each time the pregnancy, real, tubular or hysterical, is over.

Every twenty-eight days you play it. Russian Roulette. Are you pregnant? If so, who's the father? If you know, how are you going to tell him? You're not seeing him anymore. It was a one-night stand. He's married. He told you a million times he doesn't want a baby. You've had four or five abortions. Every time it gets worse. You want to have a baby more than anything in the world but you seem to know only the wrong men who won't or can't marry you. Why can't you be like everyone else? You run the wedding fantasy by, one more time, your gown, the ring, the invitations, the flowers, the music, throwing the bouquet, the honeymoon in the Caribbean. Instead you have morning sickness, pregnant with a baby you can't have.

Your at-home pregnancy test is positive; your trip to the gynecologist a rerun.

You have the abortion, alone as always. He didn't come; you couldn't tell him or you did and he was less than thrilled. You go home depressed, promise yourself that you're going to have safe sex until you get married . . . you've learned your lesson. You wait ten days to have sex, then start the cycle again, abusing your body, mind and spirit by playing Russian Roulette every twenty-eight days.

"YEARS OF LIVING AND LOVING DANGEROUSLY," STARRING MILLIE MELODRAMA, SOAP OPERA QUEEN

When we left Millie yesterday, her world was coming to an end again. Her boyfriend John had just left her in the lurch and run off with her best friend Alice, without repaying the thousand dollars he owed her. There was no dial tone on her phone because the telephone company had shut it off because she hadn't paid her bill. She couldn't call into work to say that she was going to be late because she had an appointment to go to the dentist because the toothache she'd been ignoring for three weeks had gotten really bad. She was late for her dentist appointment because she couldn't find any clean clothes to wear and when she tried to buy some new clothes, the machines ate her credit cards because she owed money on all of them. When she finally got to the dentist after a stop at the laundromat and a hysterical battle at the dry cleaners to have them clean her clothes in one hour, and a desperate attempt to beat someone out for a cab which she lost, the dentist told her that he couldn't see her until the next day. When she finally got to work her boss fired her because she was late again.

Poor Millie. What's in store for her tomorrow?

Will John come back? Will Millie die of loneliness? Will the doctor be able to save her tooth? Will Millie be evicted from her apartment? Tune in tomorrow for the next episode of "Years of Living and Loving Dangerously," starring Millie Melodrama.

Adrenalin rushes! Anxiety attacks! Panic! Chaos! Melodrama! Worry! That's what you create every day so that you can live on the edge because that's the way it was growing up lovesick. Every day you were criticized, ignored or punished, beaten up emotionally or physically; rejected. You never knew when or why it would happen. When it did, you felt terror, anxiety or panic. Adrenalin rushes.

As a lovesick adult you're a soap opera queen in search of a daily crisis, adrenalin rushes and bad actors. Every day you act out your lovesick roles, create an Emmy award–winning performance in your daily soap opera. You're the one who loses her man, her home, her life, her job, whose friends betray her, whose husband is an alcoholic, a gambler, always in debt no matter how hard you try to change him.

You're chronically late. By now all your friends know that if you say you're going to be there by twelve you'll show up at one. You procrastinate so much that when you finally decide to get things done you don't have enough time. You overschedule your time so that you get gridlock, so there is no way you can keep all your appointments and by the time you do get to one you're in a state of high anxiety with adrenalin rushing and flowing all over the place like a virus, infecting you and everyone around you. You need a daily disaster to feel alright and if things are going right you sabotage them.

On May 19, 1962, there was to be a "Birthday Salute" to President Kennedy at Madison Square Garden in New York . . . Peter Lawford had the idea of Marilyn Monroe singing "Happy Birthday" to the president . . . Marilyn was flattered, but also very scared. She was less and less able to perform even short pieces of dialogue for Something's Got to Give. She was more and more dependent on pills, on trips to her psychiatrist, and on fantasies. She was so frightened that Joan Greenson, the daughter of her psychiatrist, gave Marilyn the children's book, *The Little Engine That Could*, and Marilyn took it with her for confidence. In a transparent dress she had to be sewn into, with a psyche held together with a children's book, pills and champagne, Marilyn managed a brief, breathy, sexy rendition of "Thanks, Mr. President" (special lyrics had been written to the tune of "Thanks for the Memory"), and then led the crowd in a chorus of "Happy Birthday." . . . It was a moment both of great vitality, with the crowd going crazy, and one of great embarrassment. Marilyn's very fear and doped slowness had created long sexy pauses. Her voluptuous body was exposed, but her mind had receded, as Arthur Schlesinger wrote later, "into her own glittering mist."

A deadly force is with you, anguish, terror, pain, worry, upset, chaos and crisis. You can't live without them. But you can't live with them. They're killing you.

LOVESICKNESS KILLS

The loneliness Marilyn felt at Mr. [Arthur] Miller's silent departure was underscored by the sudden death of Clark Gable a few days later. Gable had a severe heart attack the very day after they finished "The Misfits." Everyone thought he would recover and he seemed to be making excellent progress. Then he died. Marilyn was in shock . . . "I loved him, Lena. He was so nice to me. He was always smiling, always encouraging. If anyone in the world could have looked down on me, it was him. He was the biggest star of all. But he respected me. I just saw him. He kissed me good-bye. My friend . . . Oh, God, why is he dead?"

As upsetting to Marilyn as Clark Gable's death were the vicious rumors that she had killed him. He had a weak heart before production started. Marilyn's lateness and her fights with Arthur Miller were said to have caused a terrible tension Gable kept to himself, because he was such a gentleman . . . somehow she got it into her head that she was responsible for Gable's heart attack.

"All he had to do was tell me. I would have been up at five o'clock. No matter what. Oh, I did it. I was so selfish. Oh, Jesus, I did. I killed him. God forgive me. Oh, no!"

The nightmares started, then it became impossible for her to go to sleep without ever-increasing doses of sleeping pills . . . For days, she would lie on her bed, her eyes bulging out, wringing her hands in frustration . . . One afternoon . . . she decided to go out shopping. It seemed like a good idea, to get her mind off her troubles. It wasn't. New York was aglow with the Christmas season. Lovers were strolling down Fifth Avenue . . . And Marilyn was all alone. She came back to the apartment empty-handed and crying. There was no tree, no gifts, no cards. The place was cold and lonely . . . Something told me that I had better watch her closely. About seven-thirty I came back to see how she was . . . The curtains to one of the bedroom windows had been pulled apart . . . Furthermore, the window was wide open. Marilyn was standing before it with her white robe on . . . Both of her hands grasped the outside molding. It looked as if she might jump.

I ran over and surprised Marilyn by grabbing her around the waist. She turned and fell into my arms, "Lena, no. Let me die. I want to die. What have I got to live for?"

"Are you crazy?" I said, closing the window and curtains. "What's the matter with you?"

"I can't live anymore. What have I done with my life? Who do I have? It's Christmas! I want to have a Christmas. I never had one . . . I never will."

Lovesickness is a progressive disease that kills you little by little, every day, as you get more and more addicted to rejection and pain.

You live on high anxiety. Your judgment is off. You beat yourself up in daily bouts of vicious self-hatred. You're depressed. You suffer from the damaging side effects of cross-addictions, alcoholism, obesity, drug abuse, the trauma of frequent abortions. You anguish over your unmet needs and expectations. You're jealous, paranoid, indecisive, worried, racked with pain from excessive adrenalin rushes.

Each rejection builds on the last. The more you get rejected the more you need to get rejected. As you become more and more addicted to your rejecting partner, you feel worse and worse about yourself, more and more anxious, insecure and out of touch with reality. You feel more sick—lovesick. You're addicted to or obsessed with Mr. Wrong, or a series of them. You've squashed and buried your you, your own identity, needs, desires, feelings and spirit, giving away your own life to a rejecting man in exchange for approval that never comes. Every day is a battle. You become desperate. You try everything to make your relationship work. When it doesn't and you lose, you beat yourself up for being ineffectual, for being bad, for being you.

Your whole life centers around him. What he says, thinks, feels. You worship him. He becomes your god, your own spirit dying. If someone asks you how you are, your answer is how he is, how he's treating or mistreating you. You react rather than act. You neglect your own needs, spiritual, physical and emotional. Driven by your lovesick compulsion to get him you cut yourself off from everyone and everything else. Creativity, spontaneity, joy and beauty are crowded out of your life. You can't enjoy anything, relax, smile, laugh. Fun is a forgotten word. He has become the god of your shrunken universe and he doesn't want you. What's left?

Little by little, every day, it adds up. You've become overexposed to prolonged stress. Your spirit is suffocating. Your mind traps you in vicious games where you always lose. You're in pain every second of your life. Your body can take only so much. Lovesickness starts to take its toll. You get warnings: back pain, migraines, indigestion, constipation, constant exhaustion, insomnia, skin problems, allergies, a cold that won't go away.

As lovesickness progresses you break down, body, mind and spirit. How much rejection, pain and unhappiness can you take? More pernicious illnesses develop: ulcers, high blood pressure, heart attacks, tumors. Psychological, emotional and spiritual deterioration progress. You become more and more depressed, out of touch with reality, hopeless, exhausted, obsessed with your failures, possessed by your rejections.

Addiction to a rejecting or unavailable partner, can be terminal:

You slowly cease to exist. Your body breaks down. Your mind breaks down. Your spirit breaks down.

Lovesickness is an acquired emotional illness.

Lovesickness means that you come from a lovesick family where you did not get unconditional love so you never learned to love yourself for who you were but rather grew up hating yourself for who you were not.

Lovesick people don't love themselves, can't accept love from others and can fall in love only with unavailable or rejecting partners who can't love them back.

Lovesick people are addicted to rejection.

Lovesickness kills.

Part II

RECOVERY

1. CLEANING UP YOUR ACT

CHAPTER 4

Recovery Rules and Tools

THERE ARE GOING TO BE SOME CHANGES MADE!

Recovery begins with breaking through denial: seeing, accepting, understanding that you've been lovesick all your life, that all of your relationships have been lovesick including your relationship with hims, your family and yourself. Once you break through denial, as this process is called, you'll be able to break away from the lovesick relationships, break the old lovesick molds, clean up your act and learn to love yourself, learn how to have healthy relationships, a healthy life.

But you're going to have to make some drastic changes and this means work. You're going to have to stay open so that you can learn new ways of doing old things. You're going to have to learn to speak a new language: the language of self-love. You've been disconnected, your body, mind and spirit out of kilter, out of synch. You need to get realigned. You need to rebuild your life: how you see it, how you live it, how you experience it, how you feel it. There's a body, mind and spirit makeover in your future, a new you.

You don't have to be Marilyn! You can recover from lovesickness.

"THE ROAD TO RECOVERY," STARRING BOB HOPE, BING CROSBY, DOROTHY LAMOUR AND YOU!

The road to recovery lies ahead. It's going to be the biggest adventure of your life, a sometimes bumpy trip, a roller-coaster ride, with ups and downs, some tight spots, close calls, narrow escapes, but you're going to make it! You're going to win an academy award for the best picture; after all, you're the director, star, writer, producer! This is not a dress rehearsal this is it, this is your life!

You can do it as long as you carry along all the recovery tools with you and use them whenever you need them, keep your commitments, follow the rules and do your homework! The most important thing to remember is that you and your recovery must remain the number one priority in your life.

Roll 'em.

RECOVERY RULES

You're Number One, Recovery Comes First

> At the moment of impact in my car crash, *his* life passed right before my eyes.

> —ELLEN

You're going to have to make you and your recovery from lovesickness the number one priority in your life! Period! That's it! End of discussion. Your recovery is the most important thing you've ever done for you in your whole life. You've got to make you number one, for the first time in your life, not him, them, her or it. If you're feeling resistence to this, get that you're resisting it. It's uncomfortable. It's new. But it's still true. You have to come first.

Recovery Rule #1: You've got to make your recovery your number one priority.

The Ten Commitments

This is a series of commitments you need to make to yourself and keep:

I am commited to loving myself and giving myself unconditional love, day by day.

I am commited to my recovery as the most important thing in my life.

I am commited to respecting myself.

I am commited to believing in myself.

I am commited to taking care of myself.

I am commited to a body, mind and spirit makeover.

I am commited to loving my body and taking care of it.

I am commited to staying open to new ideas so that I can change.

I am commited to enjoying my life.

I am commited to being a winner.

Recovery Rule #2: You'll keep your ten commitments.

My Open Door Policy

I'm going to break my lifelong lovesick patterns and change them by learning new healthy ones.

I'm going to stay open to change, no matter how big, radical or different it will be. I believe that I can change. I'm willing to fly blind and make quantum leaps of faith, believing it's going to turn out all right. It will. Whatever I do now has to be better than what I've been doing.

I'm going to have a positive mental attitude. I'm going to make it. I'm committed to doing it.

Signed _____ Dated _____.

Recovery Rule #3: You'll keep your open door policy.

RECOVERY TOOLS

Recovery is a tall order, a lot of work. You need to do the work. This book is set up with specific exercises, affirmations, and visualizations to be used exactly when they appear. These recovery tools have been developed through group work, networking, interaction with members of the group, and working with Susan. They work but you have to do the work, your homework.

You can't do it alone. You're going to need all the help you can get, a net to catch you and a network, a buddy and a support system to help you through the rough patches.

Friends or Foes

As a lovesick person you can't differentiate between who's good, who's bad for you. That's not just men, it's all the way across the board, with your friends as well. You may not know who's a friend, who can be a buddy. Here's your first homework, some exercises that will help you break through denial to help you determine whether your friends are friends, whether or not they can be buddies.

One of the first exercises I asked Susan to do was to evaluate her friendships and take a close look at who was supportive of her recovery and who was not.

—E.M.

Elizabeth suggested it was time to clean out my closets, get rid of of all my so-called friends, like old clothes that no longer fit but I was keeping around like a bad habit, cluttering my life. I'd have to toss them all, the hangers-on, the takers, the users, the ones who didn't approve of me, everyone who was rejecting. She gave me this exercise to do.

—S.I.

Breaking-Through-Denial Exercise: Are Your Friends Friends?

Make a list of your current best women or men friends, buddies, pals, acquaintances, people who are in your life on a fairly regular basis no matter where they live or how long you've known them. Go down the list asking yourself the following questions about each. If you get stuck on an answer, remember a specific incident:

Does she approve or disapprove of you?

Is she critical of your actions?

Have you had incidents with her where she flirted with your man or made you jealous?

Has she ever taken advantage of you?

Are you the one who's always giving?

Would she be there for you in a crisis?

Can you be honest with her or do you feel you have to be on your best behavior to get her approval?

Do you feel better after you talk to her or worse?

Is it healthy for you to be around her or do you get into trouble with her?

Is she addicted to alcohol, substances, sex?

Is she interested in recovering or not?

Don't be surprised if it turns out that the majority of your friends aren't friends; this is a typical lovesick pattern.

What should you do about it?

It's not healthy for *you* to be around anyone who's not on your side, who's not rooting for *you* and your recovery.

If you see that the friends you thought were friends are enemies, then put your relationships on hold. You may need to cool it with some of them in marginal cases, drop the ones who aren't on your side. You can do this actively or passively. You can call them up and tell them that you're starting recovery and you need to be alone for awhile. If this feels too radical, take the passive approach, stop chasing them, calling them, feeding them dinner, etc. You probably won't hear from them anyway. Remember the old line, "With friends like these, who needs enemies?" You don't.

Recovery Tool #1: My Buddy, Your Net

Remember the buddy system in life saving? You had a designated partner, a buddy, and the two of you watched over each other; each made sure the other one didn't go under, didn't get hurt. We recommend that you find a buddy to do this recovery work with, someone who's on your side, is rooting for you and your recovery, someone you can call up any time of the day or night, who'll be there for you, someone who can be a net so that if you fall you don't hurt yourself, someone to help you, someone who loves or cares about you.

If you find someone on your list who passes the test, know someone who's already in recovery or interested in starting recovery, approach her. Ask if she'd like to be your buddy. Make an agreement with her that you'll recover together, that you'll be there for each other. Agree that you can call her anytime when you feel you're going to slip, ready to fall off the high wire and you need a net. Seeing each other constantly is not a necessity but phone accessibility is.

Almost no one on my list was a friend except beautiful Margie, my new buddy. She had begun to play a key role in my life. We were on the phone two, three or four times a day, whenever either one of us needed to talk, for whatever the reason, to make it through. We were in this recovery thing together, a survival team. If I was in a situation where I didn't know what to do or say, if I'd made a slip, was about to make one, or just felt unbelievably lonely, no matter where I was, who I was with, I would call Margie, my lifeline.

I went to an art gallery opening in Soho on a Saturday afternoon and met a very cute guy. He bragged about his fabulous Porsche and gave me his card. I called him that Sunday morning, as ever alone and in panic about being alone on a Sunday morning. He told me to take an hour and a half subway ride to his apartment on the beach in Brooklyn. He'd cook me brunch, we'd take a walk on the boardwalk at Coney Island, he had some great smoke, I could stay overnight with him or if I insisted take the subway back to New York alone that night.

"I'm not going to take the subway back alone at night, are you crazy, I'd get killed, it's not safe."

"Then you can always take a cab—it's only about seventy bucks."

"Why can't you drive me back in your Porsche if it's so fabulous?"

"I don't drive on Sunday, especially after I get stoned."

"Oh."

"Are you coming or not?"

"Do you mind if I call you back? I have something to take care of first."

I called Marjie and told her the story, "What should I do?"

"What would a healthy person do?" (This was the question Elizabeth had suggested we ask each other if we didn't know what to do.)

"I think a healthy person wouldn't go under those circumstances, no matter how cute he is. He could put himself out one way at least. You don't want to smoke and you certainly don't want to stay over with him. A healthy person would never do that."

"Thanks, Marjie. I was afraid you'd say that. I'm not going."

I didn't go. "What would a healthy person do" was a very big question. Until I figured out the answer, I'd have to keep on picking up the phone.

—S.I.

Recovery Tool #2: Support Groups, Your Network

We recommend joining a support group while you're in recovery. This can be a twelve-step program like ACOA or CODA or a local Women Who Love Too Much Group. Please look in the back of the book for a complete listing of our recommendations. If you've not been able to find any friend to be a buddy, a support group will put you in touch with other women in recovery programs—exchanging telephone numbers there on a first-name basis is part of the program. This will also allow you to form a recovery network for yourself so that you have more than one possibility for learning, talking about and understanding the recovery process. Open dialogue with other people in the same boat saves you from sinking.

Turning Off Your Mindspeak Station

I was playing softball one morning, hanging out with a good friend. After the game he said, "Do you realize that we've been together now for almost three hours and you haven't said one positive thing?"

"What do you mean? What are you talking about?"

"You've complained about what number you were up, your hitting, my hitting, the weather, the opposition, how tired you are, how hung-over you are, how much you'd rather be swimming than playing ball. Are you sure you really like playing ball?"

"I love playing ball."

"Doesn't sound like it to me."

He was right; I started to apologize and tell him how bad I was for being so negative.

"There you go again. See what I mean?"

—S.I.

Your mindspeak station, the voice that you hear in your head, has been stuck on Station S-E-L-F-H-A-T-E. All day, all night, all your life, you've been beating yourself up with, "You're bad, you're stupid, why can't you ever do anything right, how could you have done that, what's the matter with you, you're alone and never going to get married, he's going to leave you."

One of the first steps in your recovery is to be able to identify this negative voice, your mindspeak station. Get conscious of the amount of time during the day, every day, you spend putting yourself down, battering, beating yourself up.

Recovery is about turning off this lovesick mindspeak station.

Recovery Tool #3: Affirmations

You can learn to turn off your mindspeak station, ac-cen-tu-ate the positive, e-lim-in-ate the negative, start having a positive mental attitude about yourself with positive self-talk, affirmative declarations, or affirmations, as they are called. Affirmations can be done anywhere, spoken silently or out loud. The more you use them, the more real, solid, true and alive they become.

The most powerful way to use an affirmation is to repeat it out loud in front of a mirror while looking directly into your own eyes. All the negative thoughts and feelings which keep you from fulfilling your affirmation will probably surface. Keep on going, no matter what!

Try these affirmations:

I am worthy of love.

I am open to change.

I choose to make my recovery the number one priority of my life.

I am the most important person in my life and I deserve to be well.

I'm a winner and I'm going to win.

Recovery Tool #4: Visualizations

One day my friend, blithe spirit Lili Townsend came back to town after a year out and about the planet. She was concerned about ecology, the rainforests, saving the dolphins, the future of the earth, the spiritual domain. We discovered that in the past year, although she'd traveled thousands of miles and I hadn't moved, we'd both been working on recovery each in our own way. "I'll tell you what's bothering me, Lili. I'm sick and tired of always being in my head, I think too much. I admit it, I'm stuck. Even I, confirmed cynic that I am, have to have a spiritual side somewhere. I'd do anything to find it. I can't be the only person who's ever lived who's too logical to believe in God."

"Want to try something I've been working on?"

"What is it?"

"Visualizations."

Over the next two years Lili inspired and cocreated the visualizations in this book.

—S.I.

Visualization is a tool of recovery that allows you to create positive visions of things you want to accomplish, like receive the love you always wanted or let go of someone that's hurting you. The purpose of a visualization is to bypass, fool your lovesick mind into quiet submission for long enough to get in touch with your you and do the healing work you need to do to recover.

When you breathe to a state of peacefulness and relaxation you can still the voice of the mind, thus enabling you to hear the voice of love, of wisdom, of your you, of the higher self, of God within. Learning how to breathe and visualize allows you to let go so you can connect with what's always been there: you, love, your loving you.

The visualizations presented in this book are original work. They were created as recovery tools to heal specific aspects of lovesickness. They have been very successful in group and individual work. We simply ask you to try them.

You may have some favorites. Return to them, do them again. If you don't like one or another, that's natural, too. Use the ones that work best now, try the ones that didn't work at a later time. You may not be sure what you get because this is uncharted territory. It doesn't matter what you think, what your mindspeak station says, whether you understand exactly what you're doing, you'll benefit just by doing them. You'll get it! These recovery tools work!

FINDING THE RIGHT SPACE

From time to time we'll have a visualization for you to do. In preparation for it you need to find the right space. That means a place in your home where you can feel safe and private. It could be your bed, a favorite chair, the floor. It's a place where you can be comfortable for a period of a half hour or more. When you find it, practice breathing there. Loosen your clothes so that nothing is constricting you. Breathe slowly in through your nose so that your belly inflates with air. As you exhale through your nose, let your belly go. Inhale through your nose, let your belly expand, exhale through your nose, let your belly collapse. Do it again that way. And again.

When you're ready to do a visualization, go back to the same place. You may want to close the blinds and light a candle and in your own way ask Spirit to be present, represented by the candle flame. (In this book for clarity and brevity we refer to what's widely called God as Spirit. Other terms that you may want to use are Great Spirit, the Goddess, the force, Nature, the Universe, your higher power.) Follow the instructions, stay open, keep breathing, see what happens, enjoy the ride.

VISUALIZATION:
THE TEMPLE OF LOVE AND HEALING

This is the time to create your own sacred space you can return to again and again. Before doing a visualization it's always a good idea to move your body so that any tight places or negative energy that's being held in the body can be released. Start to stretch. Feel where your body feels tight. Move into the tightness until you feel little releases in your body, little clicks. Turn the opposite way to an unfamiliar position. Breathe in energy and light, more oxygen to your body, breathe in through your nose, feel your belly expand, breathe out and let your belly collapse. Breathe in a sense of well being and excitement, the joy of being alive. Feel at the same time a wonderful quiet, peacefulness growing within you. When you're ready, light a candle and dedicate this to Spirit.

Lie back in complete comfort, close your eyes and begin a slow, steady, breathing pattern. Imagine breathing in golden sunlight, breathing out any tension in your body, in through your nose, out through your nose, your tummy expanding on the inhale, collapsing on the exhale.

Visualize your Temple of Love and Healing on a mountain top overlooking a lush forest. Take time to create the interior of your temple. Notice the portals, the floors and ceilings, the walls. See that there is a comfortable place to sit, another to lie down. Through the mother of pearl columns, you can see a pathway leading to a meadow, a stream curving through the greenery to a lagoon, another pathway leading down to a sandy white beach and the shimmering sapphire sea. Along the beach are graceful trees and vibrant flowers. Volcanic peaks are visible in the distance.

Breathe in sparkling golden light. Feel the oxygen and energy flooding into your head, your body with each breath. Breathe out the shadows within, feeling a sense of relief with each exhale. Feel the safety and love present in your space. This is your place for insight, recognition, release and change. Imagine that you are exploring this new land, finding secret places where beautiful birds and animal allies can be seen and heard. Feel surprise and wonder as you find a waterfall flowing into an emerald pool, a circle of magical stones, a field of fragrant flowers. Come to your Temple of Love and Healing often for the refreshment of your whole being.

CHAPTER 5

Fifty Ways to Leave Your Lovesick Relationship

Here comes some bad news. **You have to leave him.** Why? In order to recover, you have to break your lovesick addiction to the unavailable, unattainable or rejecting man in your life.

You may be saying to yourself, "Jim is so wonderful, he's not unavailable or rejecting, why should I leave him?" This is called *being in denial*. You're denying that Jim could be bad, nasty, unkind, selfish, rejecting, unavailable or unattainable. Denial is part of being lovesick. Denial is part of that fantasy bond. As a matter of fact, the more dysfunctional, lovesick your original relationship was with your family, the more you denied it, the more you deny that there's anything wrong with your current relationship. "Jim is wonderful, there's something wrong with me." The reality is that the only men you've been able to bond with are rejecting, emotionally or physically unavailable, unstable or unable to love you. Every relationship you've ever had, whether it's with your current boyfriend, your husband, your ex, the man you're living with, sleeping with or slept with has been lovesick. On the other hand, as a charter member of the Groucho Marx Club you've rejected anyone who's loved you, anyone kind, stable, reliable or interested in you. Nice men bore you as in *nice guys finish last*. It scares you if a man is available to you emotionally and physically.

Just as an overweight person decides to go on a diet because she doesn't want to be fat anymore, or an alcoholic decides to go on the wagon because he doesn't want to be drunk anymore, you have to make the decision to leave the unavailable, unattainable or rejecting "him" of your life. This is the only way for *you* to continue *your* recovery. This is the only way you can stop perpetuating your addiction to rejection, to pain, to lost causes.

He isn't going to change—he can't. You're the one who's going to make the changes—you can!

GARDEN-VARIETY TYPES OF UNAVAILABLE, UNATTAINABLE OR REJECTING MEN

If you're lovesick, by definition, the man you're living with, married to, in love with, just dating or obsessing over is either unavailable, unattainable or rejecting and you're addicted to both him and the rejection. Here are the telltale signs that help you spot a him:

He lives with you and doesn't sleep with you or sleeps with you and goes home to someone else.

He wants what he wants when he wants it no matter what you want.

He's interested in talking about him, forget you.

He's unreliable, inconsistent and keeps you guessing. You never know when or if he's going to call you so he keeps you hanging on.

He criticizes you, is a put-down artist.

He has all the control over the money, fulfills his needs, ignores yours.

He controls bed, makes all the decisions about sex, fulfills his needs, ignores yours.

He's physically violent.

You never know what to expect or where you stand.

He's incapable of dealing with, talking about or coping with the truth, anything controversial or anything that makes him feel uncomfortable.

He won't see you on weekends.

He's got problems, is always depressed.

He's a drug addict, pot head, alcoholic, gambler, overeater, shopaholic, workaholic, sportsaholic.

He's commitmentphobic. He sees you occasionally, takes you out once in a while, but the "when" is on his terms. When you do see him you don't know when or if you're going to see him again.

You're afraid of him.

He's got to be in the driver's seat, in control. Spontaneity scares him to death.

He's mysterious, secretive, you don't understand him.

You can't count on him, he's never there for you.

THE REMEMBRANCE OF THINGS PAST

In the beginning of every group, I'd hand out a list of lovesick problems which we'd read together out loud. There were fifteen points.

—E.M.

There were two points which made me nervous, scared me to death. "You are addicted to unavailable men." "You are not attracted to men who are kind, loving. Nice men repulse you." Could this be? I decided to find out. Elizabeth suggested I list all the men in my life, "the ones something significant had happened with." Just writing their names gave me an electrical charge. My stomach turned over. I reexperienced the heartbreaks, my dashed hopes, the pain as they rejected me . . . they all had. Memories. No, nightmares. They'd come back to haunt me over the years, living reminders of my failure; they'd all married other women. As I continued to write down the names of my long lost or obsessed-over loves, I thought about each relationship. There had been so many rejections. So many loves who didn't love me. So much pain. All my life. A series of old wounds reopened . . . bleeding. I'd been only thirteen when it started, gone from one to another to another, the same patterns, over and over. All the loves of my life were Men Who Had Rejected Me without exception. Shocking. It was nauseating.

My Rejects column made me feel worse . . . guilty. Every time a man had fallen in love with me I'd rejected him. Cruelly. Inexplicably. I'd hurt so many wonderful men, whose only mistake had been to love me. Pinpricks to my conscience. I should have married any one of them. If only I had. Too late now. They'd never forgive me. I didn't blame them. I'd rejected every single one of them for the crime of loving me.

There it was on paper without exceptions. Another thunderbolt! There were two kinds of men in my life, the nice ones I ran away from and the bastards I chased. I was addicted to relationships with rejecting men, worse, or equally horrible, I couldn't accept love. "I love you," the three little words I'd waited for all my life became a death sentence to any man who dared utter them. Why? What was the matter with me?

—S.I.

BREAKING-THROUGH-DENIAL EXERCISE: WHO'S WHO AND WHAT'S WHAT IN YOUR LOVE LIFE

Try this exercise: it will give you a perspective on your love life. Make three headings: Your Rejects—Men Whom You've Rejected;

Men Who've Rejected You or Who Were Unavailable or Unattainable; Crossovers—Men Whom You've Been In Love With and Pursued But When They Began to Love You, You Rejected Them.

Now make a list of all your exes, the major loves, boyfriends, husbands, lovers, sweethearts, fiancés, any man you've ever had a relationship with or obsessed over and put them in the three columns.

When you're finished you'll have a picture of your lovesick life.

The results will probably upset you. This is a thunderbolt to your consciousness but that's the whole point, to get you to become conscious of your patterns. You've been chasing the same hims, recreating the same old lousy relationship time after time, whether you've had five or five hundred "hims." The only variable has been the duration, one night, one month, one year, ten years. You know that expression, "If you've known one, you've known them all"? Well, now you can say that about your relationships. You've spent your life addicted to falling in love with, chasing and having relationships with bad guys while rejecting good guys.

Recovery from lovesickness is not just about giving up one him but about giving up all the hims, the need to be rejected and the inability to accept love.

Men Whom Marilyn Rejected—Her Rejects

Johnny Hyde

Kindness is the strangest thing to find in a man or anybody. Johnny's kindness made him seem the most wonderful human being I'd ever met.

. . . Johnny Hyde's kindness changed the outside world for me but it didn't touch my inner world. I tried hard to love him. He was not only kind, but loyal and wise and devoted. . . . He was the first man I'd ever known who understood me. I'd never met anyone like him before. . . . He made me happy and kept me believing in myself. I didn't run around the studios job hunting anymore. Johnny did that. I stayed home and took dramatic lessons and read books. My heart ached with gratitude and I'd have cut off my head for him. But the love he hoped for wasn't in me. . . . He took me everywhere. People admired him and accepted me as his fiancee. Johnny asked me to marry him. It wouldn't be a long marriage, he said, because he had a heart condition. I never could say yes.

. . . "Tell me again why you won't marry me," he would smile at me.

"Because it wouldn't be fair," I'd answer him. "I don't love you Johnny. That means if I married you I might meet some other man and fall in love with him. I don't want that ever to happen."

... "I'm rich," he said to me. "I have almost a million dollars. If you marry me you'll inherit it when I die."

I had dreamed of money and longed for it but the million dollars Johnny Hyde now offered me meant nothing. ... Joe Schenk argued with me to do it. "What have you got to lose?" he asked.

"Myself!" I said. "I am only going to marry for one reason—love."

... The person I wanted to help most in my life—Johnny Hyde—remained someone for whom I could do almost nothing. He needed something I didn't have—love. And love is something you can't invent, no matter how much you want to.

—MARILYN MONROE

Marilyn's Unavailable, Unattainable or Rejecting Men

Fred Karger

Marilyn Monroe wanted to marry Fred Karger; however, he did not consider her to be an appropriate wife and/or mother material.

There was only one cloud in my paradise, and it kept growing. At first nothing mattered to me except my own love. After a few months I began to look at *his* love. I looked, listened and looked, and I couldn't tell myself more than he told me. I couldn't tell if he really loved me.

He grinned a lot when we were together and kidded me a lot. I knew he liked me and was happy to be with me. But his love did not seem anything like mine. Most of his talk to me was a form of criticism. He criticized my mind. He kept pointing out how little I knew and how unaware of life I was ... I never complained about his criticism, but it hurt me. His cynicism hurt me, too.

... Alone, I would lie awake repeating all he'd said. I'd think, "He can't love me or he wouldn't be so conscious of my faults. How can he love me if I'm such a goof to him?" I didn't mind being a goof if only he loved me. I felt when we were together that I walked in the gutter and he in the sidewalk. All I did was keep looking up to see if there was love in his eyes.

Joe DiMaggio

Marilyn married him January 14, 1954. The following is from the transcript of the divorce, nine months later.

Your honor, my husband would get in moods where he wouldn't speak to me for five to seven days at a time. Sometimes longer . . . I would ask him what was wrong. He wouldn't answer, or he would say, "Stop nagging me" . . . He didn't want to talk to me. He was cold. He was indifferent to me as a human being and as an artist. He didn't want me to have friends of my own. He didn't want me to do my work. He watched television instead of talking to me.

Arthur Miller

When Marilyn first met Miller he was married. She fell in love at first sight, married him six years later. Their marriage ended in divorce after four years.

It started out so beautifully. I was terribly in love. I wanted children, a happy home, a loving husband. It all seemed so simple and possible, like a birthright given to everyone. Now there is nothing left between us.

Whenever they ate together, there was little discussion, only longing looks on Marilyn's part. "I wish he'd say more to me," she confided. "He makes me think I am stupid. Gee, he almost scares me sometimes . . ."

Dr. Greenson [Marilyn's psychiatrist] advised Miller that his wife needed unconditional love and devotion, that anything less was unbearable to her. But the advice was impossible to follow, or too late, or both. Marilyn turned to Yves Montand, for the attention and reward of a new affair, Arthur Miller turned more and more inside himself . . . Dr. Greenson believed Miller genuinely wanted to help Monroe but was not able to control his anger that expressed itself as a rejection of his wife.

John F. Kennedy

I made it with the Prez.

Robert F. Kennedy

Kennedy in 1962 had been married for more than a decade, had seven children and had recently been named America's father of the year.

Bobby Kennedy promised to marry me.

In the heat of an August weekend, as Marilyn's last day began, Marilyn tried unsuccessfully to reach Bobby Kennedy in the San Francisco area where he was staying with Ethel and four of their children.

Dr. Greenson revealed that on that fatal Saturday afternoon, "she expressed considerable dissatisfaction with the fact that here she was, the most beautiful woman in the world and she did not have a date for Saturday night." Greenson said that Marilyn had been expecting to see one of the "extremely important men in government . . . at the highest level . . . whom she'd recently had a sexual relationship with." She had called Dr. Greenson when she learned the meeting was off. Marilyn died, Greenson said, feeling rejected by "some of the people [she] had been close to."

ARE YOU IN A LOVESICK RELATIONSHIP NOW?

This exercise is about the him in your life. It's a series of questions. The answers will help you determine whether you're in a lovesick relationship. If you're not currently seeing or with someone, you can use this questionnaire to see if your past relationship(s) were lovesick.

	YES	NO
Are you unhappy with your relationship?		
Are you jealous of other women in his life?		
Is his behavior inconsistent?		
Does he criticize you constantly?		
Are you afraid to talk to him honestly about your feelings?		
Does he make love to you inconsistently?		
Are you afraid of him?		
Are you afraid that he's going to leave you?		
Is your big daily fear when or if he's going to call, when he's going to come home, when he's going to meet someone else?		
Is he unpredictable?		
Are you constantly depressed, moody and down since you started being with him?		
Do you feel you give and give yet get nothing in return from him?		
Are you hoping and waiting for him to change?		
Does he ever abuse you physically? Mentally?		
Do you think about him all the time?		
Do you feel lonely, uncomfortable and nervous when you're alone?		

Add up your answers, scoring one point for each yes. The higher the number of yes answers you gave, the more lovesick your relationship is.

If you scored zero points and are patting yourself on the back because you think you're in a healthy relationship, you may still be in denial so take this test again—on a bad day, or a week from now. Compare your scores.

TRUTH GAMES

#1—The Carton-of-Milk Exercise

This is another test to determine if he's rejecting. Ask him to do you a favor, something slightly inconvenient to him like pick up a carton of milk on the way home, mail your letter, pick up a paper or a prescription. Ask him to give you a lift that takes him a little out of his way, maybe two or three blocks. If you're afraid to ask him in the first place or would rather walk two blocks in the rain than ask him to give you a lift because you legitimately fear putting him out or his anger, then he's not as nice as you think he is. Be brave, ask. See what happens. Review past incidents where you were afraid to ask.

If he yells at you, lectures you, finds a way out, makes you feel uncomfortable for asking, does the errand but makes you pay for asking, ignores you, he's not as nice as you think he is.

#2—You Know Something For Sure

You know something for sure. By accident you saw him eating lunch with his secretary or you noticed two ticket stubs in the wastebasket. Ask him, "Did you eat lunch with your secretary the other day? Did you go to the theatre the other night?" If you get, "Are you crazy, of course I didn't blah blah blah . . ." then you know that he's not being honest . . . ever.

#3—Communicate A Real Feeling

Create a situation where you're vulnerable. Tell him something you really feel. "I feel sick or afraid of something." See how he reacts. Notice whether he notices it or ignores you.

#4—What Does He Say To You

Notice what he tells you about you. How does he make you feel about you? Does he say; "You're too fat or too skinny, too pushy, too shy, too stupid, too young, too old? If he's always putting you down one way or the other, then he's reinforcing your negative self image, which is very unhealthy for you, and he isn't as nice as you think he is.

WHAT'S SO GOOD ABOUT YOUR RELATIONSHIP?

Make a list of the good things about your relationship. If this is the world's shortest list, if the good things about it are negatives like, "it's better than being alone," or "it's better than starting over" or "it's better than having Jim be with Jane," then your relationship may not be as perfect as you thought.

SOMETHING'S WRONG,
NOW YOU SEE IT, NOW YOU DON'T

Breaking through denial is a process. You get it then lose it. You have a vague sense that something's wrong, but then it disappears. You see how bad it is, then you panic; "how can I leave him? I'm better off the way I am." "I'll be alone forever, I'll never met another man."

If you're in a constant state of anxiety, feeling pain, depressed and obsessed, barely able to get through your day, getting sick all the time, feeling angry most of the time, alienated, have worn out all your friends with your war stories and yourself with your unhappiness, you're in a lovesick relationship.

THE LONG GOODBYE:
BREAKING UP IS SO VERY HARD TO DO

We were in the room one night and he started talking about our future. "I've thought of us getting married," he said, "but I'm afraid it's impossible."

I didn't say anything.

"It would be all right for me," he said, "but I keep thinking of my son. If we were married and anything should happen to me—such as my dropping dead—it would be very bad for him."

"Why?" I asked.

"It wouldn't be right for him to be brought up by a woman like you," he said. "It would be unfair to him."

After he left, I cried all night, not over what he said but over what I had to do. I had to leave him.

The moment I thought it, I realized I'd known it for a long time. That's why I've been sad—and desperate. That's why I had tried to make myself more and more beautiful for him, why I had clung to him as if I were half mad. Because I had known it was ending.

He didn't love me. A man can't love a woman for whom he feels half contempt. He can't love her if his mind is ashamed of her.

When I saw him again the next day I said good-bye to him. He stood staring at me while I told him how I felt. I cried, sobbed, and ended up in his arms.

But a week later I said good-bye again. This time I walked out of his house with my head up. Two days later I was back. There were a third and fourth good-bye. But it was like rushing to the edge of a roof to jump off. I stopped each time and didn't jump, and turned to him and begged him to hold me. It's hard to do something that hurts your heart, especially when it's a new heart and you think that one hurt may kill it.

—MARILYN MONROE (breaking up with Karger)

How can you possibly break up; abandon him and leave your relationship? That's what you ask yourself day in and day out. What will he do without you? He'll go and find someone else, that's what. The same day. What will you do without him? Be alone, lonely, depressed, unhappy and miserable. You'll have to start dating again, go out there to the war zone. Somewhere in the dim recesses of your brain you realize that your relationship is killing you. But you love him. He is you. You're connected. You have so much together. You're between the proverbial rock and hard place. You'll die with him. You'll die without him. He could be so perfect, so wonderful. If only he would change. If only he would listen to you. You know what's right for both of you. But he can't. He won't. He hasn't. You're in failure. Finally you admit it. Then you deny it.

You change from one second to the next, oscillate like the wind. You hate him, then love him. You call everyone and ask them what to do, then don't listen to what they're saying. You withdraw, then get determined. You must do something. What? During this whole time you haven't said a word to him. Your relationship is in trouble but you'll never tell, he'll be the last one to know. You get increasingly anxious, depressed and on edge. You start to smoke, overeat, drink. You can't work. You can't concentrate. You cry at the drop of a hat. Anything sets you off. Then the fear comes. It begins to strangle you, the rope tighter and tighter around your neck: "What will people say? How will I ever find another man? What am I going to do about money? My life is over. How will I survive? Maybe I should try again."

You wake up one morning and do it. Make the break. You get on a plane to anywhere, move back with your parents, sleep on the couch in your girlfriend's living room. You tell him to leave, it's over, this time you really mean it, tears rolling down your cheeks, clenching your fists in pain.

You call to see how he's doing, give him your telephone number. When he doesn't call, you go crazy. You forget why you've broken up and start obsessing about the other woman he's sleeping with. You call him and hang up at four o'clock in the morning, just to check. You're miserable without him, more miserable than you were with him. You beg him to take you back. If he gives you the slightest hint that he misses you, you're on the next plane, or bus, or train or cab, back to him, back to the trenches.

Your second honeymoon lasts for a day or two, a week, a month. Then there's another party and you catch him flirting again. He doesn't call you when he promised. He starts insulting you, calling you names, drinking or asking you for money. You really thought he was going to change this time, but he's the same old b—— he used to be. You leave again.

Your long good-bye can last a year or years for you suffer equally by now, with or without him. The longer it lasts the more lovesick you become. It's time to bite the bullet and do it, leave!

STALLING TACTICS:
MY DOG ATE MY HOMEWORK

You make the decision to leave. It could last only three minutes or three hours before you change your mind. Don't beat yourself up for waffling, indecision, or sheer panic. If it were that easy you would have left him already. Some of the feelings that might come up for you are:

If you leave him someone else will get him. If you leave him you'll lose all your friends. You can't leave him because he needs you. You feel sorry for him. You can't leave him because it's Valentine's Day, Washington's Birthday, Lincoln's Birthday, Easter, The Ides of March, Passover, St. Patrick's Day, Memorial Day, July Fourth, Bastille Day, Labor Day, Columbus Day, Halloween, Thanksgiving, Christmas or New Year's Eve and you don't want to be alone.

Things you'll probably do to avoid leaving him:

Call all your friends and ask their advice about a decision that you've already made hoping that one of them will try and talk you out of it. Binge, act out or go on any spree or binder that you normally do with whatever you're addicted to. Go to an astrologer, have your tea leaves or your palm read. Hopefully they'll tell you how great he is. Go to sleep. Get depressed. Cry a lot. Feel anxious.

After all is said and done you still have to leave him.

MAKING THE BIG DECISION

You feel like you're going to die if you leave him but the reality is that you'll die if you don't! Harsh words? You bet. It's that bad. You may feel like you're going to lose your arm or your leg, that leaving him is like diving from a high board into a teardrop or walking on a high wire without a net. You say to yourself, I can't do it. Yes, you can.

Think of it as if you were going on a diet. How do you do that? You wake up one morning, put on your jeans, but can't get into them. You look into the mirror and say to yourself, you have to go on a diet.

Think of it as if you were going on the wagon. You wake up one morning with a killer hangover, realize you're drinking too much and say to yourself, you're going on the wagon.

Decide that you're going to break your lovesick addiction, the one that's killing you. You're going to leave him. You've been waiting for him to change but he's not going to do it. You're the one who has to make the changes. The way to make this decision is to realize that you deserve a better life and you can have one. You don't know how or when but in order to get there you must leave him. Making the decision to leave him is the first baby step to health, although it's going to feel like a giant step. You're going on the wagon, on a diet with your relationship.

AFFIRMATIONS

Say to yourself as many times as you need to every day:
I deserve a better life and I can have one.
I let go of what's not working in my life.

I have the courage to choose a better life.
I am choosing to change. I am choosing me.
I am going to make it.

FIFTY WAYS TO END A LOVESICK RELATIONSHIP

Making the decision to leave him starts with staying aware, conscious of what's going to happen *to you* if you don't do it. You've got to keep coming back to *you*. What will happen to *you* if you don't leave? What will happen to *you* if you stay? What is he giving *you*? How does he make *you* feel? No matter how uncomfortable this feels, *you* are the reason you're leaving. Repeat that affirmation. "I deserve a better life."

Making this decision is a giant leap of faith. It goes against all your patterns, conditioning and everything you've ever experienced in your life. If you're obsessing about him, whatever the situation, he's not a good guy for *you*. Whether you're married, living together, chasing him, fantasizing, sleeping with him, dating, or being the other woman, you must do it. You don't obsess over "good guys." There's no other way. He's not going to change, you are.

Be prepared, like the boy scouts say. Have a way out. Plan ahead. Put as much preparation and effort into doing this as you did trying to get him in the first place. Whatever works is the best way.

It's best to have an escape route or a physical place to go especially if you're married or living together. If you're dating it doesn't hurt, either.

Call up your mother, girlfriend, sister, brother, father, uncle, aunt, grandmother, grandfather, best friend and let them in on it, ask them if you can stay on their couch for awhile ahead of time. Make a hotel reservation. Buy a plane, train or bus ticket.

I hit bottom on a Sunday. I looked at him, the temptation that I couldn't touch, an eternal rejection slip . . . never, never, never. You can't have me, ever. I was in hell eternally bound to a man who didn't want me, drowning in my own emptiness. Lonely. Rejected. Depressed. Hopeless. Stuck. I wanted to die.

I had to leave him. How could I? He was my life. He was me. We were attached, bonded together by some magical power, from the moment I looked into those sapphires four years ago. I was dying. Caught in between Scylla and Charybdis. I couldn't live with or without him.

Suicide? An asp? Sleeping pills? What difference would it make if I died? He wouldn't notice anyway. Probably be relieved. No, I wasn't the suicide type but I knew I'd die if I didn't leave him.

I tiptoed into the living room and called my friend in Santa Fe. She got my S.O.S, "Come, right now, amiga, hurry." I woke him up. "Goodbye, I'm leaving." I was out the door before he could hypnotize me with the sapphires again.

—S.I.

Have a specific rational reason to leave him, like you're sick, you can't tolerate him having an affair, it's not working for you, he's bad for you, you can't support him anymore. Have a specific irrational reason to leave him like he hates animals, you don't like being a sports widow every weekend.

Decide when you're going to do it: the next time you have a blow up or a fight, the next time he puts you down, the next time he doesn't call you when he said he would, the next time he flirts with someone else, the next time you don't believe his feeble excuse for being late.

Tell him in person, "I'm leaving—it's over." Be brief. Don't discuss it. Call him on the telephone and tell him you're leaving. Again, be brief. Don't discuss it. Don't let him engage you or rope you into a conversation under any circumstances. There's absolutely nothing to discuss. You are leaving. Period!

Call him when you know he's not there and leave a message on his machine. Write him a letter. Serve him with papers. Make a long distance call from your escape place once you're there and safe.

Do whatever you have to do, whatever works. If you're afraid to do it in person, then you're probably right, you can't.

My whole life was centered around him. Sporadically he'd arrange a date at his convenience, late in the afternoon or at the last minute late in the evening so he could stop over and make love. That drove me crazy. It also drove me crazy not knowing when I would see him again. He never said he loved me but our lovemaking was so passionate that I thought we both felt the same way. My friends kept asking me why I was so crazy about him. They said to accept him the way he was and to have fun when I was with him. I couldn't do it. The silence of the non-ringing phone drove me crazy. I was getting more and more depressed, more and more angry. The pain in my chest was unbearable. After about a year I couldn't cope with the situation any longer. I realized that I never saw him on weekends. He kept reassuring me that I was the only one in his life but it didn't feel right to me.

I called his summer house the day he was supposed to go to Europe just to hear his voice on the recording. I was shocked to hear a woman's voice saying, "Darling it's for you." Oh, God, I'll never forget that pain. I was so jealous and so much in pain that it was even hard to get angry at him . . . I wanted him so badly anyway. But I knew it was sick. I had to get away from him.

I planned it. I put my answering machine on and as I expected he started calling the moment he supposedly came back from his trip. For the first time ever I didn't call him back. He called and called and called and finally, for the first time, he called me at work. I gave him the line I'd practiced for hours. "Don't call me anymore. It is over." I hung up. Then he became compulsive about calling me and phoned ten to fifteen times a day. I never spoke to him. It was shocking when I finally realized that the only way to get his attention was to reject him.

—JOAN

YOU HAVEN'T SEEN THE LAST OF HIM

Finally I left him, and two days passed and I was still away. I sat in my room watching myself.

"Stick it out another day," I'd say. "The hurt's getting less already."

It wasn't, but I stuck it out a third and fourth day. Then he came after me. He knocked on my door. I walked to the door and leaned against it.

"It's me," he said.

"I know."

"Please let me in," he said.

I didn't answer. He started banging on the door. When I heard him banging, I knew I was through with my love affair. I knew I was over it. The pain was still there but it would go away.

"Please," he kept saying, "I want to talk to you."

"I don't want to see you," I said. "Please go away."

He raised his voice and banged harder.

"But you're mine," he cried at me. "You can't leave me out here."

The neighbors opened their doors. One of them yelled she'd call the police if he didn't quit making a disturbance.

He went away.

—MARILYN MONROE (final goodbye to Karger)

Expect him to try and come back and pull you back into his net or web. He'll promise to reform or change, say anything he needs to say to get back into your good graces and relationship again. This is a very dangerous moment. Watch out! You'll say to yourself, he really loves me after all, look how much he needs me, he's so miserable without me. You'll confuse his addiction to you with love. Make no mistake, it's not. The tragedy is that your rejection turns him on, not your love! Give him a few hours or days and he'll be back being his good old bad self and you'll get stuck with your good old bad relationship again.

IF AT FIRST YOU DON'T SUCCEED TRY, TRY AGAIN

Don't be hard on yourself if you don't or can't break up or leave him the first, second, third or even fourth time. Just do the best you can on your own timetable. Don't beat yourself up if you leave him then beg him to forgive you, you made a mistake, would he please come back. It's part of this pattern. You're breaking your addiction to someone. It takes courage to leave a "him." Pat yourself on the back for even trying. Don't get down on yourself for failing. Sooner or later you're going to be able to do it and stay away.

NO, YOU CAN'T TAKE HIM BACK: NINE HE-CAN'T-COME-HOME-AGAIN TOUGH RULES

1. You can't see him once you've left him.
2. You can't talk to him.
3. Don't call him. Put a note on your phone to yourself for bad moments, "Don't call John on pain of death."
4. If he calls you tell him "Please don't call me," and mean it.
5. Write down the reasons that you left him, all the bad stuff, since for sure you're going to forget.
6. Don't try and get in touch with him.
7. Stay away from his friends, family and business associates.
8. If you have business or family dealings together make a deal that you'll talk through another party.
9. Don't go any place that's his territory, where you know you'll bump into him, from a restaurant to the gym to a party given by mutual friends.

You have to be the tough one now.
Note: If you're truly so upset you can't function seek outside help.

CHAPTER 6

Après He

Breaking up is going to be hard. Just as bad as if you were breaking your addiction to alcohol or drugs, except you're breaking your addiction to a person who's no good for you.

Giving him up is going to feel like the worst thing that ever happened to you in your whole life. Giving him up is going to be the best thing that has ever happened to you in your whole life.

Keep coming back to this no matter what happens. This is the only way, the only road to recovery no matter how bad you feel, how difficult it is to break your addiction to him. The amount of pain you're going to feel is no indication of how much you love him but rather how much you've been addicted to him.

You can expect some time-honored, well-documented stages as you go through the separation from your lovesick relationship.

The first stage is called Shock/Denial.
The second stage is called Depression/Anger.
The third stage is Understanding.
The fourth stage is Acceptance of the Loss.

In order to complete the experience of loss, to acccept it, no matter how tragic it may feel, you must go through each of these stages in order to come out the other side. There are no ifs, ands or buts about this, although there are many variations of how you may go through these stages. You may have a brief experience with one and a prolonged experience with another, feel very intense about one and not the others. You'll slide back and forth between stages at random. There's no set course, no right or wrong way to do this, no right or wrong time. Each stage is natural and necessary. You need to go through them all. The only way out is to go through it. You're going to make it.

MORE AFFIRMATIONS, APHORISMS,
A HUG AND A PAT ON THE BACK

It's never too late to make a change, the longer you wait, the more time wasted.

If he's going to be the same five or ten years from now, do you still want to be with him?

What you see is what you get so stop hanging on to the hope that you can change him; you can't.

If he says, "I don't want to be tied down," "I'm not ready for a relationship," "I don't want to divorce my wife," believe him.

Your obsession with "him" is not enough to make your relationship work.

Loving is healthy but being in love with someone who doesn't love you back isn't.

You deserve a pat on the back and a hug. You've picked up this book and stayed with it so far. It means: You're committed to your recovery and you're keeping the ten commitments. You're choosing to let go of your addiction to "his" rejection or you're choosing to let go of "him." You're willing to change. You're choosing to change. You're letting go of self-hate and are on your way to self-love.

Here's a pat on the back, a hug. You deserve it! Keep up the good work.

STAGE 1: SHOCK/DENIAL,
DEAF, NUMB AND BLIND

"I Can't Believe He's Gone, I Don't Believe It's Over"

We spent three weeks in limbo packing up our lives together into separate cartons tied up with unbreakable cord. Then all of a sudden it was the day. He was moving to a friend's place, I was leaving town to put thousands of miles between us. I told him on the street as we waited for a taxi, tears running down my face, "I love you. I love you. I want you. I can't live without you. This is a mistake. We belong together. I'll change. I'll make it up to you. I'll never meet anyone like you again. I can't live without you."

"Goodbye. You're going to miss your plane." He slammed the taxi door closed and that was it.

—S.I.

The pain will be extreme. All you'll be able to think of and obsess over is "him." His reactions. His feelings. You may feel like dying. You'll repeat to yourself, "I can't believe he's gone," "I can't believe it's over" and for those moments you really won't believe he's gone or that it's over. You're in shock. You may also say, "I can't live without him" or "I'd rather die than live without him." You may also be feeling numbness, disorientation, feeling off-center. You'll probably forget why you were really separating from "him" in the first place. This is a kind of temporary memory loss that happens when you're in shock. You'll fear that you're going to be alone forever, while he, of course, will find someone else in three seconds. You'll feel down and depressed, cry a lot, may even feel a pain in your chest. You may feel immobilized. You may want to sleep a lot or not be able to sleep at all, suffer insomnia. You may lose your appetite or overeat. You'll feel empty. The black hole will yawn and gape. In general you'll feel as if you've lost a part of yourself, that something has been wrenched from you. This can last for a day or a month, but rarely longer.

It helps to admit to yourself that you're hurting, that being without him is going to be difficult, *but* remember that no matter how hard you tried your relationship did not work. Accept that failure. Congratulate yourself if you left him and have a good cry. Feel all the pain if he left you. Although you may feel frightened by the pain, the best thing to do is be with it. Don't deny it or try and cover it up by acting out, or running away from it. You're in the middle of your own Greek tragedy so play it for all it's worth. You're entitled. The pain is not bottomless or endless, nature is on your side and there will come a time when it's over, the healing will happen; it's happening right now. The end will come. After all, by giving up what did not work for *you*, you are choosing *you* over "*him*"!

I made a decision to give Johnny up just for two weeks so that I could get a sense of what it might feel like to really separate. I had no idea how hard it was going to be, how much pain I was going to suffer. The first weekend was horrible. I felt like I was dying. I had terrible waves of fear about being totally alone. I cried for hours. I wrote and wrote in my diary about how lonely and terrible and miserable I felt and how angry I was at Johnny for not giving me what I wanted. That helped. After those two nightmare weeks I discovered that somehow or other I had survived and that I could deal with the crisis of giving him up. I also realized that the choice between giving him up or remaining in my bad relationship meant that I was choosing between anxiety (being alone) and depression (being with him). Depression meant death. I could deal with anxiety.

I kept repeating to myself, "I am a survivor. I am going to make it. I am going to be strong enough to give Johnny up. I claim my birthright to happiness and love. I'm letting go of my need for rejection. I choose love."

I got back with him after those two weeks. After two more attempts I finally went through with leaving him for keeps.

—PEGGY

SOME AFFIRMATIONS TO SAY TO YOURSELF:

It's over. I'm ready and available for something better in my life.
I am a worthwhile lovable person.
I am willing to change.
I am willing to heal and be healed.
God loves me. My friends love me. I love me.
Life works for the better.

HOW TO STOP OBSESSING AND REMOVE THE TRIGGERS: BURN HIS LETTERS, TOSS HIS PICTURES, GIVE AWAY HIS CLOTHES

Now that you've left him or he's left you, you're going to start obsessing over him. These obsessive thoughts are withdrawal symptoms while you get off him.

No matter what happens, how low you get, how depressed you feel, remember you're the one in charge, you made the decision to leave (if he did so much the better), this is for your own good even if for the moment it may feel bad.

In order to make it through this period you have to remove the triggers, the things that make you think about him or remind you of him.

In a memorable scene from "An Unmarried Woman," Jill Clayburgh, who's husband has left her for another woman, tears up, breaks every picture of him, then tosses all his belongings out the window. She's getting rid of all the triggers.

Looking at his side of the bed, having breakfast without him but with his favorite coffee can trigger your yearning for him. Just staying in a place full of memories, if you've lived there together, can also be loaded with triggers, bring on more obsessing about being with him. Make some changes. Do anything you can to change your old routine that involved "we" and start a new one that centers around the most important person in the world, you!

CHANGING PLACES

If you can leave your home, get away while the getting is good. If you can afford to sublet, sell or rent your place, do it and move to a new one. If you can't, then redecorate and clean out your old one, buy new sheets, new pillows, new bedding for sure!

Don't go places where the two of you went as a "we" together. Find new ones. That means restaurants, hangouts, bars. Avoid memory lanes at all cost because places where you spent time together trigger bad memories.

Don't walk, drive, take a bus or cab any place that you know he's going to be, might be or ever has been.

Take a trip to a place that you've never been to before or always wanted to see. Under no circumstances return to a place where you've been together, especially where you've been on your honeymoon. You'll miss him more. Try a place where you can keep busy, a spa or Club Med. Travel to a place that's challenging, where you don't know the language. Take a photographic safari. Try something adventurous like mountain climbing, or athletic like cross-country skiing. Learn a new sport. Go to tennis camp. Anything new will take your mind off your old problem.

If you're away and obsessing about him, don't write him long letters, send him the "Wish you were here" post card, or shop for his gift.

A FEW OF HIS FAVORITE THINGS

Gather up everything that reminds you of your ex, object by object, memento by memento, broken dream by broken dream and burn them, toss them or give them away. That means records, tapes, the photograph of the two of you on your piano and every other picture, they're the worst offenders.

You may want to have a good riddance to bad rubbish ceremony. "I herewith get rid of you and all your baggage. I am free of you. I am free to be me, to have a life without you, to have my own life."

HUNG UP ON HANGING UP

The telephone, as we already know, is the worst problem, because you can't tear it off the wall and toss it out the window. Dialing him late at night just to hear the sound of his voice one more time and then hanging up is the oldest trick in the world. The problem is that since it's the oldest trick in the world he'll know it's you. All you've done is torture yourself with the fact that he knows it's you or worry if there's someone else sleeping next to him. The small triumph of hearing his voice one more time or waking him up in the middle of the night because you know he's a bad sleeper and won't be able to get back to sleep is meager beside the shame. Try putting a note up on your phone, DON'T CALL HIM ON PAIN OF DEATH. Make a deal with your buddy that every time you get the urge to call him you'll call her no matter what time of night or day.

AFFIRMATIONS

I can live without him better than with him.
I'm a winner. I'm going to win.
My life gets better every day.

STAGE 2: FROM MAD TO SAD

"I Didn't Know Who To Kill First, Him Or Me"

The second stage is a roller coaster ride of extreme mood swings as you speed along at one hundred miles an hour between depression and anger. You won't be able to decide whether you want to kill him or you. You'll shift from black depression, inertia, feeling sorry for yourself, wanting to sleep your life away, even contemplating suicide, to anger directed at him, the new her if there is one (there usually is), real or imaginary, to you and life in general.

You'll feel extraordinarily vulnerable. You'll cry suddenly for no apparent reason, go to sleep in the middle of the day, not be able to sleep in the middle of the night, feel irritable and short-tempered, snap at friends, co-workers, or anyone who's trying to be nice to you, blow up at the poor unsuspecting soul who just happened to wander into your path at the wrong time. Remember that this is only a stage and it will pass.

THE UNDERCOVER STORY

No more Michael. No more relationship. No more dinners with him, breakfasts with him, sleeping with him, God, did I love to sleep with him. He was gone. It was over. I went to sleep, laid out for days. It wasn't worth it to get up because I had nothing to get up for, I had nothing to do, no one to think about and when I thought about Michael I wanted to cry. I was totally alone in the world, no one knew I was alive.

I began to fantasize about sex with him. I started to call him up on the phone, broke out into a cold sweat and hung up when I heard his voice. I began to cry, called my buddy instead, "Molly please help me cut off my fingers so that I can't press my touchtone. I'm dying to have sex with Michael. Do you think he'd consider having a sex-only relationship? After all he kept telling me how great I was in bed. What do you think?"

"I think you're right. You should cut off your fingers. Are you kidding? a sex-only relationship with him? That ——? You left him, remember? He's not good for you, remember? Okay, let's make a compromise. You don't have to cut off your fingers but you do have to cut off your nails. Get it? Don't call him. He doesn't want to hear from you and you don't want to talk to that dirty, rotten ——."

"You're right, he is a dirty, rotten ——. Thanks, Molly. I'm going back to sleep now. I'm exhausted. Oh, Molly, could you call me later so I can remember what it sounds like when the telephone rings?"

—BETH

You're going to want to get your security blanket out, get into bed and stay there undercover, sleep your life away. You're depressed. It takes too much energy to get up and face the world and why bother, it's come to an end anyway. Don't beat yourself up if you feel like hibernating. This is only a stage of loss. Other people feel the same way. Expect it. Keep in touch with your buddy and your network. Ask them to check in with you. Make regular phone dates with them and keep them. That's all you have to do and you can do it.

ANTILONELINESS INSURANCE PLANS

> Sundays were the loneliest. You couldn't look for a job on Sundays or pretend you were shopping in stores. All you could do was walk as if you were going someplace.
>
> —MARILYN MONROE

Watch out for sunset, evening, for the night. As the sun goes down, depression will set in. You can handle it as long as you plan ahead. Plan to be with someone at sundown. Keep busy. Buy an appointment book and fill it up with dates. Have a movie date. Go out for dinner. Go to a meeting. Cook dinner for a friend. Go to a support group. Take a class. Exercise. Go to a concert. Do volunteer work. Keep moving, plan ahead, fill your book up with two weeks of wall-to-wall dates so you're covered.

There's nothing worse than a case of the lonelies on the weekend. Don't fall into the "everyone in the whole world has something to do on Saturday night, except you" trap. Do not under any circumstances leave yourself high and dry on the weekend. Plan ahead. Buy an organizer. Start clipping interesting things to do, places to go, new restaurants, art openings, films, anything that's happening, and put it in the book so that when the weekend starts to yawn empty on Monday, you can plan something interesting to do from Friday to Sunday.

LITTLE VICTORIES

> What helped me to fight my depression was my "Broken Heart Recovery Agenda Plan." It meant that every day I would set up a goal for myself. Something very small but necessary. Then I would make sure to complete it. In the beginning, just making a phone call a day felt like a real struggle but I would keep to my plan, forcing myself to get at least one thing done. Filing insurance forms or paying bills would take me a week, but I did it. Having a plan of action to keep to helped me get through.
>
> —ALICE

In this stage you may be having trouble keeping up with your life as you suffer from inertia. Doing simple things like bills, returning phone calls, correspondence, dry cleaning, house cleaning, doing the laundry, even shopping for food may seem like climbing Mount Everest. Alice's Broken Heart Recovery Agenda Plan works. Call it the Winner's Plan, or Yes, I Can Do It. Create a small daily goal for yourself, something that you can really get done. It can be just not calling him. Buy yourself some gold stars and give yourself one, every time you get something done like not calling him. Every little victory will make you feel like you've climbed Mount Everest.

HIDDEN ANGER

You may not be aware that you're angry. You may have trouble identifying your feelings because they're frozen, buried, hidden. Symptoms that signal the presence of hidden anger are: prolonged depression, being accident-prone, irritability, erratic sleep patterns, constant self-flagellation.

If you can't feel your anger here are some ways to get in touch with it.

GET-ANGRY EXERCISE: THE CRIME SHEET

List all the reasons why he's no good, lousy, rotten, terrible, mean. Once you start you'll find plenty of examples of the thoughtless things he did to you: He left you. He flirted with other women. He always said mean things to you. He was a liar. He was never there for you. He hit you. He charged a gift for another woman on your charge account. You waited hours by the telephone for calls that never came.

Every time you slip into a romantic thought about him say to yourself, "Yes, but . . ." and either bring out the list or write in new entries.

GET-ANGRY EXERCISE:
YOUR FRIENDS REMEMBER

If you catch yourself in a wave of nostalgia and you feel like you're going under again, call up your friends and ask them to remind you of all the horrible things you've told them about "him." The time he didn't show up until the next day, etc.

GET-ANGRY EXERCISE: THE LETTER

Write him a good-bye letter and don't send it. It's a good way to put a period at the end of the sentence (no pun intended).

VISUALIZATION:
UNDER THE VOLCANO, FIREWORKS!

This visualization was created to allow you to release your hidden anger, blow your top. Do this whenever you need to vent your anger. Allow yourself to really feel it and get into it. Let yourself go.

Light a candle to invoke Pele, Goddess of the Volcano. Lie down and make yourself comfortable, begin to breathe slowly. Glide into your Temple of Love. Beyond the columns, the green hillside flows down to the sparkling blue sea. Turn your attention to the smoldering volcanic peak rising up in the distance. As you breathe in fiery red flames, exhale fiery breath, imagine that you are One with the volcano. Take some time to breathe the flames from the top of your head all the way down to your toes. Exhale fiery breath.

Imagine the man who fills you with rage and fury. See him clearly before you as you remember how he lied to you, hurt you, rejected you. Feel those feelings as you breathe the fire through your body. It's safe to feel the molten anger now, to feel the hurt and the pain, the broken dreams, disappointments, dashed hopes, disillusions. Breathe into it. Allow sounds of fury to come from deep within, growl and rage. See and feel the lava in your belly filled with pulsing tension. You are Pele, the Goddess of the Volcano. You are powerful! You feel the rage of a woman scorned by a man who does not love or see how beautiful you really are. Breathe the fire in more rapidly now. Imagine it is gathering force in your lava belly. Remember how he treated you. Let those feelings fan the flames within. You are gathering rage, passion, anger for a grand volcanic eruption.

When you have gathered the force of fury, unleash it in a giant exhalation. Let the inferno blaze and burst upwards. Flames and lava spew forth from the top of your head, the top of the volcano. Pele speaks as you roar with rage, ignite in anger. It is magnificent. The molten fire explodes into the night, fireworks light up the black sky. You are magnificent. Those flames purify your whole being. Every cell burns brighter.

When you are ready, invoke healing rain, tears. Allow yourself to cry. Feel the healing tears as clouds of ash drift down upon the mountainside. Healing rain and ash begin to make the soil fertile. The volcano subsides as you relax your whole body. Feel the relief as a rainbow appears. Breathe in the rainbow. The colors restore balance and peace within you. You are whole and strong, stronger than you've ever been. You are a phoenix rising from the ashes.

When you are ready, open your eyes.

RED FLAG WARNING

This stage is very dangerous. Watch it! You may have the urge to get drunk, stoned, overeat or have sex, your usual, time-honored escapes. Anything to ease the pain. You may even develop a new one. Beware. We call this the Changing Seats on the Titanic Syndrome. (We'll talk about this more, later.) The bottom line is that all of these escapes add more guilt and upset and you still hit the bottom.

STAGE 3: I UNDERSTAND

"It Wouldn't Have Worked If I Had Jane Fonda's Body"

As the pain of your loss subsides you'll have a strong need to make sense of what's happened to you, get things straight, understand. You'll start to analyze what went wrong and when you do you'll probably blame yourself for it then slip right back into denial that there was anything wrong with him in the first place. It was your fault. You'll say to yourself, "What happened? How could I have been so stupid? Where did I go wrong? If only I had been fatter/thinner/richer/poorer/older/younger we would still be together." Beware of self-blame. Stay

away from self-destructive anger directed at your favorite target, you!
If you find yourself starting on the "if onlies" remind yourself that your
relationship would not have worked anyway.

EXERCISE: I UNDERSTAND #1

If you begin to slip back into denial look at your Crime Sheet.

If you find yourself on a crash diet because he would have loved you
if you weren't so fat and when you're thin it's going to work, say to
yourself, "It wouldn't work if I did aerobics twice a day and had Jane
Fonda's body! Keep repeating that to yourself. Substitute Raquel
Welch or Cher.

EXERCISE: I UNDERSTAND #2

The answers to these questions are a profile of your relationship:

1. How did the relationship start? Who was the pursuer?
2. Who seemed to control when and where you would get together?
3. What was the emotional tone of the relationship for you? Loving?
   Angry? Depressed? Romantic? Desperate? Painful? (Did you
   feel rejected or loved most of the time?)
4. Did you get your emotional needs satisfied?
5. What was the sexual relationship like? Were you happy with it?
   Unhappy? Angry? Did you feel abused? Did he satisfy you?
6. How did the relationship end? Who ended it? Why? What were
   the feelings of each of you about its ending?
7. In the cost/benefit analysis, was what you got out of the relationship worth the price?

If you answer honestly, you'll be able to see a clear picture of what your
relationship wasn't rather than staying in denial about what it was.

THE LAST DITCH ATTEMPT, A SLIP

You've done everything right, you're well on your way to recovery and
you wake up one morning, lose it, slip and try and get back with him,
all in the twinkling of an eye. Beware. The reason you'll lose it is that

it's very difficult to give up your relationship, the dream, even though it's been a nightmare. You'll say to yourself everything will be wonderful when I go back and life will be beautiful again. It won't. You're going to try and mess yourself up because feeling all right is so scary, so new. Don't do it.

If you find yourself on the verge of a slip, say to yourself:

There's no ray of hope. The relationship will never work. He is not the last man on earth. I'm doing fine without him. It's true, you are.

It happened nearly a year after my traumatic break up with Andrew. I was doing very well, when I got a telephone call from my friend in San Francisco telling me that Andrew was in New York with his new girlfriend. In a split second I lost it. I put down the receiver and my whole body started to shake. I grabbed a telephone book and began to call all the hotels in New York City determined to find out where he was registered and with whom. After calling at least fifteen hotels I finally got the courage to call the Plaza which used to be "our hotel," hoping that he wouldn't take her to our sacred place. Much to my surprise he was registered there. I'll never forget that endless ringing hoping to hear his voice. He was out. My crazy scenario was born.

I spent the next five hours taking everything out of my closets trying to figure out how he would like me to look. My plan was that I would get dressed to kill and show up unexpectedly passing through the lobby of his hotel. I would make sure to be there as he walked in. He would see me looking so gorgeous that he would leave her for me.

I went to the beauty parlor and invested five hundred dollars in a makeover session, new makeup, a new hairstyle, a perm, a set of artificial nails, a new me. With my roommate's fox draped over my shoulder (he loved fur), my new outfit, hairdo, silky legs and a dramatic mysterious smile I practiced in the mirror, I left for the lobby of the Plaza. I jumped into a taxi, fighting rain, traffic and my own compulsion to get him back.

When I got there I discovered that he had checked out two hours before. I just couldn't believe it. I went to the bathroom in order to calm down. My heart was racing. My hands were shaking. I looked at myself in the mirror. I couldn't believe how I looked. I didn't look like me at all. I looked horrible. All of a sudden I started to laugh. I had an overwhelming sense of gratitude for not meeting him there. I thanked God. I realized how powerful my illness was; if I didn't watch it, it could take over and change the way I would think, feel and act. Trying to see him again to prove how much he was missing by being with her and not me would have been a Pyrrhic victory. I would have lost far more than I gained. I'm much better off without him. I'm doing fine with me.

—JEAN

STAGE 4: I ACCEPT THAT HE'S GONE

"Yes, I Can Go It Alone. It's Better Without Him."

When you can finally say without horrible pain, he is no longer in my life, I can go forward and move on without him, you're on your way to full-scale recovery and in the last stage of loss. You'll begin to feel stronger and more independent. You're able to go back to your daily routines. You can start to rebuild your life on your own. Accept that you'll have happy days as well as some sad ones. Rebuilding is like learning to walk again after having broken a leg. You've mended but you need to build your strength. You need to stay away from him.

At this stage you'll be able to see what you've gained and what you've lost because the relationship will finally be in perspective.

EXERCISE: WHAT I'VE LOST, WHAT I'VE GAINED

Make two columns. What I've Lost is one, What I've Gained is the other. List all the things you've lost now that you're no longer with him and all the things you've gained.

YOUR FRIENDS OR HIS

When you separate from someone you've been with for a significant amount of time, it's inevitable that besides splitting up your possessions, you have to deal with whether your friends are going to be your friends or his. Don't expect to keep all of your friends. Not all of them will remain faithful to you. Don't take this personally, another put-down, another it's-your-fault-they-don't-love-you routine. Not every-one of your friends is going to be on your side or stay with you. They can't. Some of them may just feel that you're wrong or that they like him more. Some of them may have been his friends long before he met you. You've been in the same situation yourself. It's awkward, for everyone.

Don't go after the ones who can't be there for you. You'll be able to tell. They won't return your phone calls or will be critical of you.

Choose not to see them! Choose only the friends who are going to be
loyal to you and support you. If you feel awkward about being with
friends who knew you as a "we" then don't be friends with them and
don't beat yourself up for losing them. Choose not to see them. Let
them go.

Call up any old friends who you haven't seen because of him. Call up
any exes that you've become friends with. Call up the friend you've
been meaning to call for ages but just haven't gotten around to calling.
Get a new telephone book and start over. Take your old telephone book
and make a list of all the people you'd like to see at the same time
eliminating anyone who won't be there for you. Make new friends.
Start your life over without him.

VISUALIZATION: THE HEAD BALLOON

This visualization has been created to help you stop obsessing about
him, holding onto your memories. And move on with your life. Use
this as often as you like to with women, too.

Light your candle and dedicate this ceremony to Diana the Moon
Goddess. Close your eyes and start breathing slowly. Go through the
columns to your Temple of Love. It is night. There's a full moon.
Imagine that you are breathing in the glow of silver stars and breathing
out red-hot air: anger, pain, hurt, any negative feelings about him. As
you breathe in silver starlight and moonlight, let each breath heal your
wounds. As you exhale red-hot air, imagine that every breath begins to
fill up a balloon. On the balloon is a picture of him. As you breathe in
starlight and out red-hot air, imagine that the balloon gets bigger and
bigger, his head gets bigger and bigger. Go through your body, from
your head to your toes, breathing in starlight, full moonlight, breathing out red-hot air as you release the rage, all the hurts, all the painful
memories. Now see that this enormous balloon, his inflated head, is
tied around your finger by a red ribbon. All his baggage, painful
memories, despair, depression, obsession are in the balloon ready for
you to release. When you release it, he'll be gone forever. Breathe in
silver starlight and moonlight. Breathe out the last of the anger. Untie
the ribbon, hold it in your hand. Ask for assistance from the Universe
to release him. When you feel ready say, "I release you from my
consciousness. I release you from my body. I release you from my
spirit and I release you from my mind. I let you go. Thank you for the

lessons." Let the balloon go. Watch it go into the Universe and as it gets smaller and smaller say, "Good-bye, adios. Up, up and away." Watch it disappear. When it's gone, breathe in silver starlight and breathe out moonlight. Feel the peace.

When you're ready, open your eyes.

"You Deserve a Medal, You Have the Chest to Put It On"

As you proceed without him, your thinking will get sharper, your concentration will increase, you'll start to feel better about you. You'll wake up one morning and feel happy. You've made it through the war. You deserve a medal for courage, bravery, for keeping your commitment to your self. Congratulations!

Take a few moments out to remember what you've learned in this process: You can survive on your own. Being without him is much less painful than being with him. You don't need him. You are healing from your hurt. You are a whole and complete being without him. You can enjoy your life again. You've taken responsibility for the need to change your life. First you recognized that your lovesick relationship was not working for you, now you've done something about it by leaving him, no matter how hard it was. Congratulations for choosing you over him, it's the first giant step in your recovery. Now you're ready to proceed along recovery road with a lot less baggage to hamper your progress.

AFFIRMATIONS FOR A NEW LIFE

The past is over.
My life will go on in a healthier way.
I'm open and receptive to a new way of living away from pain, struggle, rejection, depression, unhappiness and unhealthiness.
I'm ready for a new life.
My being is complete.
I am happy in my relationship with me.

CHAPTER 7

Oops! A Slip

PYRRHIC VICTORIES: BACK DOWN TO THE LOWER DEPTHS

Recovery, especially in the beginning, is a very precarious state. At any stage of your recovery you may slip and try to get back together with him against all rationality. We call this a slip because it's slipping back into your old lovesick patterns. A slip is a Pyrrhic victory, for whatever you do was not worth the price.

When you have a slip it feels like you've jumped off the top of the Empire State building and hit the bottom at full force. That bad! So bad you can't believe it. You were doing so well and then you blew it, how can you face yourself. A slip hurts so much. That's why having a slip feels like a shock and you start to shake from it. The slip is snapping you out of your fantasy trip, waking you up.

WHAT IS A SLIP?

Slips are allergic reactions to old feelings, returns to addictive behavior. Slips are about slipping back into denial, forgetting how bad it was to have him in your life. A slip is about losing you, losing control and giving it back to him. Recovery means gaining control of your life. A slip is a reminder from the Universe, designed to put you back on your healing path. It shows you what it was like when you were with him being in the House of Pain twenty-four hours every day. It reminds you how destructive his presence in your life was, when you fixated only on him, totally neglecting you.

Slips are an important part of your healing because they allow you to

101

see your addiction with all its danger, in all of its ugliness. Slips teach you that you do indeed have the power to snap out of it and come back to reality. The reality is that you can't be with him.

When you're in constant pain, adding one more painful event doesn't make that big a difference. When you're in recovery and your body, mind and spirit have started to heal, to feel different, any strong pain from a slip is going to be experienced as a major violation of your functioning, a loud warning signal that something is off, wrong, something is not agreeing with you. If you feel that way pay attention to it. Listen to your body, your mind, your spirit. What are they telling you?

A slip is a reminder of the destructive power of your lovesickness. A slip is there to warn you how easily you can get thrown off balance and get sucked back into self-destructiveness if you're not careful. A slip reinforces why you and your recovery have to be the number one priority in your life. A slip is a major growth opportunity.

Slips call for your undivided attention. They are designed to make you humble. A slip says this is why you have to protect yourself against him. This is why you can't go back with him. This is why you have to stay conscious. This is why you need to heal.

A slip is the only way to keep you in line by showing you the bottom line, the naked truth of your illness and the choice between him (death) and you (life). You don't have any other choice. You can't have both. Ultimately slips are cosmically designed to give you a taste of what will happen to you if you go back and how much you've gained by leaving.

I was in Boston and everything was arranged for me to see my family for Thanksgiving at six. I called my answering machine in New York. My ex, Edward, had called. I'd been working on giving him up for a year, done everything in my power to cut myself off from him including a move back to Boston. I told myself it was to get a better job but it really was to make sure I didn't bump into him on purpose on the street. I called my machine back to double check . . . to make sure I wasn't dreaming, but no, it was true. My body started to shake when I heard that tone in his voice. I knew I'd lost it. I called him back right away.

He asked me how I was doing. I bragged and said I was doing fantastically and everything was great. I told him I was making a lot of money. He said he was broke and since I was doing so well, asked with "that voice that I always give into and he knows it," if I could give him some cash because he needed to go to Atlantic City. He added that he really wanted me to be with him. All of a sudden seeing him was the most important thing in the world. Nothing else mattered. I could see him in my mind . . . I needed to touch him so badly, I wanted to feel him holding me. I didn't want to tell him that my New York City number was a scam, that for the past year I'd been living in Boston (not across the street from him any more), that I was there now, that my parents were expecting me for dinner. I told him I'd meet him at Atlantic City at ten o'clock. I didn't tell him I was broke. I called my mother and made a stupid excuse why I couldn't come. She got furious. Then I started calling all my friends, desperate to borrow money to support his addiction, gambling, my addiction him and my lie. One of my friends came through. I rushed madly to Atlantic City driven by the demons of reawakened hope. Maybe he had changed. Maybe he'd left his new girlfriend. Maybe he'd see after not seeing me for a year how wonderful I was. Maybe. Maybe. Maybe.

Ten minutes after I met Edward at the casino he made his final bet and lost all the cash I'd borrowed. Twenty minutes later we were in a hotel room I was paying for, totally broke, without even five dollars to take a cab to the airport. He was cold, distant, withdrawn, staring at a baseball game on T.V.

I tried to say something but everything I said only made him angrier. First he told me how much he hated to be bothered by me. Then he told me how gross I looked, how much weight I'd gained. I felt the same old horror. My body started shaking again and I felt like the most disgusting person in the whole world. I didn't even know if I was going to make it through the night. He ignored me totally and then said I was so disgusting that he didn't even want to get into the same bed with me, I should sleep on the couch, which I did. By two o'clock he was asleep in the bed and I was in pain so strong that I had to leave the room. Everything hurt.

I wandered around The Trop World in despair. I saw a man eyeing me at the bar. He asked me if I wanted to have a drink, said I looked lonely. I prostituted myself with him for two hundred dollars. I'd have to make the rest back another way. Edward didn't even notice I was gone.

When I finally got home the next day I knew I was in serious trouble. I couldn't call my family because they'd never talk to me again if they knew the truth. I called my friend Sarah. I told her everything, the shame, the guilt, the pain! She said that I'd had a slip but it was only a slip, not the end of the world. She told me about a slip she'd made, too. She was reassuring. I felt better.

It took me about two weeks to get over it, to come back to myself. What I learned from that slip is that seeing him is like taking poison. He makes me sick. Crazy. In a split second I revert back to old feelings and patterns that terrify me. It's like being in a nightmare in the middle of the day. I hate the person I become. I can't afford to feel that way, I'm working too hard on liking me.

—NANCY

TRIGGERS

There are as many different kinds of reasons as there are kinds of slips. Here are the most common causes, the things or thoughts or feelings that trigger slips:

Exhaustion: If you allow yourself to get overtired or in poor health you increase the danger of a slip because you don't think straight and can more easily give into needy thoughts about him. If you feel this coming on sleep on it!

Weight gain: Whether you gain an ounce, a pound, five, ten or fifteen pounds, a physical change that you experience for the worse, it has the power to increase your self-hatred and precipitate a slip. It's the "I'm fat, what's the difference if I call him or eat more" blues. Focus back on you and positive action, losing the weight.

Getting high: Calling him when you're high, whether on mood-altering substances or alcohol, is one of the easiest and most frequent ways to promote a slip. It gives you fake courage, that second wind to do all the wrong stuff that you know you shouldn't do. We call this the Forbidden Fruit Fantasy Slip, "I'll call him even though I know I shouldn't and then when I see him everything will be *so* wonderful again." Call your network or your buddy, tell yourself not to do anything while you're stoned or high. No, I shouldn't call. Repeat that fifty times. You'll remember why tomorrow.

Gossip: You heard it on the grapevine from one of your friends about how he's doing or the "her" in his life. Once you start to compare his new girlfriend to you, or think that he's doing fine or better without you, you let jealousy and insecurity in the door. If one of your friends starts to tell you, thank them but say you're not interested and if they're really a friend they'll keep the information to themselves.

Impatience: You get fed up with all the discipline and hard work of recovery. Why aren't things happening faster? You become impatient with your snail's progress, slip into negativity and the I'm-never-going-to-recover blues, let go of your discipline, stop going to meetings, feel alone and cut off again and then say, "the hell with it, who cares what I do," and call him. You care, that's who. Don't expect to recover in one day.

Social conflicts: Arguments with people where you feel victimized, attacked, or you lose can cause you to have a slip. It's the "everyone hates me so I might as well call him" slip. Everyone doesn't hate you and you'll hate you worse if you do. If you're feeling this way call up your buddy.

Getting even: Success with a new man, a flirtation, a date with a new man, or meeting someone new can do it. You feel that because they or a new "him" likes you, you should call him up just to tell him how well things are going for you or to make him jealous and rub his nose in "it." This is a backfire situation every time. You're the one that ends up thinking that you're sorry you let him go. Tell yourself, I don't have to get even to get better.

Dishonesty: You make excuses for not doing what you don't want to do and cheat yourself by doing what you know you shouldn't do. This is usually in the form of checking up on him, calling him and hanging up. We call this one the Pink Panther Slip because it's inevitable that you botch it. You're bound to discover what you can't bear to hear, he will be in bed with someone else. Save yourself the grief. Be honest. Admit that you're human and still care, tell your buddy that you're a hang-up artist, share your techniques with her, laugh and get a little perspective.

Comparison shopping: You compare yourself all the time to others, the ones who are married and have two kids, or the one who's always got a date or the one with the great job and the great boyfriend. Obviously you're doing worse, so you might as well call him. The way out is to stop comparing.

Victimhood: You let yourself be taken advantage of one more time by your friends or at work and then slide right into a slip. Poor me, look at all the work I did for nothing. Kill it before it multiplies or snowballs.

Resisting change: You get stuck in situations that you know are no good for you and resist changing your life. We call this the Broken Record Slip, a record that's stuck in one place and keeps repeating and repeating until you pick up the arm and change it. Staying in these old situations or finding new improved bad ones or bad guys ensures slips. Lovesick people resist change. Recovery is about going with the new flow and staying open. Change brings freedom.

Lost fantasies: They can come back at any time when you have a self-hatred attack and are usually precipitated by lost fantasy thoughts like, "I've lost the great love of my life and now I'll be alone forever," "I wish we could start over again, I'd do it right this time," "If I looked differently, was thinner, he would have loved me more." Soon these thoughts become obsessions. You make preparations in case he calls. You wonder where he is and who he's with. He's taking her to the restaurant you loved so much, he's making love to her. You check into your answering machine five hundred times a day in case he called, fantasizing that he'll leave you the message, "Darling, I love you, I can't live without you a day longer." You pray to get him back. When you can't stand it a second longer you call and plead, beg, cajole him to get back together with you. Don't do it. Call your buddy instead.

The Holidays: Holidays do it every time. It's a foolproof reason to have a high anxiety attack and a slip so you have to fool it. Instead of giving in to the "what am I going to do alone, without him, it's Valentine's Day/Christmas/New Year's Eve/Memorial Day/Labor Day," plan ahead! Make a date with your buddy. Call up your friends and invite them over to dinner. Call up your friends and tell them you're an orphan and invite yourself for dinner. The best possible thing to do is to get out of whatever town or city you live in and go somewhere else. Save up your money and commit yourself to a vacation or a weekend away from everyone else's anxieties.

High Anxiety: If you're under pressure, in a stressful situation, have to face something new or difficult in your career or social life, starting to succeed, excessively worried or anxious about something over which you have no control you could have a slip. Recognize that you're anxious and trying to sabotage yourself. Structure your day so that you make yourself do things to relax. Prepare. Do your homework. Do a visualization, say an affirmation, work out, go to a meeting, call your support system, tell your buddy how uptight you are. Get some distance.

Life without Peter if not exciting was at least satisfying. Out of nowhere one day, my boss gave me a major promotion, told me they were making me a vice president . . . showed me my new office. I was shocked. Out of nowhere I became obsessed, "wait till I tell Peter" was my first thought. How would he react to the news? It wasn't news without his knowing. I had to tell him how well I was doing . . . how stupid he was for not wanting me . . . how much he was losing by not being with me.

Possessed, obsessed, in one afternoon, three hours and fifteen minutes to be exact, I spent my raise on an executive makeover, including new clothes, makeup, a new hair color and style, and sexy new underwear—all for the moment when I would see him and reveal the new improved, successful, rich, me. Before I knew it I was on the phone calling him. When he finally took my call, after I'd left six messages, his voice was cold. He told me he couldn't care less about my new job. Nothing had changed. I felt totally sick and angry at myself for forgetting that he was a b——. He hadn't cared about my last job so why would he care about this one? I dragged myself to group and told them about my expensive slip. Suddenly I realized that my obsessing about him had to do with sabotaging myself. My fear of success had overwhelmed me. I'd obsessed about Peter to run away from facing my new job, replacing fear of success and the unknown with that old familiar feeling, failure with him.

—MARSHA

MAKING YOUR OWN ANTI-SLIP KIT

What helped me a great deal apart from taking a trip for a week was delaying the urge to call him, which was so strong. I knew that if I called him I would ask him to come back so I made myself postpone the urge five to ten minutes, then fifteen minutes to a half hour, as long as I could. Finally it helped. The longer I stayed away from him and didn't call the better I felt. I was in control of my life again. I also made sure to reward myself with something special each time I won.

—IRIS

A slip is always triggered by irrational thinking. If you start feeling that you want him back, you're experiencing a loneliness attack or you're trying to sabotage your recovery. You can prepare for a slip ahead of time, while you're rational and feeling strong so that when you start to have that old feeling of falling you can take out your Anti-Slip Kit and be prepared. Make a commitment to yourself that before you do anything bad you'll pull out your kit and read it. That means that if you get the urge to call in the office and your kit is at home, you'll have to go home and read everything in the kit before you call him. That kind of a commitment.

Buy yourself a folder. Label it Anti-Slip Kit. For emergencies only. Your kit should include the following:

1. The Crime Sheet of his faults.
2. The phone numbers of your buddy and all the people in your network that you've made a commitment to call before you call him.
3. A short statement about your recovery when you're feeling good, safe and together: the reasons why you've left him, why he's no good for you, why you are in recovery.
4. A letter to your lovesick self from your healthy self in case you feel a slip coming on. Write this to yourself on a good day and promise that you'll read it on the bad day:

"Dear _____(fill in your name):

I love you. I know how much you want to see _____ (fill in his name) again and hear his voice but you know how bad it is for you to call him. He can't give you what he doesn't have to give. If you call him up and try to see him you're going to feel terrible. Just thinking about it makes you feel nervous and anxious. It's something that isn't good for you in the long run. You don't want to hurt yourself and feel that old pain again. Don't do it. Don't give in. You can live through this moment. Yield not to temptation. He doesn't make you feel good. You don't need to feel bad. Hang on! You can do it. You're a winner. Call _____ (fill in the name of your buddy) instead. Thank you for listening. Love, _____ (your name)

5. Include this questionnaire in your kit. Make yourself a deal that you'll answer these questions before taking any further action:
   What am I trying to get out of seeing him again?
   Is it worth it?
   Do I really want to see him or am I running away from something else? What is it? Is it worth it?
   Which part of me, healthy or lovesick is acting out?
   What do I really need right now to calm down and fill the black hole?
   What has set me off?
   How will I feel tomorrow if I do it today?

6. Include these affirmations and make a commitment to read them and say them out loud before you do anything:
   I've learned all from my relationship with him that I've needed. I am ready to move on.
   I am opening myself up for a brighter future. I am letting go of my past need of being rejected.
   I am all right without him.
   I am letting in love and life to heal me.
   I deserve something better.
   I am choosing to heal.

7. Repeat the Head Balloon Meditation. Make a commitment to do it before you call him.

8. Write yourself a weekly newsletter for your time of need and mail it to yourself when you're feeling healthy. Keep it in the kit. This could include some of your big wins of the week, anything from doing the laundry to not calling him three times. Make yourself a deal that if you're going to slip you'll read all your letters before you do anything else.

9. **Let the Good Times Roll Visualization.** Promise yourself that you'll do this before you call him. Remember a good time in advance. Anything that you did with total self-confidence that made you feel wonderful. The time you won a tennis match, the time you had a brainstorm at work and then were able to translate it into action, the time you cooked a gourmet dinner, the time you harvested the first tomato after working on your garden all summer, the time you took a walk on a beautiful beach on a sunny day and you felt great about life. Write down the memory. When you open your kit read the memory to remind yourself. Lie down, close your eyes and visualize doing it. Recreate the mood, the feeling, where you were, the kind of day it was. Breathe in and out slowly as you remember that feeling. Now visualize calling him and his picking up the phone on the other end and being unhappy or angry at you for calling him. See how you feel when he hangs up or is rude or won't take your call or is angry. Feel his anger. Feel how you feel about his anger. Keep breathing. Now feel how good you feel by not calling him. Keep breathing. Feel the good feeling. When you're ready, feeling good, open your eyes.

AFTER A SLIP

The first time Richard called me for money, begging in this pathetic, needy, desperate voice, somehow or other I was able to say no. I felt like I was dying but I hung on, called my support system and got through it. Over Christmas, a year after we broke up, he showed up at work and I gave him two hundred dollars. I got sick over it. I felt so confused, guilty for giving him the money, but he needed it. Now I've learned that I can't give him money, it makes me sick to do it. He hasn't changed but I have. It's my sickness to give him money and his sickness to ask.

—TINA

The most important thing to do after a slip is be kind to yourself, kinder than you've ever been before because this is the time you're going to hate yourself the most. You can't afford to fall into that trap because that will trigger another slip. Don't listen to that same old broken-down mindspeak record, "you're bad, you're bad, how could you have done it." Shut it off. Break the pattern, the patter. Do something good for yourself, instead. Say some affirmations. Take a

bath, take a walk. Forgive yourself. Accept that you had a slip. Don't
beat yourself up for it. Call your support system to discuss it. Write
down what you learned from your slip. Put it into the Emergency Kit.

A slip is there to remind you that you can't go back because you've
made so much progress recovering. It does not mean that you've lost
again. Think of how far you've come. Think of the gains you've made.
Of course you're not perfect but you're doing better . . . a lot better.
Recognize that the process of disengaging yourself from him is much
faster after a slip than after the original breakup or after you first go
cold turkey. Instead of going through the process painfully for months,
you've recovered so much that this time it will only take days or even
hours to get back on track.

Make a deal with yourself that the next time he calls to see you for
his fix, sex, money or whatever he needs, you'll put a limit on it. You'll
only give him five dollars, you'll have a drink but won't go to bed with
him, you'll not return his phone call for two days or you'll call your
support system instead of him. Set the limit in advance so you're
prepared. Make a deal with yourself that the next time you feel like
you're slipping, you'll remember how you felt when you slipped before
and ask yourself whether or not it's worth it again.

Don't get terrified if you experience a very strong emotional or even
physical reaction to having had a slip. If you're normal you're going to
slip, be upset; it's part of the healing process, part of recovery. Don't
despair, your recovery has not gone up in smoke. On the contrary, the
slip is there to give you a lesson, a growth opportunity, it will show you
that you're getting healthy and help you to see that he hasn't changed
but you have!

AFTER-A-SLIP EXERCISE #1: WHAT'S THE LESSON?

Write down the answers to the following questions:

What triggered the slip? You're a good detective, see if you can
reconstruct the moments preceding your slip and get to the root of
your slip. Who were you talking to, what you were doing, where were
you, when was it? Was it a phone call, a conversation, a fear, real or
imagined—a perceived put-down, argument, anxiety attack, adrenalin rush, rejection? You felt something upsetting, what was it?

Was there a moment when you could have stopped yourself? Was
there something you could have done before you slipped in order not

to slip? Could you have called your buddy instead? Gone to a meeting? What did you learn from your slip? What was the lesson?

How can you protect yourself better in the future?

VISUALIZATION: SUNFLOWER POWER

This visualization is written to help you stop obsessing when all else fails. Use the sunflower when you have an attack of the hims and he starts to haunt your day, your night like a melody that you can't get out of your head. It will help you stop the music.

Go to your sacred space, light a candle and bless, dedicate this visualization to Gaia, Mother Goddess of the Earth. Breathe in sunlight, breathe out green mist. As you breathe in sunlight go from your Temple of Love and Healing down the pathway to an open meadow where there are wildflowers growing, butterflies dancing. Sit down on a soft cushion of grass. In front of you is a bare patch of rich, dark soil. There's a seed in your hand and you can feel the life energy pulsing in the seed. State your intention: to use this sunflower seed to clear your mind of your obsessive thoughts. Dig in the soil, plant the seed in the earth, water it. Breathe in sunlight, breathe out green mist, the obsessive thoughts, down your spine into the earth. Feel your roots grow deep. Identify any places in your body that are tense. Put your hand there and ask your body what it is that is hurting you. Is it an obsession? A thought? A judgment? What is it? As you breathe out, let the answer flow down through your body, through your roots, into the soil and into the roots of the sunflower. Watch it sprout up from the earth and begin to grow. Clean energy flows up into the stem, into a leaf. Each thought, pain or anxiety becomes a leaf. Breathe in sunlight, breathe out green mist. See the plant begin to grow upward and upward. Breathe out your obsessive thoughts, each thought is a leaf. Breathe in sunlight, out green mist, and as you continue the process the stem grows taller and taller.

Put your attention on a person who has caused you pain. As you concentrate on this person see a bud form. As you breathe in sunlight allow the bud to grow and grow into a grand yellow sunflower. As the sunflower reaches its maximum growth, you notice the enormous circle of brown seeds surrounded by yellow petals. Watch the face of the person appear in the center of the sunflower. Speak to him, saying, "I release you from my thoughts, from my life. I release you from my heart, body, mind and spirit. I bless you and thank you for the lessons you have shown me." Now notice the machete that is lying next to you in the grass. Pick it up, get the feel of it. When you're ready, brandish the machete in the air, and cry out loud, "Off with your head" and cut off the head of the sunflower in one swoop!

Notice if any of the other buds have faces. If there is another face, repeat the process. Do this until a sunflower grows without an image, only a pattern of seeds. Thank the plant for helping you to release, to turn over a new leaf. Feel the relief. Feel the gratitude. When you're ready, open your eyes.

CHAPTER 8

Your Parents are Lovesick, Too

In order to continue your recovery process, it's time to deal with the source of your lovesickness, why you became addicted to hims in the first place, your lovesick role model, your relationship with your lovesick parents.

Wouldn't he have ever wanted to see how I was, how I turned out, didn't he care at all? I kept thinking, hoping when I was at strange homes, that one day a nice man would come and say, "I'm here to take my daughter" then I would be saved . . . I kept hoping. Sometimes I remember even dressing up in whatever clothes I had, thinking that this was the day he would come. I wanted to be ready. But he never came. No one ever came.

When they passed Riverside, she pulled onto the shoulder and stopped.

"I'm going to do it . . . I'm going to see my father. I'm going to call him . . . I can't just barge in on him this way."

A woman, probably the third Mrs. Gifford, answered the phone, and Marilyn asked if Mr. Gifford was there.

"Who's calling him?" the woman asked.

"This is Marilyn . . . I'm his child . . . I mean the little girl years ago. Gladys Baker's daughter. He's sure to know who I am."

"I don't know who you are," the unfriendly voice replied, "but I'll tell him you're on the phone."

Minutes later, the woman returned. "He doesn't want to see you," she said. "He suggests you see his lawyer in Los Angeles if you have some complaint. Do you have a pencil?"

"No." said Marilyn. "Good bye."

When she walked back to the car, she slumped over the wheel.

—Marilyn Monroe

113

OF FANTASY BONDAGE

You have a fantasy bond with your parents, idolizing them, putting them on pedestals; the more unattainable, unavailable, rejecting they are, the harder you try to get their love, the more addicted you become to their rejection.

In order to recover you're going to have to sever this fantasy bond, break the mold, destroy the blueprint, cut the cords that bind you to your lovesickness. You became lovesick because your parents were lovesick and could not give you unconditional love; you remain lovesick because you continue to have a lovesick relationship with your parents. You cannot feel, give, accept love until you do this. They aren't going to change, they can't. You're the one who's going to make the changes, you can!

You're going to have to divorce your parents as parents. This is the only way for you to stop perpetuating your addiction to rejection, to pain, to lost causes, to not getting love, to not loving yourself.

This may be shocking, an upset, perhaps the most difficult thing you've ever faced in your life. Please don't skip this chapter because this doesn't apply to you (especially if you want to skip to the next chapter); it does.

It's possible that your parents are no longer living, one of them, both of them. It's also possible that your parents divorced, remarried, that you were raised by a single parent, that you were raised without parents, by your grandparents, aunts and uncles, by surrogate parents, that you were adopted, or like Marilyn, in and out of foster care homes. No matter what your situation, please read this chapter and do all the exercises, all the work. It works.

> I was a mistake. My mother didn't want to have me . . . I probably got in her way. I know I must have disgraced her. I know that a divorced woman has enough problems in getting a man but one with an illegitimate baby has even more . . . I wish . . . I still wish she had wanted me.
>
> —MARILYN MONROE

Be aware that the death of a parent will tend to color your memories, reinforce your denial. You'll remember only the good things, idealize, keep this parent on a pedestal, fearful of "waking the dead." It's not desecrating the memory of your dead parent or violating a living parent to come to grips with the reality of your lovesick relationship with him, her or them. On the contrary, it's necessary for *your* life, for *your* recovery.

The purpose of this is not to blame your parents, point the finger at them, make them into bad guys; it's to give you the opportunity to cut the lovesick cords that bind you to your lovesick parents, dead or alive—to your lovesickness.

AND NOW ANOTHER MINDSPEAK BROADCAST BROUGHT TO YOU BY DONNA DENIAL

"Oh, no my mother is perfect and I love her, my father is perfect, I love him, don't you dare point a finger at them, don't you dare insinuate that something's wrong. You're talking about something sacred, the ten commandments, honor thy mother and father, this is sacrilege."

The more you protest, the more you deny, the more upsetting this is, the more lovesick your relationship is with your lovesick family.

The more lovesick your family was, the greater your denial that there was anything wrong with your parents, the more responsibility you take for things being wrong, the more self-hatred you feel, the more lovesick you've become. No matter how hard this is please keep going.

GARDEN VARIETY TYPES OF LOVESICK/ DYSFUNCTIONAL PARENTS

Here are some ways to help you spot dysfunctional, lovesick parents:

They want what they want when they want it no matter what you want.

They're unreliable, inconsistent and keep you guessing. You never know what to expect.

He or she criticizes you constantly.

He or she controls you with money.

He or she is incapable of dealing with the truth, anything controversial or anything that makes them feel uncomfortable, which is almost everything.

They start fights with you if they're angry with someone else.

He or she is always depressed.

You're afraid of him or her.

He or she has got to be in the driver's seat, in control. Spontaneity scares them to death.

He or she is mysterious, secretive, you don't understand him or her.

You can't count on him or her, they're never there for you but demand that you're there for them. They never hug you, tell you how much they love you. They're cold, withdrawn, rigid.

BREAKING-THROUGH-DENIAL EXERCISE: CLIMBING YOUR LOVESICK FAMILY TREE

This exercise requires sleuth work, the kind that you've been so good at in the past when it came to tracking down something about a him. Should your grandparents or parents no longer be alive, talk to their friends, your aunts and uncles, nieces and nephews, children, anyone who knew them, remembers. Answer these questions to the best of your ability:

Your Mother:

Is your mother an alcoholic, a workaholic, a cleanaholic, a shopaholic, a fearaholic, a drug abuser, a pill abuser, a foodaholic, a sportsaholic, a gambler?

Repeat this exercise with your father, then with your grandparents on both sides, great grandparents if you can go back that far. If you discover that you have a history of addiction or cross-addiction running in your family the probability is that you've inherited lovesickness.

BREAKING-THROUGH-DENIAL EXERCISE: THE REMEMBRANCE OF THINGS PAST

Your Childhood Relationship With Your Parents

This exercise is to assist you in remembering what it was like to grow up in your home with your parents. Don't get discouraged if you can't remember. Put this down, pick it up a few days later and work on it then.

Answer these questions first about your mother, then about your father.

Did your mother tell you she loved you on a consistent basis?

Did she hug you?

Do you remember being told that you were a good child consistently?

Were you afraid of your mother?

Did she beat you?

Did she abuse you verbally?

Do you remember feeling frightened or abandoned?

Do you remember being criticized?

Did your mother tell you often that you were a bad child or worthless?

Were you punished often psychologically or physically for things you didn't feel were wrong?

Did you feel neglected? Did you feel smothered?

If something went wrong, was she there or did she criticize you?

Do you remember any psychosomatic illnesses on your mother's part?

Was your mother often unhappy, angry, frustrated with your father?

Did your mother have a negative attitude toward life?

Did you have to take care of her?

Was your home a happy place? Was your mother able to take care of your home, herself and you, manage her responsibilities?

Did your mother ever allow you to do the things you wanted to do or did you feel that she was controlling and you had to do things her way?

Were you frequently sick as a child?

Were you sexually abused?

Did your parents argue, fight or quarrel consistently? Did you feel responsible?

Did you feel that you were welcomed or did your mother make you feel that you were an accident that had destroyed her life?

Did you ever fantasize about or attempt suicide?

Was your mother's behavior consistent, did you know what to expect?

Could you trust your mother with your secrets? Did she keep her promises?

Did your parents separate or divorce? Did they remarry, and if so, did you feel welcome by your new step-parent? Did one of your parents die early?

Add up your answers, scoring one point for each yes. The higher the number of yes answers you gave, the more lovesick your relationship is.

If you scored zero points and are patting yourself on the back because you think you're in a healthy relationship, you may still be in denial so take this test again, tomorrow or a week from now. Compare your scores.

BREAKING-THROUGH-DENIAL EXERCISE: WHAT'S WHAT WITH YOUR RELATIONSHIP WITH YOUR PARENTS

I went to visit my mother in California. All she did was criticize me for an endless list of things that didn't amount to pile of beans. There was no way to avoid her poison darts. I felt like those pictures of St. Sebastian, the martyr, smiling bravely, with five arrows stuck into him. I'd tried to stay calm and cool but every time she said something nasty, I reacted by screaming back at the top of my lungs to defend myself. We fought every day, all day, the arguments, as always, out of proportion to the subjects.

"With all the nice clothes you have do you have to wear that outfit?"

"I like these pants. What's the matter with them?"

"They look old. I won't go out of this house with you looking like that!"

"We're only going to the movies. Who's going to see us?"

"I'm going to see you, that's who."

"Then I won't go!" At this point I lost it, became a nuclear reactor, called her some names, slammed the door and went to sleep until the next day, next fight. Then I felt guilty. It was my fault. If I were a better daughter, we wouldn't be fighting.

—KATE

This exercise is about your present relationship with your parents. The answers will help you determine whether you have a lovesick relationship with your parents. Answer first about your mother, then your father.

Do you always know where you stand with your mother?
Do you feel that you can't please her no matter what you do?
Is her behavior inconsistent so you never know what to expect?

Can you ask her for a favor without fear of the consequences?

If she does something for you does she make you pay for it?

Can you be honest with your mother?

Do you feel defensive all the time around her, as if she's going to attack you at any minute?

Do you feel that somehow you're always wrong, can't ever win?

Do you inevitably have to do it her way, from fear of disapproval, fear of the consequences, whether she's right or wrong, no matter what?

Are you afraid of your mother?

Does she ever hug you?

Does she criticize you?

Is she supportive?

Do you feel like crying often when you're around her?

Does she control you with money?

Are your conversations with her composed of threats?

Are you afraid to talk to her honestly about your emotional life, afraid to admit that you have troubles, problems, addictions?

Does she still treat you as a child?

Do you fight with her on a constant basis?

Are you afraid of provoking her?

When you try to talk to her about your feelings, your problems, your fears, do you feel as if you're banging your head against a stone wall?

Do you worry if you have to go and see her, spend time together?

Does she insult you, put you down or show lack of interest in your life?

Does she want you to be different from the way you are?

Does she constantly scold you, tell you how many things you do wrong?

Do you overdo around her (drink too much, smoke too much, eat too much) when you're with her or after you've seen her? Do you often feel bad, depressed, angry, crazy, powerless, rejected, sick after seeing her?

Does she support your recovery or are you afraid to tell her about it?

Add up your answers, scoring one point for each yes. The higher the number of yes answers you gave, the more lovesick your relationship is. If you scored zero points and are patting yourself on the back because your relationship is healthy you may be in denial so take this test again tomorrow or a week from now. Compare your scores.

BREAKING-THROUGH-DENIAL EXERCISE: COMPARISON SHOPPING

Take a blank piece of paper and divide it into columns. Answer yes or no for your mother, father, the hims in your life, past or present. The purpose of this exercise is to compare your lovesick relationships.

Unable to show love?
Addicted to _____?
Emotionally frozen?
Dishonest?
Controlling?
Depressed?
Negative?
Moody?
Unpredictable?
Irresponsible?
Not there for you?
Rejecting?
Demanding?
Rigid?
Abusive—physically or mentally?
Critical?
Needy?
Manipulative?
Authoritarian?
Weak/vacant?
Disrespectful?
Emotionally/physically absent?

Are there similarities? Your lovesick relationship with your parents is the blueprint.

BREAKING-THROUGH-DENIAL EXERCISE: A WEEK IN YOUR FAMILY LIFE

Buy a notebook and make notes about all telephone conversations, visits, interactions with your family during a week. Note the following:

How you feel before, during and after. Did you fight? Did they criticize you? Did you feel angry? Did you cry, have a tantrum, yell, scream, rage? Did you get depressed? Did you feel uneasy, upset? Were you afraid? Did you want to binge out, drink, smoke, or whatever you usually do to escape after you were with them or talked to them?

If you didn't call them or see them was it because you didn't want to see them, because you made yourself unavailable, because you live thousands of miles from them, because it wasn't worth it, etc. Did you feel guilty that you didn't call them, see them, visit, etc.?

BREAKING-THROUGH-DENIAL EXERCISE: FINANCIAL DEPENDENCE

Are you financially dependent on them? This quiz will help you answer.

Do your parents support you financially?
For how long have they been supporting you?
Is there any good reason why you can't support yourself?
Is there a job you could get that would enable you to make enough money to support yourself?
Can you see any connection between your need to remain dependent on your parents and your inability to find a job?
What is keeping you from being able to hold a job, or support yourself?
Have you made an attempt to get work in the last six months?
Do your parents want you to become financially independent?
Do you feel controlled, unable to say no because they support you?
Do you feel they own you?
What is the cost of your financial dependence? Is it worth the price?

BREAKING-THROUGH-DENIAL EXERCISE: EMOTIONAL DEPENDENCE

Take this quiz first for your mother, then your father:

How often do you see your mother?
How often do you call your mother during the day to ask her advice?
When you have to make a decision, do you call your mother up, ask

her to decide for you? Do you become immobilized if they're not around to tell you?

Are you part of your mother and father's every day emotional life? Do you know every detail of their day? Do they know the details of yours?

Do you worry, obsess over, spend all your time thinking about them, their problems and their life?

Does interaction with them cause you to get stressed out?

The more yes answers you have the greater your lovesick relationship with them, the greater your lovesick dependence on them.

TRUTH GAMES: ASKING FOR HELP

Do this exercise with the parent you fear the most:

Tell your mother (father) about something that makes you feel vulnerable, upset, nervous, anxious and for which you would like to get her sympathy and understanding, support or help. "I feel sick or afraid of something." "My boyfriend hasn't called me for three days, what should I do?" See how she reacts. What does she say? Notice whose side she's on. Does she put you down? Does she make you feel worse? Does she make you feel victimized, sorry that you told her in the first place?

BREAKING-THROUGH-DENIAL EXERCISE:
HEARING THEIR VOICES,
WHAT THEY ARE REALLY SAYING

Take your notebook and keep track of all your interactions with your parents the next few times you see or speak to them. Write down all the things they tell you, that you react to.

Notice what your mother/father tells you most often. Does she say you're too fat or too skinny, too shy, too stupid? Does she tell you that you should be doing better, that you're not doing as well as ———? Notice if she ever says anything at all, notices you, your new apartment, haircut, job. If she seems to be oblivious, notice that.

If your parents ignore you, aren't there for you, interrupt you, belittle you or your problems, are drunk, stoned, withdrawn, unavailable, mentally or physically ill, emotionally withholding, preoccupied, rejecting or self-involved when you talk to them, note this down.

Now look over your notes, remember the tone of her/his voice, mark down the following categories: Was it a put-down? A criticism? A loaded remark? A veiled threat? How did these exchanges make you feel? Listen to that voice. Hear it. Reexperience your feelings, your reactions. Be aware of the impact it had, has on you. How long does your reaction last?

YOUR RELATIONSHIP WITH YOUR PARENTS IS LOVESICK

"Now You See It, Now You Don't."

You may just have discovered that your relationship with your parents is lovesick. This is devastating news, so upsetting, in fact that you're going to slip back into denial, get depressed, angry, very, very angry. Be prepared! Your mindspeak station is going to start blasting away trying to protect your fantasy bond, resisting. "You're an ingrate, a bad child, after all the things your parents have done for you. How could you think that anything's wrong with them, something's wrong with you." You're going to have to get tough, shut it off, remind yourself every time you slip back into denial that yes, it's true, sad, but true, terrible, but true.

After all, the things your lovesick relationship with your mother/father is doing to you is the problem, the core issue of your lovesickness; it's preventing you from loving yourself.

CUTTING THE CORDS: TIME × SPACE = DISTANCE

In order to recover from lovesickness you must break your addiction to your lovesick relationship with your parents. This means separating, cutting the lovesick cords so that you get enough distance from them to love yourself, to renegotiate your relationship with them as people.

Breaking your addiction to your parents is no different from breaking your addiction to him. You can't see or speak to, hang out with, visit your parents just once right now without getting totally plugged in to their rejection, control, to your lovesick relationship. You can't see them until you have the distance you need for you to heal, for you to change. In order to get the distance you need space and time. It doesn't have to be forever, but long enough for you to feel good enough about yourself. This means that for a while, a nonspecific amount of time, you're going to have to take time off from your parents, divorce your parents as parents. You're buying time to change the dynamics of your lovesick relationship with your parents so that you can neutralize the electrical charge between you, let go of the negative force that has kept you lovesick, unable to connect with anything positive in your life.

You need time off, your own space to get the distance.

Time off × your own space = the distance.

CUTTING THE CORDS IS SO HARD TO DO

The situation between Mother and me deteriorated. The treat she'd planned for us, a matinée of "Anything Goes," turned into a pitched battle in the DMZ zone. We fought before, during intermission, and after. We had to do something or we'd kill each other. I suggested a ceasefire. Elizabeth suggested a divorce.

"Divorce? I can't divorce my own mother."

"But you've got to separate from her for a while. You need to experience what's it like to live on your own, without her criticisms. Otherwise you'll never grow up."

"You've got to be kidding. How long is a while?" (This was the way I handled any new concept, rigid and fearful about making changes.)

"A while could be three months, maybe more. You'll know it when you can be around her without getting upset. When you've learned how to do things for yourself."

I called Mother. In the fearful voice of a ten-year-old child, I told her that I couldn't see her for the summer.

"Why? What's gotten into you? What's wrong?"

"Nothing. I just need some time alone now, some space."

"That's ridiculous."

"Mother, please. You have to leave me alone, I mean it! Don't call me either." My heart was breaking. My resolve quavering. I was a rotten, ungrateful child. How could I do this to my poor Mother? It wasn't fair. I'd die of guilt. I didn't have the courage to tell her why. I kept losing it. The why. Maybe I didn't want to know or understand. I went on automatic pilot. Repeated over and over to myself, "She's going to be all right. She isn't going to die. Anything is better than the constant fight that's been your relationship. You have to do this for yourself." For myself. For me. Me, the most foreign word in my vocabulary."

—S.I.

Separating from your parents is going to be tough. You've had the same old bad relationship with them all your life, you've become addicted to it, to the pain and now all of a sudden you have to separate from your parents. Your parents!

This is the core issue of your recovery. No matter how odd, strange, upsetting, unnatural, painful, against all of your instincts it may feel, no matter how difficult it is, how guilty you become, you still have to break the fantasy bond if you're going to recover. You need to do this for *you*. You can't have a part-time relationship with them. You can't be a little pregnant. The point is to learn how to differentiate between who they are, what they want you to be, what they think of you and who you are, who you need to be, what you think of yourself. Yes, you have to cut the cords. There is no other way.

Giving yourself a chance to be you, not your mother or father's lovesick daughter, is what recovery is all about.

The more you've been addicted to your relationship with your mother and father, the closer your relationship to your parents, the more difficult you may think this is going to be. This however, is about cutting the psychic connection, the invisible umbilical cord between you. This is about changing your early programming. You can and must do it for you.

> After a solid eight months of group, I finally began to see the connection between staying in my bad marriage and calling home. Each time John would get violent with me I would call my mother. She would say, "No wonder he's losing his temper, you've been impossible all your life. Why don't you try harder to please him." I wound up in the hospital with serious injuries after he beat me up. During the month it took me to recuperate I realized that I had to give both of them up. Between them, they were killing me."

—NINA

VARIATIONS ON A THEME OF LOVESICK PARENTS

There are many variations of lovesick relationship with your parents. Whatever the variation, you still need to cut the cords and you can: They could both be dead. They could both be alive. One could be alive, one dead. They could both be alive and well but separated and remarried, one, the other, both. You could have a good relationship with one and not the other. You could have a good relationship with the other not the one. One of them may be controlling, rejecting, in charge, around too much. One of them could be a wimp, not there, not around, absent. One or both of them might be an alcoholic, a work-aholic, drug addict, foodaholic, be addicted to something, anything, everything. You could be living with both of them, one of them. You could be taking care of one, or both. You could be dependent on them financially. You could be dependent on them emotionally. You could live thousands of miles away from them. You could live next door. You could speak to them five times a day. You could speak to them five times a year. You could not be on speaking terms.

Whatever the variation, you still have to do it—cut the ties that are strangling you, keeping you lovesick.

You can accomplish this no matter what your situation is. You can get creative, do this work no matter where you are, who you're living with, what your circumstances. If you want to do it you can do it. The more daily contact you have with your parents the more you have to separate literally, physically. For example, if you talk to your mother twice a day, separating from her is going to be very different than if you speak to her once a month or once a year. The more lovesick your relation-ship, the more dependent you are on them, the harder it's going to be to accomplish this, the more you need to do it. Things to remember:

She or he isn't going to change. You can't change them. This is not about changing them. It's about changing you.

This is not about blaming your parents, making them wrong for a lifetime of your lovesick troubles and woes; it's about cutting your lovesick ties with them, your emotional addiction to getting hurt, not getting their approval, feeling unlovable, unloved, or being wrong. It's about taking the negative charge out of your lovesick relationship with them, neutralizing it so that you can bring positive power back to you.

CHAPTER 9

Divorcing Your Parents as Parents

CUTTING THE CORDS

"Activate Your Support System, Call Your Buddy"

You can't do this alone! Call your buddy, activate your support system. Tell them that you're planning to separate from your parents, explain why. Ask for their support. Make sure you have their permission to call when you need them morning, day, evening.

YOUR OWN DECLARATION OF INDEPENDENCE

Write your own declaration of independence, your reasons for needing to become independent from your lovesick parents. You can start with this abridged version of the 1776 one:

When in the course of human events it becomes necessary for _____ (your name) to dissolve the lovesick bonds which have connected you with your parents and to assume among the Powers of Earth, the separate and equal Station to which the Laws of Nature and of Nature's God entitle you, a decent respect to yourself requires that you should declare the causes which impel you to the separation:

My parents were unable to give me unconditional love and I therefore am unable to give myself unconditional love, am addicted to rejection.

My lovesick relationship with my parents does not allow me to love myself, to recover.

I GOTTA BE ME

I_____ (your name), in healthy body, mind and spirit, declare that I am cutting the cords with my lovesick parents to enable me to have a healthy body, mind and spirit makeover.

I do not mean this in any malicious way, but it is necessary to end my unhappy relationship with myself and to begin a new healthy relationship with myself. I recognize that they did the best they could. It's up to me to heal the wounds from the past. It's my commitment to myself to learn how to give myself unconditional love.

I gotta be me and I need to separate from them to do it!

YOUR BILL OF RIGHTS

Write your own Bill of Rights. Use this one as a start. Add any amendments or modifications as you see fit.

I have a right to life, liberty and the pursuit of happiness. If any relationship threatens these fundamental rights, I have the right to terminate it.

I have a right to say no to or refuse to do anything or have any interaction that does not feel right, is manipulative, controlling, or forces me into compromising myself.

I have a right to say no to anything that threatens my integrity, my fundamental rights as a human being.

I have a right to express my feelings, thoughts, attitudes without hearing that I am wrong.

I have a right to say no to control, manipulation, rejection.

I have a right to choose what's good for me.

I have a right to life, liberty and the pursuit of happiness.

I have a right not to be lovesick.

WRITE A LETTER

If your parents don't leave you alone, interfere with your life, are on your case all the time, write a letter to your family. Explain to them that for a while you need to separate from them. Tell them that you're working on yourself, that you're feeling fine, that you would appreciate it if they did not try to get in touch with you. Assure them that you'll send postcards or letters from time to time letting them know how you are doing. Make sure that you do!

MAKE A PHONE CALL

Call up your parents and tell them that you need a little time off. Tell them that this is something you're doing for yourself. It has nothing to do with them. (It doesn't, this is your life, your move!)

IF YOU'RE FINANCIALLY DEPENDENT ON THEM . . .

If your parents are supporting you because you have no income, can't seem to make it on your own, the probability is that your reasons for maintaining this financial dependency are lovesick. There's no way you can separate, grow up, cut the cords, assume the responsibilities of an adult, and recover if you're living off your parents, if they're paying your bills, supporting you. You lose your vote, lose your independence, your rights, your you. How can you have a differing opinion about anything when your mother/father is paying for you? You're not entitled to disagree as along as they're footing the bills. It's basic Economics 101. Financial dependency *costs* and you're the one who has to pay. Recovery is about taking responsibility for your own life, paying your own bills. It's time to cut the financial cords that bind you to your lovesick parents:

Get a job. Or two. Open your own bank account. Open a savings account. Apply for your own credit cards. Go back to school and get that degree. Take courses at night. Learn how to run a computer, type—basic business skills. Do anything you need to do to support yourself.

IF YOU'RE LIVING WITH THEM . . .

If you're living with your parents for whatever the reason, because you have no income, because you can't find the right apartment, because you're afraid of living alone, because you can't run a household, shop, cook for yourself, because you can't bear to live in a hole in the wall when you have such a nice room in their house, because they need you, would be lonely without you, and you're a healthy grown-up over the age of twenty-one, the probability is that your reason for staying home and living with your parents, needing to be around them, feeling incapacitated without them is lovesick.

Living with your parents costs you your independence. It's time to cut the cords that bind you to living with them:

Start budgeting your money so that you can afford to move out. Move out. Get an apartment on your own, with a roommate or roommates. Move in with a friend, your sister or brother or other relatives. Look in the paper for people advertising for roommates. Get a job out of town that will relocate you. Apply for a scholarship to a college or university. Apply for a student loan, apply to college. Go to a meeting and put it out there that you're looking for a roommate. If you're paying rent to your parents, find a replacement.

If you can't move out then at least get and pay for your own telephone, pay rent on your room, contribute to food, utilities, household expenses.

NICKNAMES—CALLING NAMES

I'm going to call my mother, "Mommie dearest" because every time I ever had a boy over to the house, my mother flirted with him and tried to take him away from me.

I'm going to call my father, "Hitler." Everything has to be his way and if I've ever disagreed with him he punished me. I'll never forget the way he abused me as a child.

—The Group

One of the best ways to avoid slipping back into denial, to get some distance is to nickname your parent. Pick the character or the characteristic that most represents your lovesick parent and nickname them that. Some of the other nicknames that came up for the women in group were: the Boston Strangler, Medea, the Wicked Witch, the Great Dictator. Start using that name when you discuss your parent with your buddy and your support network.

SET BOUNDARIES, WHAT'S OFF LIMITS,
OUT OF BOUNDS, OPERATIONAL GROUND RULES

The following may sound like drastic measures. They are. You're the betcha-can't-eat-just-one girl, remember? Right now you can't have any contact whatsoever (unless there's an emergency) no matter *what* because just one slip will put you back three spaces.

Don't call home no matter how much you miss them for whatever reason you cook up.

Don't call you mother up and ask to borrow the car, go shopping with her, ask her to help you do the laundry, pay your bills. Call your buddy instead—ask *her* which shoes to wear, if she'll go shopping with you, how to make chicken soup, and if she doesn't know try her recipe for pasta. Use the yellow pages to rent a car, find a laundromat if need be. Figure out a way to do these things, the things you've always relied on your mother or father to do yourself. Courage! You can do it! Recovery is about growing up, becoming independent and learning how to do things for yourself.

Don't visit them. No dinners, lunches, brunches, cocktails, overnights, drop ins, pop ins. In other words don't see, hear, listen to, have any form of contact with them except through the mail.

If you live with them or have to talk to them for a very good reason:

Don't discuss anything even remotely controversial. Don't tell them anything that can be used against you. If everything you say has been used against you don't tell them anything, period!

Don't ask them for anything that feels uncomfortable.

Don't confide in them if you fear their reaction or response. Trust your intuition, yourself.

Don't share anything with them that will give them an edge, an advantage, a wedge into manipulating or disapproval.

Don't ask for their advice no matter what you do.

Don't introduce them to anyone important to you if you fear their disapproval or have to worry about what they will do, say, or think.

Don't tell them any of your secrets, dreams, hopes, plans.

Don't discuss your recovery with them if you feel that they will be threatened, unsupportive or critical.

Don't tell them you are lovesick because they didn't give you unconditional love as if you were blaming them. It wasn't their fault, remember?

STORMY WEATHER:
HURRICANE AND GALE WARNINGS POSTED

The marine forecast is that there's going to be stormy weather ahead high seas, hurricane winds, tidal waves because you're rocking the boat of your lovesick relationship with your parents. The closer your relationship, the more difficult cutting the ties with them is going to be, the stormier their reaction. If you're in the habit of calling your parents once or twice a year and you stop calling them they may or may not notice but if you're used to being on the phone five or six times a day with your mother and you stop, you're rocking the boat of your lovesick relationship, the one that your family has been sitting in since you were born and you can bet that she/he/they are going to react. They'll do anything to stop the Bad Ship Lovesick from sinking; they have a lifetime investment in maintaining your lovesick relationship status quo. If it were okay for you to be you, to be different from them in the first place, you wouldn't have become lovesick!

There are a range of things you should expect from your parents at this time—forewarned is forearmed!

Anger: They're going to throw the book at you, tell you you're acting crazy, criticize you for going off on one of your dumb tangents one more time, complain, insult you, the old "you're bad, you're bad, you're bad"!

Guilt and Gang War: The whole family will unite against you. They're going to tell you that you're killing them, your mother will say, "how could you do this to your poor father after all the things he's done for you;" your father will say, "how could you do this to your poor mother after all the things she's done for you all your life." Your brother will call you up and say, "Are you crazy? How can you do this to poor mom and dad after all the things they've done for you."

Blame: They'll blame your new friends, your old friends, your therapist if you're seeing one, suggest that you go to one if you're not, blame your group, your boss, your boyfriend, your husband, your ex, your children.

Guerilla Warfare: They'll go behind your back and call your new friends, your old friends, your therapist, your group, your boss, your boyfriend, your ex, your husband, your children and tell them that you've lost it, that something's gone wrong, that they're really worried and ask whomever it is that they finally nail for help in getting you back, back on track!

Threats: They may threaten to cut you out of their will, take away the car, your apartment, stop taking care of your children, the dog.

Material manipulation: All of a sudden your parents will find the extra money to give you what you've been dying for and they know what it is. Your mother will ask you to go to Paris with her, she just happens to have an extra ticket, how about going shopping for the new dress you need, anything to buy you back.

The more they try to get you back the more you have to stand your ground. Keep coming back to *you*! Remember: If it had been all right with your parents that you change in the first place you wouldn't be lovesick. A lovesick family will sabotage any effort on your part to become different, break away, be you. A healthy family will support you, give you unconditional love, allow you to be who you are no matter what!

This may be one of the most terrifying experiences of your life, heartwrenching, guilt provoking, sad. You're saying no for the first time in your life to your parents, only you're not two years old, you're a grown-up. Keep coming back to why you're doing this—it's for you. Stay aware, awake and conscious of what's going to happen to you if you don't do it! You've got to keep coming back to *you*. What will happen to *you* if you don't do it? The answer is that *you* will remain lovesick.

JUST VISITING (AS IN MONOPOLY)

There's only one right reason to visit right now: because of an emergency, illness, or unavoidable family commitment like a wedding or a wake. Any other reason is a wrong reason to visit.

Variations on wrong reasons to visit:

Because your mother calls you up and wants you to visit her and you say no and five minutes later she calls you again and you say no again, but the third phone call makes you feel so guilty that you crack.

Because you try to prove to yourself that you can do it without having your normal reaction and then you end up by having it anyway, beating yourself up for your slip.

Because you're supposed to visit once a week like it or not and if you don't like it you're afraid they won't like you if you say no, but the problem is that if you go, you won't like yourself.

Because you'll feel guilty if you don't visit.

Right reasons to visit: It's in your own best interests.

If you have to visit, make it on your terms: Visit on nonholidays. Avoid those days loaded with pain and bad memories, everyone else's anxieties, plus your own holidays. There's no place like home for the holidays to slip!

You can decide to stay in a hotel or with a friend if you feel nervous about spending too long a period of concentrated time with your family with no escapes. Stop by for tea, a short lunch, brunch rather than a long-term overnighter. If an overnighter is unavoidable, bring a friend along. Invite them to visit you on your turf, on your terms. Make it easy on yourself. Help them to behave themselves. Suggest dinner, lunch, brunch out at a restaurant, neutral territory instead of their home ground where the same old arguments, upsets, attacks bring you to your knees.

IF YOU HAVE TO VISIT

Avoid certain loaded topics: Your recovery. Your support group. How well you're doing kicking an addiction they didn't notice you had. How well you're doing in therapy kicking your addiction to them. Telling them that they are dysfunctional and lovesick and giving them some pointers on how to change like, "All you have to do is work on giving yourself more love." Asking them why they never told you they loved you or hugged you is a loaded topic sure to create a heated argument if not a nuclear explosion. Your mother will protest too much. She'll feel shattered, use it against you, make you feel guilty—after all the things she's done for you.

Your personal life; this includes *everything*: your boyfriend, your new friends, your latest obsession, your buddy, why you're not seeing your old friends, why you're not seeing _____ (fill in the blank) anymore. In other words, anything that you're vulnerable about and can give them a cutting edge. Give them an inch and they'll take a mile—at your expense.

Stay in the present. Stand fast!

OOPS! A SLIP

If you slip back into denial and want to call them or give into their pressure to see or speak to you and you call, see, visit your parents at this precarious time it's almost 100 percent certain that you'll have a slip within the first fifteen minutes. You'll have an argument, a fight, a confrontation. They'll put you down, criticize you, try and control you, ignore you, same as it ever was. Only this time you'll hear their criticisms, put downs, control, those voices, "you're wrong." That voice pushes all your buttons, triggers, detonates your raw nerves, you explode, blow up, go off the deep end, the explosion out of proportion to the cause.

Like any slip, you'll feel worse than you've ever felt before, reexperience the pain of separating one more time, the why-me's, guilt, anger, resentment, sadness, depression. Don't beat yourself up for it. Get back on track.

What's the lesson? Your parents still have remarkable power over you. You're not ready to see, speak, or deal with them yet. You don't have the distance.

VISUALIZATION: CUTTING THE CORDS

This ceremony will help to free you of your lovesick emotional attachments with your lovesick family. You'll be able to cut the psychic negative cords that have kept you lovesick.

Light a candle and ask Spirit to bless this healing.

Lie down and make your self comfortable. Imagine the warmth of the sun surrounding you, caressing you. Breathe in sunlight, breathe out tension and fatigue. Breathe in light and breathe out shadow. Imagine now that you pass through the columns and enter your Temple of Love and Healing. Imagine sparkling sunlight filling your head, circling downwards through your neck and shoulders.

Breathe in golden light, breathe out gray smoke. Fill your chest, your heart. Feel the warmth spreading down. Imagine the golden sunlight energy accumulating at the base of the spine. Breathe in golden sunlight once more sending the energy down your legs to the soles of your feet.

From this point of deep relaxation picture your father in your mind's eye. Call his name out aloud four times. Invite him to be present at this ceremony. See him dressed for a grand event. Explain to him that at this point in your life it's important to sever old lovesick bonds between you . . . this is a healing process that allows you to let go of any pain and negativity. You may wish to tell him that growing up as his daughter was painful or hurtful and that you need to express this to feel complete. It's safe for you to feel whatever you feel, say any words, make any sounds that will release you, growl or hiss until you experience a feeling of emptiness. Express your willingness to forgive him and accept his need for forgiveness, too. Thank your father for bringing you into the world. See if you are ready to tell him that you love him. Ask him to stand by while you call forth your mother.

Picture your mother. Call her name aloud four times. Invite her to be present at this ceremony. Observe how she is dressed for this grand event. Notice what emotions her presence brings up within you. Keep breathing in golden light as you recognize what issues you need to address. Explain to her that you're at a point in your life where it's important to sever old bonds between you . . . this is a healing process that allows you the time and space to let go of any pain and negativity. You may wish to tell her that growing up as her daughter was painful or hurtful and that you need to express this to feel complete. It's safe for you to feel whatever you feel, say any words, make any sounds that will release you, growl or hiss until you experience a feeling of emptiness. Express your willingness to forgive her and accept her need for forgiveness, too.

Thank her for bringing you into the world. See if you are ready to tell her that you love her. When you feel complete with your mother, ask your father to step forward. Ask your grandparents, all your relations, any special friends to be present. Invite them to witness a ceremony of forgiveness and love. Know that this ceremony will flow like healing sap through all the limbs and branches of the family tree.

Now it's time for the ceremony. Notice what you're wearing. Call forth an esteemed teacher to be the mistress or master of ceremonies. Notice what he or she is wearing. This Being carries a pair of golden scissors sparkling with jewels in one hand and in the other carries a short sword surrounded by a blue flame.

The Mistress of Ceremonies speaks, "Divine Spirit we ask for your blessing at this important moment in our personal history." As you stand before your father, see two umbilical cords between you. The green one is positive, the red one is negative. Bless these cords. Feel love, light and forgiveness pulse through these cords as you count to thirteen outloud. Address the negative cord that contains all your lovesick attachments. The Mistress of Ceremonies asks you, "Are you ready?" When you are, choose an implement and on the count of three, cut the red cord! Ask yourself what you would like to do with the positive cord, cut it or let it remain. If you choose to cut it, do so on the count of three. See the Mistress of Ceremonies apply a rainbow patch to heal the places where the cords were cut on you and your father.

Repeat this process with your mother, finishing it with the rainbow patches. This blessing goes back through all the limbs and branches, all the generations of your family tree. Imagine that everyone congratulates you on becoming you. Today you're whole and complete. Feel the sunshine, the joy, the love within. You're free to be you.

When you're ready, open your eyes.

THE CORDS ARE CUT, NOW WHAT?

You can expect the stages of loss and separation as when you cut the cords with "him," because what you're doing is exactly the same, breaking an addiction, your lovesick relationship with your parents.

With any separation or loss, you need to go through these stages in order to complete the process and accept the loss.

STAGE 1: SHOCK/DENIAL, FLYING BLIND

You're going to be in a state of shock. Your mindspeak station is going to start blasting, "I can't believe this is happening to me." "I always thought that she was such a good mother, that he was the greatest father, that they were perfect, that I was flawed." "How could this be?" "I must have been on another planet all my life. How could I have been so blind?" "This can't be true, it's too terrible to be true." "Oh God, it's true."

You'll cry, feel sorry for yourself, try to run away, do anything and everything not to face reality. You'll fantasize that all of a sudden one day you'll wake up and your parents will be perfect, you won't have to go cold turkey, separate from them, deal with *their* lovesickness, they'll have changed. This is the same old fantasy—somehow, some way they'll love you.

Your big question will be "Couldn't I see them just once?" If you start to slip back into denial and you might, do one of the Breaking-Through-Denial exercises again.

Affirmations

I'm doing this for me.
I am successfully cutting the lovesick cords that bind me.

I am divorcing my parents as parents so I can reconnect with them as
people.

STAGE 2: DEPRESSION/ANGER/GUILT

This stage is like walking through a mine field, at any time you could
blow up, be blown up, it's just a question of when, where, why! This is
it, you're in the trenches with major mood swings from anger to
depression to anger, back and forth, back and forth. You'll feel on edge,
snap at almost anyone for almost anything. You'll go from being *so*
angry you can't believe it at your mother for controlling you, for your
father for not being there, abandoning you, leaving you at the mercy of
your mother, to feeling guilty about how angry you feel, to beating
yourself up for feeling angry in the first place. Then you'll panic at
these mutinous, heretical, terrifying thoughts and feelings, then you'll
cry feeling more pain than you've ever experienced in your life, even
from losing a him, as you begin to remember, experience, what was/is
real, not fantasy.

"Why Me? It Could Have Been So Nice—I Was Robbed"

As you begin to peel away the layers of denial, confront the truth,
you'll feel ripped off, robbed, unlucky, deprived. You're going to start
thinking, "Why me? Why did this happen to me? Why couldn't I have
been lucky enough to have been born to nice, normal parents like
everyone else? Why was I born into such a miserable, lovesick family?
Why didn't father notice that mother was smothering, strangling me?
Why didn't he stop her? Why did he let her control me? Why wasn't
he there for me? Why didn't he protect me from her? Why was I the
one dealt the bad cards? It could have been *so* nice if I came from a
normal, healthy, loving, apple-pie family like Ward and June Cleaver,
then I wouldn't have so many problems and I would be married and
living happily ever after, not having to struggle so hard with my
recovery. I was robbed.

It would have been so nice but it wasn't. That's the reality. It wasn't
and nothing you can do will ever change the past. This is about
changing you in the present so that you can heal your you, so that you
can take your life back into your own hands and divorce your lovesick
parents as parents.

Don't Get Even, Get Angry

Allow yourself to feel angry, very, very angry, furious, enraged. It's healthy to feel it. Go for it! Your mother is a b——! Your father is a b——! Your mother, whom you worshipped all these years, is a selfish, self-centered, manipulative woman who cannot love you or anyone else. Your father, whom you idolized all these years, was absent from your family life, unable to show love, to be intimate, to tell the truth. Neither one was ever there for you.

These are very powerful feelings! You can be just as angry at your father for not being there, as you are at your mother for being there too much or vice versa, however it worked in your family! The probability is that you'll get angry at them both, although it's harder to feel anger at the not-there-when-you-needed-them parent because you can hardly remember their presence, interaction with them, intimacy, talks, sharing. The more this parent was withdrawn or absent the more you tried to get his or her attention, the more you overidealized him or her. If you worked very hard this person on a pedestal, this god, would notice you. It was "your fault" if he or she didn't. Now you understand that you were working hard at getting water from a stone, that no matter what you did, or how hard you tried, this parent didn't, couldn't, be there for you, talk to you, hug you, love you.

Either way, whatever the combination, whether your parents are dead or alive, this is it, the original anger you repressed when you made that fantasy bond switch and changed angry feelings about your parents into angry feelings at yourself, changed "their fault" to "your fault," changed "they're wrong" to "you're wrong." This is the anger you feel at your parents' inability to love you the way you were; their not letting you be you, ignoring you, not being there for you.

This anger has been buried for a long time in the black hole! Now all of a sudden it's going to emerge, come out, hit you with hurricane force, take your breath away. This is going to be very unsettling, upsetting. You're going to feel like a human grenade, your nerves raw, open; anyone, anything can pull your pin, make you explode, detonate your anger. You'll be on a short fuse, blow up at anyone who crosses your path, overreact. This is a powerful, healing reaction.

You're going to blame your parents for everything that's ever happened to you in your life. Finally, the fantasy bond broken, "your fault" has turned to "their fault." It's their fault that you can't have relationships, that you're a loser, that nothing in your life works—your own parents have cheated you of your birthright, made you lovesick, your own parents are the villains in your life, they did it to you, they are bad news, they're wrong, they're wrong, they're wrong! Now that the fantasy bond is broken you'll begin to fantasize about getting even, intricate revenge plots to kill off your parents, make them suffer, tell them off, confront them in a public place so that everyone will know how bad they are, Mommie and Daddy dearest.

There are many ways to express this anger in a healthy way in order to get rid of it. *Do not confuse this anger with reality and act it out.* If you start to feel that you're overwhelmed by your fantasies and can no longer differentiate between fantasy and reality you need professional help. Call a doctor, a psychologist, a therapist and ask for help. It's nothing to be ashamed of, you have a lot of anger that's been buried for a lifetime and it may feel overwhelming to deal with it alone right now!

Exercises: Getting Angry, Not Even

Make two columns in your notebook. Your Mother. Your Father. List all the things you're angry at them for since you were born. "I'm angry at my mother because when I was seven she never came to see me in the school play." "I'm angry at my father because his work was more important to him than I was and he never came home on weekends." Everything that comes up, no matter how small, how petty, needs to be released.

Write a letter to your parents and tell them all the reasons you're angry at them. This letter is for you, not for them. It's not meant to be mailed or sent, it's merely a way for you to express your anger.

Buy yourself a padded bat (Bataka) and let'er rip, take a tennis racket and bash pillows. Smash. Bang. Hit. Pummel. Say out loud, "You're a wimp, Dad! Totally controlled by Mom. I'm furious at you for not being able to stand up for yourself or for me. You wimped out!"

Turn yourself into a ferocious beast and growl till you feel empty. Throw pillows or kick them. Say out loud, "This one's for you, Mom, for all the times you told me I was wrong." Scream underwater in a swimming pool or your bath tub. Punch a punching bag. Get into it. Bang away to your heart's content. Go someplace isolated and scream. Exercise. Overdo it for a day—swim till you drop, run till you drop, walk till you drop, bike thirty miles, take two aerobic classes, play three sets of tennis, play softball and have an hour batting practice.

Do spring cleaning in winter, summer, fall or spring. Clean everything you can lay your hands on including glasses and silverware. Clean out your closets. Buy Play-Doh and make images of your parents, then destroy them. Paint a picture of your mother, your father, and shred it. Call your buddy and complain about your parents. Go to a support group and share that you're angry at your parents.

SOON TO BE A MAJOR GUILT TRIP

After you get angry, then you're going to feel guilty, very guilty, the heaviest guilt trip of your life. This guilt, the other side of feeling angry, can and will stab you in the back, suffocate you, put you through hell. This is the death rattle of your mindspeak station, beating you up within an inch of your life in an almost unbearable harangue. "You're a bad seed, a bad child, evil!" "How can you think such monstrous things about your parents, *your* own parents?" "You're going to be the death of them." "You're going to kill them." "If they die it's your fault." There are moments when you won't be able to stand it a second longer, feel an incredible urge to call them, apologize, make sure that they're still alive, that you haven't killed them. You'll want to do anything to get back in their favor again beg, plead, wimper, apologize. Don't do it! This is as low as you'll ever feel, the loneliest, but you can't go home again! Not yet! This is the moment of truth, of separation, of pain from cutting the cords. It's the death struggle of your lovesick you.

Watch out for this guilt trip! If you start to feel overwhelmed, change your environment. Get out of the house. Exercise. Take a walk, a bike ride. Go to a movie. Say some affirmations. Pray. Tell your buddy you're feeling guilty, talk about it, admit it. Go to a meeting, share it in a meeting. Remember, you are not alone. You're feeling the pain of separating from your parents. You are at the bottom. This is what it feels like to cut the cords of your lovesick fantasy bond.

CRY, BABY

As you begin to remember all the pain, the rejections, the sadness, the loneliness and you become more and more conscious of the Greek tragedy that has been your life your mood will shift from anger and guilt to Depression with a capital D. You'll cry a lot, feel drained, wiped out, withdrawn, unable to cope with anyone with your life, want to escape from it all and sleep a lot. Now you'll realize that you've been depressed and unhappy all your life, made all the wrong choices, done all the wrong things, been with all the wrong people, a life victim and you've hated yourself all the way through. The sun is never going to shine again because these were your parents who you loved; your own parents did this to you. Unthinkable. Intolerable. Your parents have toppled from their pedestal and crashed into thousands of little pieces around you, and like Humpty Dumpty, "All the king's horses and all the king's men couldn't put Humpty Dumpty (your parents) together again."

You're depressed. Accept it. Don't beat yourself up for it. If you need to cry, have a good one. Let all the tears from all the years come forth to heal you. Don't try to stop yourself, encourage even more tears. This, too, will pass! This is just a stage, the intensity of these feelings will abate. You have to go through this to keep on going, to recover. You're going to make it! Your healthy you is going to triumph over the lovesick you! The anger and guilt will subside, the sorrow melt away, the depression lift.

STAGE 3: I UNDERSTAND

"It's My Life, Not Theirs"

In this stage you'll finally understand that you couldn't get love from your parents and it isn't a matter of how hard you tried, it's a simple fact, they did the best they could but they couldn't give you what they didn't get from their lovesick parents, unconditional love. They didn't have it to give and it isn't their fault. It's also not your fault. You'll analyze it and reanalyze it, the whys and wherefores of what went wrong, all your lovesick patterns that came from all their lovesick patterns but when all is said and done, this stage is about taking responsibility for what you can do about it now, about taking responsibility for your own life, understanding that they were lovesick, they brought you up lovesick but you don't have to continue to be lovesick. You don't have to stay that way!

How you lead your life on a daily basis is your responsibility, not their fault! Being victimized, always trying to get what you can't have, never getting what you want and not wanting it if you get it, able only to recreate rejection, unable to accept love because you feel you don't deserve it, are only lovesick patterns, not your life; yes, you have them but no, you don't have to continue them, you can break them. Now that you've cut the cords with your lovesick family, you can begin to take responsibility for living your own life, start over with a clean slate aware that you have the power now, not them.

You can choose to be healthy, you can choose you, you can choose life, you can choose not to be lovesick.

Taking the Ball Back Into Your Own Court

You've cut the cords, gone through shock, broken through denial, grieved, become *so* angry you could hardly breathe, then guilty, depressed because you come from a lovesick family. The past is past, it's history, it's over, you can't change it, rewrite it, redo it. All you can do is understand it, put it to rest, move toward accepting that although you've come from a lovesick family and you've been lovesick, you can break the pattern and take responsibility for the present and the future. The ball is in your court. You can take control of your own life in spite of your lovesick conditioning. You don't have to be lovesick. You can choose to be healthy. You have all the talent and natural resources to play a great game of life. All you have to do is play. It's your choice! The ball is in your court! You can choose to recover, win, beat it!

STAGE 4: ACCEPTANCE OF THE LOSS

Reentry into New York after four months in the country was a series of "How am I doing?" tests. Would I fall back (no pun intended) to my old bad habits? Get lonely and sleep? How would I do without a boyfriend? How would I do with Mother? She was expecting a reconciliation, the summer was over.

Mother and I did "a power lunch." We acted as if nothing had happened. Same as it ever was. No matter how crazy things were, we continued our game of "Let's Pretend." After exchanging banalities (I was too much of a chicken to come clean with what was really going on) I asked her if she'd give me a party for my upcoming birthday. She complained, "Why do you need a party? Someone else should throw you a party, why do you have to be so social? Where do you get that from, anyway?"

I held my breath, bit my tongue and didn't react. This was a test. If I didn't allow myself to be a target, her darts couldn't get me. "Yes, Mother, I am social. Yes, I love parties. Yes, I'd love it if you threw me party. Nothing elaborate."

"But your apartment's a dirty mess. I'm ashamed for anyone to see it. You don't know how to throw anything out, those papers, your closets . . ."

Same tape she'd been running for years. I was social (a sin). I loved parties (an outrage). My closets were a mess (a misdemeanor, life imprisonment). I didn't know how to throw things out (the crime of the century, death penalty). All those papers (firing squad at dawn). No, I wasn't perfect and I did have a penchant for paper piles but that didn't make me wrong or bad, just messy, different from her. She'd tried to make me the same as she was all my life, criticized me and made me wrong for being different. I wasn't okay the way I was. I had to be the way she wanted me to be. Mother had not been able to love me the way I was, she wanted me to be the same.

In the middle of this revelation I forgave her, it wasn't her fault. Her mother hadn't loved her the way she was, had tried to control, mold her, too . . . there wasn't a generation gap, just a continuum. Mother couldn't ruin my day by telling me how messy I was as long as I saw her criticism for what it was. "You're messy" didn't mean that I was no good. I didn't have to take Mother personally.

—S.I.

You've gone through the wars and come back home, battle weary, tired but triumphant. You're going to start to feel better. There will be moments when you try and try but can't think of anything wrong. There's a tiny little ray of hope, a cinder ignited inside you that will never go away and you begin to trust that it's there for keeps. You've come to terms with your lovesick parents.

You accept that you put your parents on pedestals and became addicted to their rejection. You accept that you felt unlovable, because your parents were lovesick, couldn't give you unconditional love. You accept that you have only been able to obsess over rejecting, unavailable or unattainable men because of your original relationship with your lovesick parents. You accept that you have been trying all your life to get love for being who you are not rather than for who you are because you felt empty, unlovable.

You accept that you've been recreating being a victim and victimized because it was a family pattern. You accept that many of your rejecting, negative friends, bosses, people in your life have been patterned after your lovesick, rejecting parents. You accept that you have controlled, become a caretaker in your relationships, trying to change your partner because you were mirroring, recreating your lovesick relationship with your parents.

You accept that your parents never gave you unconditional love but you can give the love and care to yourself. You can recover.

THE WHITE BUTTERFLY, A PRAYER

Beloved Divine Mother and Father:

Please forgive me for the dramas that have clouded my perception. Thank you for the lessons.

Dear God I ask that you fill the black hole in my heart with your spirals of sunlight and moonlight.

I release the pain.

I release the disappointment.

I release the anger and hurt.

I breathe in healing love.

I breathe in your infinite compassion for my journey to growth and wholeness.

I affirm Divine Right Action in my life.

I ask that your wisdom fill me so that I may move into the light of love and truth.

I choose metamorphosis from a caterpillar into a radiant white butterfly. I celebrate my flight. I celebrate my beauty. I am free.

I give thanks. I give thanks. I give thanks.

CHAPTER 10

Kicking Your Great Escapes

THE CHANGING SEATS
ON THE TITANIC SYNDROME

I woke up in the morning with a hangover of hangovers . . . the tympani section from the Philharmonic was practicing the Anvil Chorus in my head. I walked into the kitchen to make myself a cup of coffee and there on the dining room table was a business card. I picked it up and panicked. Whose card was it? What had happened last night? For a while I couldn't remember anything. Then I got it. I'd gone to a party last night and bumped into my ex, Eric, with his new wife wrapped around him. I felt so jealous I couldn't breathe. Then I met that handsome guy, a friend of Eric's. He must have taken me home. I was having a blackout! I'd never had one before. I felt gross, dirty, disgusting. I obsessed over whether I'd done it with the guy all day.

I couldn't wait to confess to group that night. I raised my hand, "Please don't think I'm a bad girl but . . . I went to a party last night and I think I went home with a man because he left his card on the table but I can't remember anything . . . I'm having a blackout."

Group tried to comfort me. They'd all been there before.

Elizabeth asked, "Were you drinking at the party?"

"Well, I, um, had a glass of champagne, smoked a joint, and it was a dinner party so I ate." Mendacity. Come on tell the truth. Bite the bullet. "Actually, I drank more glasses of champagne than I can remember, had two or three joints, ate until I couldn't eat anymore."

Elizabeth didn't seem shocked. I was.

—S.I.

"Susan, did it ever occur to you that you are cross-addicted?"

I watched Susan's face, saw the thunderbolt strike. She began to cry, to talk, to release, "I've been running away all my life! Sex. Pot. Alcohol.

146

Food. Men. I've been cross-addicted to everything I could find and I have been all my life."

It was a big moment for her, a breakthrough that would lead to the next stage of her recovery.

—E.M.

Now that he is gone from your life (no matter who rejected who), and you've separated from your parents, the black hole is going to yawn and gape. You're going to have the overwhelming sensation of feeling empty. You may also feel anxious, out of control, off balance, lonely, terrified, fearful of your life, lost. Time to run away . . . escape.

You've felt this way before . . . that you were empty and you had to run away from that feeling. You've been running on empty all your life, escaping your depression through addictions, him, other hims, overdoing sex and drugs and rock and roll, food, working, pills, shopping, exercising, cleaning . . . you name it. You've used them separately or together, one at a time, all at a time. These are your usual timehonored great escapes. The more lovesick you are the more crossaddicted you've become. We call this the Changing Seats on the Titanic Syndrome.

Cross-addictions are the symptoms of your lovesick relationship with yourself. They keep you trapped, unable to feel love for yourself or anyone else. They end up owning you, prevent you from recovering and reclaiming your right to self love by keeping you addicted to selfdestruction and self-inflicted pain.

Recovery is about being good to you, addictions are about being bad to you. The only way out of the black hole is to fill it with self love!

Recovery is about learning to love yourself. You can't recover from lovesickness while you're addicted to pain and keep abusing your body, mind and spirit. You can't find you when you're spending all your time getting lost in your addictions. No matter how hard you try, you can't fill up the black hole with a chocolate chip cookie, a bottle of champagne, a joint, a line, a new pair of boots or all of the above. You can only find more self-hate.

You can't recover from lovesickness without cleaning up your act, kicking your great escapes, breaking your addiction to pain. There is no other way!

I had a horrible morning with my mother shopping for clothes. All she did was complain about how fat I'd gotten. She was relentless. Why was I a size 14 when we both knew I should be a size 10? Listening to her complaints, trying on clothes and having to look in the mirror at myself, that fat, ugly, disgusting person, was torture. How I hated myself. If only I could peel off my body the way I could take off the clothes. I began to sweat. I left her in a terrible state. I called Dennis from the street asked if I could come over. I went to his house and we made love. I went home, but I was so lonely that I called David who asked me over. I left him after we had sex, still unsatisfied. I called Charles from the corner and went over to see him. We smoked a joint, polished off a bottle of wine and went to bed. I left him late that night and walked home. I had this weird feeling that nothing could fill me up.

—CYNTHIA

CATCH 22

1. Something happens that consciously or unconsciously triggers you. You have a jealousy attack, a friend is getting married, having a baby. He doesn't call. No one calls. The wrong one calls. Someone criticizes you. You gained two pounds. You were late to work again. You lost your wallet again. The spot in your favorite blouse won't come out. Your hair looks terrible no matter what you do. Something's wrong. You begin to obsess over it. Suddenly you begin to feel empty, depressed, uncomfortable, wired, down or put down, rejected, uneasy, anxious, worried, upset . . . very upset. Your mindspeak station goes haywire. "You're never going to meet anyone, ever again, you're going to be alone for the rest of your life, you'll die alone. You don't have a date for Saturday night. He didn't call you back."
2. You can't handle it, deal with it, stand it, cope.
3. You begin to obsess about something else instead. You visualize a glass of champagne, chocolate cookies, your favorite lover, your stash of pot, that pair of shoes you saw in the window. You gotta have it. Then you lose control. If you have them you "do" them, if you don't, you go get them.
4. You overdo everything, smoking, drinking, eating, having sex, shopping, working, working out, trying to find love, relief and salvation in a candy bar, a drink, a joint, a new lipstick, sex, a marathon run or all of them together.
5. For one minute, fifteen minutes, an hour, a day, a night, you go unconscious, block the feeling, stop the mindspeak, fill the black hole, lose control, black out, get numb, escape.

6. Right after the high there's a low; after the up, a down. The black hole feels empty again. Your mindspeak station starts blasting again, "How could you have done that, you gained five pounds in three minutes, fatty, you were fat to begin with, you don't remember what you did, you were drunk, stoned, sloppy, you can't afford what you bought, you're bad, you're bad, you're bad." You feel even worse about you . . . you've created more pain.

7. You do it again and each time you need more to fill the bottomless black hole. Each time you do it you're trying to feel better, each time you do it you find more about yourself to hate.

It's a paradox. Catch 22. The Changing Seats on the Titanic Syndrome. The more lovesick you are, the greater your self-hatred, insecurity, the greater your inner pain . . . the greater your need to run away to escape that inner pain . . . to fill up the black hole . . . the more escape routes you take, the more lovesick you become.

All of your addictions are self-destructive, add more guilt, more pain, more upset and then you still hit bottom. You can't afford to keep changing seats on the Titanic, you're going to have to sail straight. There is no other way!

SHE'S GOTTA HAVE IT

If there is one thing I have a weakness for, it's champagne.

—MARILYN MONROE

In the classic movie, "The Lost Weekend," Ray Milland plays an alcoholic. There's a scene where he's in the audience supposedly watching an opera but instead keeps visualizing, flashing to his coat pocket. Then he can't stand it anymore. In the middle of the performance, he gets up, pushes through a row of people, runs to the coatroom, gets his coat and what's in his pocket, a bottle of booze. He's been obsessing over having a drink.

He had to have it. You've gotta have it. That's the big problem. You can't eat just one, either. It's the whole bag, then another. The whole bottle, the whole anything until you go unconscious, until you get away from it all. You're a charter member of Club Getaway as in "let's get away from it all." How many times have you visualized "the bottle in the coat" (whatever that means for you), then become so obsessed that you couldn't do another thing until you had it. You can and have done unbelievable things to get the "it" that you crave when that craving comes on. You've taken trips, journeys underground in the middle of the night to strange places, to meet dealers, to find an after-hours club that serves booze, or a store that's open all night to buy junkfood. You shudder, beat yourself up the next day when you think about it, if you remember, or maybe you get lucky and black out.

> As for his patient's attitude toward men, Dr. Greenson was to note Marilyn's increasing trend toward random promiscuity. In her last months she was to tell him that she was having sex with one of the workmen remodeling her house. Once she invited in a taxi driver who brought her home late at night. An undercover investigator for the Los Angeles District Attorney, engaged on another case, told of stumbling on Marilyn having sex with a man in a darkened hallway during a Hollywood party.

That's what your life has been about—something goes wrong, you've gotta have something, you'll do anything to get it and when you get it you'll do it all until there's nothing left, gobbling up a chocolate chip cookie, then another and another, downing a glass of champagne, then another and another, having sex with someone who doesn't love you, working until you're numb, getting high till you're blind, loving someone who hates you, charging it till you're on your way to debtor's jail. Then you start all over again.

Because you can't eat just one, drink just one, smoke just one, do one line, or have just one date with him without obsessing, these addictions control you and your life in a totally self-destructive love-sick way, every day . . . because with you it's all or nothing and there's nothing in between.

Being lovesick means that you're out of control with your addictions. Recovery is about understanding that you have to break your lovesick relationship with your addictions so you can regain control over your life.

MOI? YOU'RE NOT TALKING ABOUT ME

You're not cross-addicted, not you. You can stop doing whatever you're doing anytime. Why, there have been days, even weeks when you didn't _____ (fill in the blank). An addict has to have it all the time. Of course, you're not an addict.

The moment of truth is here. You've been successful in breaking your lovesick addiction to him, to your parents, now it's time to take an honest look at the rest of your lovesick life. You can't recover from lovesickness while you're busy changing seats on the Titanic. The next step in your recovery is facing up to how you've been living your life, to what extent you've been escaping into your addictions.

Recovery is about breaking through denial of your cross-addictions, then giving them up.

BREAKING-THROUGH-DENIAL EXERCISE #1

What Are Your Great Escapes?

Make a list of your escapes. If you're not sure, put it down anyway. Go back to the list after you finish the next day and see what else comes up.

> Another exercise I asked Susan to do to help her identify her cross-addictions was to list her lifetime addictions.
>
> —E.M.

> It was the strangest list. I discovered that I'd been escaping since I was little, didn't know the meaning of moderation. I'd do, rather overdo, things in tandem. I was an "aholic." I needed a "he," or "it" to fill me up, take over my life, thoughts and actions from the moment I woke up in the morning to the time I went to sleep at night. I was cross-addicted to: overeating—in a starve/binge life yo-yo, gaining and losing thousands of pounds; drinking, smoking pot; sex. There was no difference between a bottle of Don Perignon champagne, a whole box of Entemann's chocolate chip cookies, a joint of Hawaiian sensomilia and a night of great sex, they were interchangeable, they were the same.
>
> —S.I.

BREAKING-THROUGH-DENIAL EXERCISE #2

A Week In Your Life: Binges, Bargains and Benders

Keep track of your life for a week. Write down everything you do or overdo from the time you get up in the morning until you go to bed at night. Keep track of binges, bargains and benders, sprees, what you eat, how often, how much, when you drink (alcohol), how often, how much, when you do drugs, prescription or otherwise, when you go shopping, for what, if you stay late at work and don't take lunch, who you call and why (other "hims" for a good solid rejection), when you pop pills, how often you clean, who you date, when and who you have sex with, when you smoke or snort. Note how you feel before, during and after. Be honest. Wherever you are, whatever you do, carry a notebook with you. Don't cheat, you're only cheating yourself!

LAST DEFENSES AND STUMBLING BLOCKS

One of the stumbling blocks to breaking your addictions is the shame you feel about your "problem." It's hard to accept that you're addicted, worse that you're cross-addicted. You think that addicts are bad people. Therefore this is just one more proof that you're a bad person and rather than accept that you deny it.

You're not a bad person, you're not your addictions but you are addicted. You're not your lovesickness but you are lovesick. Your addictions began as a positive impulse, a hope that you could stop the pain of your lovesickness and find relief, comfort, love. You were only doing the best you could under the circumstances. Be kind to yourself. Forgive yourself.

There are other stumbling blocks to anticipate. You may fear that stripped of your addictions, you're nothing but an empty shell, the black hole incarnate. You may fear change, anything new or unknown or out of your control. The negative talk on your mindspeak station will start blasting, "You can't do it, you can't beat it, face it you're a loser, who's kidding who, you're boring if you don't smoke, no one will like you or talk to you if you don't drink, you have nothing to say if you don't do a line. There's nothing inside you and now everyone will find out."

Your last defense is the pessimism you've built up over the years that nothing ever works, you're a loser, a life victim, you're going to fail so why even try. You're used to being a victim. You put yourself in self-destructive situations that can only lead to pain and then try to make them better by adding more pain. This is your lovesick self acting out. You recreate pain over and over, need to escape from it, then need more and more pain to keep you going. You've become addicted to the pain. It's a self-defeating, deadly cycle.

Recovery is about giving up your addiction to pain, taking responsibility for creating it, learning that there is another way to be, that you can live without it.

You can take control of your own life, give up your role model of being a victim and choose to win.

Recovery is understanding that your cross-addictions add more pain, fuel your addiction to pain, make you hate yourself more, ensure that you continue to be lovesick and maintain your loser status. You can learn how to replace self-hatred with self-respect and self-love but you're going to have to do it STRAIGHT! You can't move out of the House of Pain and learn how to love yourself if you continue to hurt yourself and create more pain.

In order to recover from lovesickness you must give up your addictions, break your addiction to pain.

WHAT DO I DO NOW COACH?
GO COLD TURKEY AND CLEAN UP YOUR ACT!

It's time to clean up your act, Susan, take a break from men and sex for a while and from the rest of your escapes, too.

"Are you crazy? How long is a while? Sure, sure, easy for you to say. Give up men, food, sex, drinking, pot. Just like that. Cold turkey. What will be left in life and will it be worth living?"

"Do you call plotting out your escapes day in and day out, every day, every night, living? Do you want to keep on hurting yourself every chance you can get for the rest of your life? Do you want to recover or not?"

This was the worst ever. She was right, g_____t, she was right. I would have to go on the wagon with my life.

—Conversation betweeen S.I. and E.M.

You can't recover unless you're straight, abstinent, sober, celibate, clean, off it, whatever you want to call it. There is no other way. You're going to have to go cold turkey. Cold turkey? Right! Cold turkey! Why cold turkey? Why give up all your addictions? Can't you keep one? Because there's no such animal as part-time addiction . . . you're either addicted or not. Once you start, it's all over, you go all the way. It's impossible for you to eat one spoonful of ice cream, have just one drink, one puff. You can't. You know it.

Bite the bullet and do it! The only way to recover is to give them all up. There are no ifs, ands, buts, maybes, compromises or in-betweens, it's a yes-or-no deal. It's going to be tough but you can do it. Cold turkey is the only way.

Your recovery comes first. *You* come first. *You* and *you* alone have the responsibility of your recovery. It's in your hands. You have the ability to stop your self-destructive behavior, to stop hurting yourself. The more you stop hurting yourself, the easier it is to love yourself.

This is not your mother or father or some authority figure telling you no, you shouldn't _____ (fill in the blank), causing you to rebel and do it anyway.

You have to go cold turkey on your addictions to recover from lovesickness. If you don't you can't. Period.

Note: You can stop most addictions cold turkey. The following are exceptions that require outside help and medical supervision: Heavy use of alcohol; any prescription drugs or substances that give you dangerous withdrawal symptoms.

YOU'RE NOT ALONE!
REACH OUT AND CALL SOMEONE

The whole country is in recovery. Everyone's getting off something, whatever it is, and they're proud of it. This is the time, if ever there's been a time, to go on the wagon with your addictions in a safe place with safe people.

Write a declaration, "I am cross-addicted to _____ (fill in the blank) and going cold turkey. Sign it. Then call in the marines . . . reach out for help, activate your network and join a twelve-step program or a few of them. Your network is the key. The buddy system wins the day.

It's impossible to overcome addictions without support! You can't recover alone!

THE COMPANY YOU KEEP

This is the time to weed out any friends or people in your life who can't support your recovery at this time. If you have a friend who over-drinks, smokes, or overdoes whatever you want to stop doing, this is not a good time to hang out with them. Once you've decided to go cold turkey, it's much too hard to be around someone who's doing it, when you've chosen not to. Make it easy on yourself. Be around people like you who can support your recovery, not your illness.

When you're in the company of others who don't judge you, put you down, criticize you or blame you, you can honestly listen, learn, feel supported, accepted, acknowledged, loved and appreciated for what you're accomplishing. Being with others who are committed to the same goal, who can share your wins, your losses, ups and downs is the way to go.

The biggest risk, however, are "other hims." Watch out! No other hims are allowed. This is a must!

BEWARE OF OTHER HIMS!

Watch out for "other hims." Being with, dating, sleeping with, obsessing over or seeing other hims is your worst problem because as a lovesick person, you'll turn to other hims to escape, once you go cold turkey on everything else. Beware! You have to go cold turkey on other hims, too. Why? It's the same problem, you can't have even one date with a him without getting addicted.

Other hims of the past. Any of the exes in your lovesick love life are off limits. X them off your list. Make sure you don't see them or call them. Every single one of them was bad for you then and will be worse for you now. He hasn't changed, you're changing by not seeing him.

Other hims of the present. Take your telephone book, rolodex, little black book and read it. List every man in it and see whether or not he is okay to see. Okay to see means that he is nice, good, boring, the kind of guy that you've avoided all your life. However, if you get that little knot of pain or anxiety when you read his name, or start to think about how nice it would be to see him, make love, any fantasy you have, you can be sure he's another "him." Make an X next to his name. Make sure that you don't see them, call them, have a date with them, much less sleep with them. Put yourself on your honor, better, do it with your buddy.

Other hims of the future. New hims are going to be everywhere! They're going to pop out of the woodwork now that you can't have them. If you meet someone and you feel hotter than the Fourth of July you can be pretty sure it's a him. Take that on faith. You won't know one when you see him but if you're attracted to him in an obsessive way then he's no good for you. The rule of thumb is, If you're not sure don't see him. You need to be on your own without any hims for a while. It's essential to recovery.

You've been addicted to hims all your life but the bottom line is that you can't recover with a him in your life. Your recovery is about learning how to be on your own, addiction-free, away from the pain of being with a him.

GOING TO MEETINGS:
THE TWELVE-STEP PROGRAMS

There's a twelve-step recovery program available to you no matter what your addiction, no matter where you live, in every city and almost every town in the country. Use them to help you recover from your great escapes. You can go to a meeting as often as you need to, whatever the time of day or evening, wherever you are, whenever you're in need. People in your twelve-step program are there for you, they'll give you their first name and phone number and ask you to call them. They mean it, call them. That's what these programs are about, that's why they *work*. The twelve-step meetings like Alcoholics Anonymous, Overeaters Anonymous, Narcotics Anonymous, Sex and Love Addicts Anonymous, ALANON, CODA, ACOA etc., work as a social, spiritual and intellectual support network. These are meetings that anyone can attend, they are free. These meetings exist to help people stop self-destructive behavior over which they are powerless, to help people help each other. They support you in going cold turkey.

Note: Joining a twelve-step program, or several, attending as many meetings as you can or need to is part of the recovery process but it is not the cure. Stopping your addictions is part of the recovery process, it is not the cure. Learning how to love yourself unconditionally is the cure!

For a total listing of nationwide available programs, see the back of the book.

TRASHING IT RATHER THAN GETTING TRASHED

One of the best ways to avoid a slip, once you've decided to go cold turkey, is to toss out, trash your escape(s). If you're going on the wagon, toss out all the booze, if you're going on a diet, don't have ice cream, cookies, or anything remotely munchable or calorie-laden around. (If you have children, make your own space in the frig and put an off limits sign on their food. "Don't eat their food.") If you smoke pot give it away or flush it down the toilet. Same with any drugs. If you're a shopaholic, consider freezing your credit cards, cutting them in two, putting yourself on a daily allowance. If you're a workaholic, plan to cut down on your work by asking the assistance of your boss, your co-workers, your secretary.

SHOWING UP FOR YOUR LIFE DAY BY DAY

To structure your life around your recovery, begin with your day. Concentrate on what you're going to do, what you're doing rather than what you're not doing! When you get up in the morning plan out your day. Anticipate any potential problem areas; down time, time alone, lunch, after work, dinner, then cover all the bases. Set rigid limits on yourself. Make a list of don'ts and live by them. Acknowledge the destructive power of your addictions. Don't tempt yourself. Avoid doing anything that makes you feel uncomfortable. Avoid loaded choices, keep it simple. Don't put yourself in any potential bad-news position like making plans to go out to a gourmet restaurant when you're on a diet and there's nothing on the menu that's less than a million calories. Don't meet your friends for a drink if you can't handle ordering a glass of sparkling water.

Call your buddy, or your sponsor, discuss your day before it begins, ask her advice about potential problems, anticipate and solve them ahead of time. Make sure that the worst times of day are covered. If dinner is a problem plan to have dinner with your buddy. Go to a meeting, go to two meetings, three. In the beginning of recovery, most people go to eight to ten meetings a week!

Whatever it takes, whatever you have to do, anticipate, plan, call, check in, structure your day around your recovery, day by day.

Put as much energy into stopping your addictions as you used to do to keep them.

This is it! This is your recovery! This is your life! This is for you! You can make it! You can do it!

THE CRAVING

Out of the blue comes a craving. You start obsessing over a joint, a brownie, a glass of champagne, that cute guy you met five months ago who never called you back. What should you do?

1. Admit that you're having a craving. "I'm dying to _____ (fill in the blank), I'm having a craving."
2. Ask yourself what's happening, what triggered this off, what just went wrong?
3. Think what you can do instead, that's good rather than bad for you. Be prepared. Make a list of things to do in case, keep it on file, pull it out now.
4. Call your buddy immediately, tell her before you act out or on the urge! Call your sponsor. Go to a meeting. Take a walk, go to the gym, take a bike ride. Do a meditation. Say some affirmations. Pray. Write. Read. Take a nap. Get a facial. Have your nails done. Buy a new book. Rent a video. Call your buddy back. Go to another meeting. Keep moving. Remember to watch out for weekends. Structure them the most carefully. Meetings and more meetings. Movies, church, temple, friends for brunch, a museum, a bookstore, exercise, go visiting if you can.
5. Congratulate yourself for beating it. Give yourself a gold star. Keep a record of your victories.

AS TIME GOES BY

As your recovery begins to progress, you'll find that you pick up signals and signs earlier that indicate you're heading for trouble. It will become easier and easier to forestall an attack, a craving. What you're really beginning to understand now is that you may be powerless over your impulses, but you have power over your choices.

You can be intensely attracted to someone and not see them or go to bed with them. Recovery means realizing that you're still going to be attracted to Mr. Wrongs, but that doesn't make you wrong because you can choose not to be with a him. You can lust after drink, a joint or a chocolate ice cream sundae and not give in. You may still have that craving but you don't have to go to the store and buy it. You can call your buddy and tell her about it, go to a meeting, take a walk, instead.

You can want something, crave it, even begin to obsess over it but (and this *but* is major) you can choose to stop it, not do it, not act on the impulse, not act out.

I had a temperature, was sneezing my brains out, my nose red from blowing, my eyes tearing, my body aching and racked with pain but I went to the dance anyway . . . it was Saturday night. I wandered around saying hello, danced one dance alone. Then I saw him. Ronny, the newspaper man. I hadn't met him but I'd heard him talk. I began to chase him around the room, staking him out, hunting him down, trying to corner him. No matter what I did he didn't notice me. A few guys asked me to dance but I turned them down. I was too busy. Then I had a sneezing attack. When I recovered I couldn't see Ronny, began to look around the room wildly—where was he, had he gone home, was he dancing with someone else? I bumped into my friend, Vicki. She told me how terrible I looked, asked why I wasn't home in bed. Why wasn't I? I began to laugh. "I'm not home in bed because I've been chasing a him around the room. You know Ronny, the newspaper man don't you?"

"Of course I know him. Everyone knows him. He hits on all the girls here. He's a womanizer. Total bad news. His wife ran him out of the house because he was addicted to sex with other partners, he even admitted that he deserved it."

"Of course he's bad news, why else would he be the only man in the room I want."

"Do you think it's healthy for you to be chasing him?"

Healthy for my cold or healthy for my head? Something snapped. The spell was broken. "Unhealthy for both. Don't be shocked but I'm giving up and going home. Thanks for the help!" I was shocked, then I felt fantastic. Best flu I ever had. I could say no to a bad guy, I could say no!

—S.I.

WINNING

My normal weight stripped on a doctor's scale, no cheating, was 128. In my ninth month of pregnancy, with my second child I hit 200 pounds on the head. After my boy was born I weighed 180 or 182, depending on how far I tipped the scale first thing in the morning, after I'd gone to the bathroom. I'd gone from pleasantly plump after the first baby, past overweight to obese.

I decided to lose the weight once again. I'd been on every diet known to man or woman. This time I did it by fasting, going on shakes. In order to do this I had to deal with the rest of my addictions. Besides overeating they were: drinking, smoking pot and pills. I gave them all up. Somehow in the next eight months I lost 55 pounds. I realized during this process that I would never be able to have a glass of wine again, that I couldn't handle it, that it made me eat more, gain weight because it made me lose control.

It's a year later now and I've kept the weight off and haven't had a drink. I go to A.A. meetings, O.A. meetings. I allow myself to eat everything else but fat.

The best thing I ever did for myself was to suspend my belief system, that life was in my hands. I choose to believe now that everything turns out the way it's supposed to so that every time something happens good or bad I look at it as an opportunity to have a growth experience. I used to feel that the world was hurtling by and I was on an obstacle course dodging, shifting my weight and balance, against the onslaught. Now I've had a few flashes of feeling complete. I even have these beautiful moments when I love myself. I feel that I'm a movie star, a good mother, responsive, nice. As long as I am myself, things are going to turn out the way I want them to. I understand that any successful people feel this way.

—CLIFFETON

How great it feels to beat it . . . to win. You wanted to do something so much but you didn't do it. You, who have given in to every impulse you felt all your life have finally done something good for you, resisted temptation. Take a moment out and congratulate yourself. This is a major league home run with the bases loaded. The pennant. The world series. That great! You're winning. Not only that, you're a winner. You are not your addictions. You are beating your lovesickness. Talk back to your mindspeak station, "See what I did, I stopped _____ (fill in the blank) and I haven't done _____ (fill in the blank) for _____ (fill in the blank). Reward yourself. Tell your buddy it's your first week or month or year or day anniversary. Keep track. Celebrate.

LEARNING TO WALK WITHOUT CRUTCHES

The hardest thing is waking up in the morning and realizing that's as good as you're going to feel all day.

—SAMMY DAVIS, JR.

Everyday living, doing normal things is a new mission and you pray it's not impossible because you think you're not well enough equipped. For the first time you're going into the trenches of life, unarmed, naked, scantily clad in your recovery uniform: head held high, eyes wide open and sober—yes, clean, dry and abstinent. It's Friday night. You're invited to a party. You shriek. You gasp, 'a party . . . with people?' One of your first missions in recovery is to go alone. You're scared but you press onward, try to look your best and chant to yourself, "I am confident, I am beautiful, I'll be okay." You get to the party . . . "oh, my God . . . you want to turn and run away. The voices are telling you, "you're not stylish enough, you're wearing the wrong dress, you're inept, different." You want to run to the bar and throw down two quick ones, fast. After all, everyone else around you is doing it, aren't they? Then click, the light bulb over your head goes on. The party epiphany: other people are just as insecure and scared as you are. This time you are opting to face it and not escape it. There's a certain satisfaction in realizing this. Maybe you don't need their approval at all, maybe you just need yourself and that's the best one can ever have.

All of a sudden you realize that you're not inept. The recovering lovesick have endless opportunities. Whether conscious of it or not you have an incredible survival mechanism, you. You're a survivor. After all, look at some of the great capers you've pulled off, are pulling off right now!

—MARY JANE

You're sober, clean, abstinent, off it, straight, on the wagon, on a diet and you're bored. There's nothing to look forward to, no wild and crazy events to get you through the day, the night. You're not having any fun. Life is a supreme drag. That's how it feels in the beginning. You're so used to getting high one way or another, of running away from you, that staying straight, living life without crutches is boring, uncomfortable, in its own way, stressful. Your mindspeak station will start up, "How are you going to get through the cocktail party straight, you're going to bore everyone, be bored when you're not drunk, stoned or high." Watch out!

Of course its going to feel strange to be straight, without your reward system, to experience a feeling rather than run from it. You're learning how to walk without crutches and you're taking little baby steps. Stay away from situations and people that can set you up for a slip. Treat yourself with kindness and courtesy. Don't push yourself or put yourself into any situation that you can't handle. This is not a test. You don't have to prove anything to anybody. If you've been doing it before using a crutch you probably can't do it without a crutch. Acknowledge it. "I can't go out drinking with my friends and not drink." "I can't go to the ice cream parlor and not have an ice cream." You are not being a wimp to say "No, I can't," you're being smart. If you take temptation away it's easier to resist.

If you start obsessing over something, call your buddy, your network, go to a meeting or two, go to the movies. Work on what's making you feel like that.

Hang on. Hang in. You can do it.

AFFIRMATIONS

Say to yourself as many times a day as you need:

I am not my addictions.
I have the power to change my life.
I'm the one who's in charge of my life.
I'm feeling good about me today.

2. STARTING OVER: A REPROGRAM GUIDE

CHAPTER 11

A Mind, Spirit and Body Makeover

RECOVERY IS THE BEST REVENGE

Recovery is a journey into the unknown, the untraveled territory of self-love, positive thinking and good experiences, a place where all things don't have to end up in crisis, a new land where a sense of self-confidence will replace self-doubt, where constructive behavior replaces destructive.

—MARY JANE

IT'S TIME FOR A CHANGE

It's time to continue down the road to recovery, time for the next steps, time for a change and you're ready. Time to ask questions you never thought of, get answers you never dreamed about, learn new patterns, new ways of thinking, of acting, of doing things.

It's time to learn to speak a new language . . . the language of self-love.

It's a time to heal, rebuild, mend, plant, reap, have fun, enjoy your life, laugh, be happy. It's time to love you. It's time for good times.

It's time to star in, produce, direct and write the script for your own feature film, "Recovery is the Best Revenge"!

It's time for a body, mind and spirit makeover.

NOTHING IS WRITTEN

In the movie "Lawrence of Arabia," while in the desert during a sand storm, one of the camel boys is lost. Lawrence (played by Peter O'Toole) notices, asks his whereabouts. One of the riders shrugs his shoulders, says, "It is written that he should die." Lawrence rides off, disappearing into the storm. Some very long time later, he reappears, his face overexposed to the sun, his lips cracked, his blue eyes triumphant, the lost boy sitting behind him on the camel. Lawrence pauses, says in a parched voice, "Nothing is written."

Nothing is written in your life. It is not written that you're doomed to be a victim, damned, eternally lost, forever lovesick, forever unable to be happy. It is not written that you have to spend the rest of your life acting out your own Greek tragedy, dying in the third act, Marilyn. You have no tragic flaw. Yes, you can break the lovesick molds and start over. You can write a new script for your life because nothing is written.

Your body, mind and spirit have been out of kilter, out of synch, disconnected, but you can start over with a clean slate and have a body, mind and spirit makeover!

YOUR MIND MAKEOVER

The Bag Lady Blues

"Good morning, this is your mindspeak station S-E-L-F-H-A-T-E with your first broadcast of the day. Didn't sleep well again? You were worrying, had one of those terrible your-life-in-review nights and realized that nothing is working, you're alone and falling apart? Well, don't worry, you'll probably never ever get a good night's sleep again unless you call up and beg your doctor for sleeping pills and you know he won't give them to you because he knows that you're addicted to them. Boy, you look terrible. Fat. Why did you eat dessert, the whole loaf of Italian bread in the restaurant, then buy that chocolate peanut butter Häagen Daz and finish it off? No wonder you gained three pounds last night. Look at those five gray hairs. Better pluck them out. You're getting old. You don't have a date for Saturday night.

"A news flash has just come in: You're going to be late again! No matter how much you rush there's no way you can catch the 8:05 and it's your fault because you reset the alarm to get fifteen more minutes sleep and you knew when you did it that you probably wouldn't have time to make the train. How could you have done that when you promised your boss you wouldn't be late again? That was his third warning so he'll probably fire you.

"Don't even bother to try and have a nice day. There's no way you can! Victims can't win, you know that! That's all for the morning news, it's Mindspeak Station S-E-L-F-H-A-T-E signing off."

You're a bag lady. You carry garbage bags around with you wherever you go filled with your lovesick debris: negative attitudes, thoughts, opinions, ideas, expectations, reverse thinking, a list of self-criticisms that you beat yourself up with, old worn-out tapes, scratchy or broken 78 rpm records that you play on your mindspeak station over and over, all day, all night, every day, every night. You live off your garbage and when you get a stomach ache from it you're so used to it that you don't complain anymore, convinced that having a stomach ache every day is your destiny in life.

Hating you, negativity, listening to your lovesick mindspeak station S-E-L-F-H-A-T-E has become a conditioned response, self-fulfilling prophecy in your lovesick life. You operate on automatic pilot, your life prerecorded on tape, whatever you do. "Play it again, Sam." You push the old recording and step into your new day. By now, as a bag lady, you've become your garbage, your lovesick mindspeak station, you are what you think and you don't let anything good happen since you've mastered the art of setting yourself up for failures and bad times, for negativity, for loss, for losing, for being a victim, for being miserable, for staying lovesick. Then you sing the blues, someone else is doing it to you, so you don't have to take responsibility for your own lovesick creations!

But there's no one else out there! You, you're the one! You're doing it to you. You're creating the rejection, the pain. You're the one who makes it happen to you, the one who recreates it. The bottom line is you are not your lovesick mindspeak station! You can cut the cords of your negative thinking patterns, change, reprogram the negative broadcasts into positive ones, toss all your lovesick garbage into a biodegradable incinerator and let the good times roll.

The only way to do it is to break through denial that you're doing it, then do it!

BREAKING-THROUGH-DENIAL EXERCISE:
A WEEK IN THE LIFE OF
MINDSPEAK STATION S-E-L-F-H-A-T-E

"What Is the Sound of No Hands Clapping?"

Keep track of everything you say to yourself, tell yourself, think, during a day in your life. Make two columns. Positive communications. Negative communications. Make notes of all your mindspeak bulletins, newsflashes, old scratchy recordings, new releases. Pay attention to everything you say regardless of what you're doing, where you are and who you're with. Don't be shocked if you come up with the world's longest list of negatives and not one positive. Whatever you've written down is your mindspeak communication to yourself.

NAME THAT VOICE

One day while I was in Greece on vacation, lying on the most beautiful beach I'd ever seen, all alone, I became conscious of a nagging voice in my head. It was telling me that I was stupid because I couldn't say one word of Greek, couldn't memorize how many drachma to a dollar, should have planned better because I wasn't going to find the right room or any room, that I was going to get too burned, that I was going to be alone and miserable for two weeks without anyone to talk to, that I shouldn't have come to Greece in the first place, that I'd wasted my airfare, on and on and on. Then all of a sudden it dawned on me, I wasn't alone on an island, I'd brought all my head baggage with me, thousands of miles from home.

It was the strangest feeling. I felt like enormous Gulliver who awakened one morning to find himself a prisoner, tied to the ground by tiny Lilliputians with thousands of tiny little ropes . . . the voices in my head. I realized that one negative thought was nothing but I never had just one negative thought. It was literally thousands and that the power of thousands of negative thoughts was enough to cripple me, bring me down, tie my life up in knots. I named them the Lilliputians.

—OLIVIA

One of the best ways to get conscious of your mindspeak station broadcasts is to name the voice or voices that you hear. The Girls. Mickey Mouse. The Voice of Doom. Chicken Little. The Bad Guys.

Your mother's voice. Your father's voice. His master's voice. After you name the voice, start to talk back to it, "Is that you again? Give me a break." "Nice try, but no cigar." "Get out of my head, Girls, I'm onto your game." The moment you get that it's only a voice is the moment you can turn off the broadcast.

A reminder: Recovery is an active process. You have to do positive things to replace the old negative patterns on a daily basis, day by day. Remember to use all your recovery tools from your fanny pack, your net, your network, affirmations, visualizations, the works. No excuses. Recovery does not happen overnight but it happens as long as you keep on doing the work and taking positive baby steps to reprogram your negative lovesick mindspeak station.

In the beginning it's going to feel strange, like you're acting, as if it isn't true or real. Eventually what seems unreal will become real as you overthrow the great dictator, your mindspeak station. Keep on inviting positive things into your life. The more you do the work, the more your life will work.

VISUALIZATION:
THE INCREDIBLE WHITENESS OF BEING

This visualization is about letting go of the psychic debris that fills your mind, the garbage, those old tapes, recordings, broken records that you keep playing, that tie you down, debilitate you, prevent you from letting a positive thought in.

Go to your space, light a candle to invoke Minerva, the Goddess of Wisdom to bless this healing. Lie down and make yourself comfortable. Imagine that you are in your Temple of Love and Healing. You can see that the sky is very blue with lots of puffy white clouds. Imagine that you are lying in the midst of a puffy white cloud. Breathe in white clouds and breathe out black smoke. Feel the white clouds coming in through the top of your head. As they float down your body, feel where you have stored memories from your past, the negative thoughts, feelings, attitudes, beliefs, mindspeak tapes that have hurt you all your life. Let yourself feel the feelings, the attitudes. As you breathe in white clouds, breathe out black smoke. Let the white clouds loosen, diffuse them. Keep breathing in white clouds until your whole body understands that these thoughts are only thought-forms that you learned, family patterns, mindspeak tapes.

Notice any tension spots in your body. Each place holds a memory, a broken dream, a disillusionment, a disappointment. Thank your body for remembering, for telling you its secrets. As you breathe in white clouds listen to the stories, allow the puffy white clouds to envelop them, diffuse their energy into your arms, your shoulders, your chest, your heart, fill your whole body through your torso, down your legs to your feet. Breathe them all out, breathe out black smoke.

Feel that your body is totally filled with white clouds. As you breathe out, sigh, feel a sense of relief, of release. Imagine that Brother Wind blows onto your cloud. He introduces himself, I am Brother Wind. Will you permit me to blow away all your old stories, all those dark clouds? When you're ready, say yes. As you inhale take a very deep breath and as you exhale make a whoosh noise. Imagine that as you exhale Brother Wind blows away all the black clouds into the stratosphere where they cannot harm you anymore.

You snuggle back in your cloud feeling relaxed, radiant, lighthearted. You are the incredible whiteness of being.

When you're ready, open your eyes.

THINK LOVELY THOUGHTS, CANDY, ICE CREAM, LOLLIPOPS

There's no pay off in pessimism.

—SIDNEY BRILL

If you find yourself saying something negative like "I'm not going to make the train," "I can't do it," "The hairdresser is going to give me a bad cut," "I'm never going to get a raise," reverse the thought immediately, "Yes, I can." "I'm going to make the train." "I can do it!" "I can learn the backhand." "Of course I'm going to get a great hair cut!" "I'm sure my boss is going to give me a raise, I deserve it." The whole trick is to catch yourself, then switch the thought to a positive, yes, I can, yes, I can, yes, I can!

Become conscious of negative images, verbs, nouns in your vocabulary and make a conscious effort to substitute a positive anytime you start to say a negative. Negative: "I'm dying to go." Positive: "I'd love to go. I'd be happy to go. I'm looking forward to going."

Keep on accentuating the positive, eliminating the negative!

HAPPY DAYS

At the end of every day remember to write down five good, happy, upbeat, wonderful, nice, *positive* things that happened to you during the day. Keep the list so that you can read your week in review, all the good things that happened to you. "I did my laundry." "I exchanged smiles with the green grocer." "I wrote a good memo." "I saw a great movie." "I had a lovely walk." "I found a penny." "I exercised for half an hour." "I bought myself anenomes." "I didn't call him up." "I saw the first snowflake."

Keep thinking happy thoughts! Keep dreaming. Keep track.

PUT ON A HAPPY FACE

You live longer if you smile. Practice makes perfect. Anytime you get tense do this exercise. It's the quickest, most pleasant way to relax.

Close your eyes. Lie down, or sit comfortably wherever you are. Breathe deeply for a minute. Smile. Starting from the top of your head, visualize sending this smile all the way down to the tips of your toes. Feel the relaxation. When you're ready, open your eyes.

YOU CAN GET IT IF YOU REALLY WANT

You can get it if you really want. This is your life. You're in charge, you're the boss. You're not your mindspeak station. You are not your mind. If you want something you can get it because nothing is written, because the only thing that has a memory of your past is your mindspeak station and you can jam it anytime you want. Stay conscious of your negativity, the more you *beep* it, the more you reverse it, the more you believe in you, the more you smile, put on a happy face, think lovely thoughts, believe, think positively, keep your commitment to recovery, to you, the more negativity and negative space will go away. The more you do the work, the more your life will work. A free woman is her own creator. You're the boss.

YOUR SPIRIT MAKEOVER

Turning On Channel S-E-L-F-L-O-V-E: Amo Meum Ergo Sum, I Love Me Therefore I Am

You've been running on empty, down depressed, desperately seeking love in all the wrong places, all your life. Optimism, enthusiasm, spontaneity, joie de vivre, high spirits—the ability to love yourself, believe in yourself or anything beyond you—have been flattened out, your feelings frozen, buried in the black hole, replaced by the Black Magic Syndrome, chronic underlying depression and its partner, pessimism. Your world has become blacker and blacker, bleaker and bleaker, smaller and smaller. You've become a tragic heroine, your life a Greek tragedy because you have a tragic flaw—there is no you, nobody's home, you're an empty shell. These negative beliefs have become the foundation of your life. No one will ever love you, nothing good will ever happen to you, there will never be a happy ending because you're unlovable.

But you are not your lovesick beliefs and you don't have to believe them. You don't have to be Marilyn. You can turn off your negative belief system, reprogram it into a positive one, toss all your lovesick scripts, write positive new ones and tune in Channel S-E-L-F-L-O-V-E where your dreams come true, where you have happy endings, where you're filled with love, where you believe in magic, where you believe in love, where you believe in you.

Your spirit makeover is about turning on Channel S-E-L-F-L-O-V-E.

Your spirit makeover is about learning how to say to yourself, I love you just the way you are.

Your spirit makeover is about finding something that's always been there inside you but got lost in the black hole, your connection with the universe.

Your spirt makeover is about finding your lost you, starting a relationship, connecting with that inner you, call it what you will, love, the higher power, your spirit, the Great Spirit, your Goddess, God.

Your spirit makeover is about taking a giant leap of faith that there's a better way to live beyond your lovesickness.

Your spirit makeover is about understanding that you are not lost, that it's only your lovesick belief system clouding your perceptions, your life, the way you experience it, the way you live it.

Your spirit makeover is about exposing your lovesick beliefs as false idols, changing pessimism to optimism, reprogramming the negative beliefs into positive ones, opening up Pandora's box to let hope in, blowing those black clouds away and letting the sunshine in!

Your spirit makeover is about believing that you can fill the black hole with self-love so you can feel good so you can feel God.

Your spirit makeover is about believing that you can fill the black hole with self-love. Your spirit makeover means giving up worshipping rejection and choosing self-love and healing in its place.

Your spirit makeover is about adding sun, fun, rainbows and miracles to your life.

Your spirit makeover is about having your dreams come true.

It's not something you can understand, it's something you will experience.

LETTING GO, LETTING GOD

I'd always hoped that life wasn't just a giant cosmic accident and there was some connection between things but somehow or other I was never able to believe in a God, anything out there, anything I couldn't see. I decided to take a course in prayer, just in case, because if there was a connection, I wanted in! Learning how to pray has been tough, perhaps the most challenging thing in my life. When I started to pray, the first thing I prayed for was a weekend house. Then I thought "No, I want to pray to end world hunger first and for a weekend house second." The upshot is that when you pray, you learn about yourself and you have to be honest because there's no point in bull——ing God. You've got to give in, let someone else take the wheel, let go of control and let the universe take over. When I pray now I say, "This one's for the universe, this one's for me." I know I'm in good hands.

—SALLY

There are many ways to pray, to connect:

Go to a church or temple, your own, someone else's. Go to Unity Church. Take a Goddess workshop. Take a Course in Miracles class. Take Yoga. Take Transcendental Meditation, T.M. as it's called. Take a course in prayer or meditation.

Take a daily nature walk to a beautiful place, sit and watch a sunrise or a sunset. Buy yourself a plant, water it every day and watch a flower grow.

Take a trip in a plane. Look out the window. Play in the clouds. Go to a planetarium. Get lost in the stars.

Spend a day with a child. Be a child. Go to the beach. Build a sand castle. Look for shells. Play in the water. Go to the river. Talk to the river. Listen to the voice of the river. Go to the lake. Watch the birds. Become a bird. Fly. Climb a mountain. Play Queen of the Mountain. Talk to the mountain. Listen for answers.

Whatever works for you is the best way.

My soul was dying. I was trying to connect with a higher power, a god, anything I could pray to because anything was better than the blackness, that feeling of hopelessness that I was alone, that there was nothing out there, nothing. It seemed so easy for others to pray.

Then one night I was watching "Heaven Can Wait" on HBO. Joe Pendleton, the Warren Beatty character, was trying to convince Mr. Jordan (James Mason) that he should be allowed to inhabit the body of an aging tycoon, so that Joe could lead the Los Angeles Rams to the Super Bowl.

That would be impossible, Mr. Jordan explained. "But don't worry, Joe, you'll get your chance. There's a plan, Joe. There's a plan for all of us."

A "plan." Maybe there was a plan for me. Maybe all the pain and despair I was feeling was a necessary part of my journey. I started praying to a plan. When I became willing to let go and follow that plan wherever it might take me without reservations, my outlook on life began to change, so did my feelings about God.

Today, God for me is simply a sense that I'm being taken care of. A feeling of "okayness." What I now view as one of the great ironies in life for me is the sense that my feelings are the truest reflection of my spirituality. What is the most real thing about me is also the most spiritual. My life is none of my business, I show up and do the best I can.

—ED BUTLER

It's all about perspective, the view from where you sit. When you step out into the margins, do something unexpected, take a look from another angle, you can get a new perspective, a new lease on life. You're not a little princess with the kingdom the size of a shrinking pea; the world's your oyster.

SOMETHING'S COMING, SOMETHING GOOD

Each day I affirm that I am connected to you, my Higher Power, and that you bring to me a high vibration of healing love and energy.

I affirm that today I will attract everything good and positive that I need for my learning.

I will live today to the fullest expression of my being.

I will fill myself with radiant light, which will bring to it beauty and fun and deep pleasure.

I welcome the luminous love that strengthens my knowing that all is well in my world.

Good things are coming to me, my world is filled with spirit and love.

Thank you for showing me the wonders of nature that expand my Being and bring peace and beauty to my soul.

Thank you for rainbows.

Thank you for starry nights, butterflies and waterfalls.

Thank you for me.

Thank you for love.

Thank you for loving me.

Thank you.

VISUALIZATION: A STAR IS BORN

This visualization has been created to help you connect with the universe.

Light a candle and dedicate this healing to Venus, the Goddess of Love. Close your eyes, relax; take three long deep breaths, inhaling relaxation, exhaling the tensions of the day. Glide through the columns into your Temple of Love and Healing. As you slowly breathe in and out, imagine that it's a clear, warm night and you are lying on a soft pink cloud suspended in the Milky Way. Just above Venus shines upon you.

As you breathe in Venus' starlight, her lovelight, imagine that you are breathing in love. A star shower of tiny little stars, that sparkle like diamonds, streams in through the top of your head. As you exhale, breathe out black smoke into the night, the dead air of self-pity, self-hate. Breathe in starlight, feel it flooding your body, filling it with love. Feel the starlight, tiny stars flash around your body, caress you. Each part of you feels their friendliness, love, and warmth. You feel safe, relaxed.

As starlight enters the crown of your head, filling your head with shimmers of stars, feel energy and light accumulate between your brows. A brilliant diamond beam forms in your third eye opening the pathway to inner vision. Starlight flows into your inner ears opening the pathway to understanding beyond words, the knowing of Divine Will.

Feel the starlight spiral down, circle your head, your eyes, your mouth, your jaw, your throat. Breathe in starlight, lovelight, exhale black smoke. Imagine the starlight circles around your shoulders, moving down your left arm, to your fingers, then flows to your left shoulder down your left arm, to your fingers. The starlight circles around your torso, your breasts, down to your hips, your legs, then streams into your toes. Breathe in starlight love, breathe out black smoke, hate, fear. Whoosh it all out.

Starlight suffuses every organ, your reproductive system, your sex organs, your digestive system, your hormone system, into your blood, lymph glands, and everywhere the light touches, a high vibration of healing begins within the center of each molecule. Each cell touched by the starlight, knows the way to be whole, to be perfect. Imagine that a halo of starlight surrounds every cell.

As you breathe in lovelight, send attention to the places in your body that need your love. As you breathe in starlight love, breathe out all your old pains, sorrows, tears, disappointments, rejections. Breathe out all your old memories, breathe out black smoke. Breathe stars into your lungs, fill them with health, with love.

Move into your heart now, and breathe in Venus love. A shower of thousands of tiny love stars collects in your heart. Breathe out pain. Stay in your heart, and as you breathe in, fill it with so much love that it overflows into the black hole filling it up with starlight, with lovelight. Breathe in love, breathe out pain, in love, out pain.

Feel how beautiful you are, how good it feels to be loved. You are perfect. You are whole. Feel the sweet love pouring into your wounded heart, into the black hole, healing all the old wounds, filling the crevices, healing with love. Allow your heart to be healed. Allow the black hole to be filled with star love. With every star breath fill the black hole up with love and exhale self-hate. Breathe in star love, breathe out black smoke, all the old stories.

As the starlight moves from your heart up to the third eye, you understand on a deeper level that nothing was wasted, that every lesson was of value in your pathway to self-love. Breathe out black smoke, release and forgive those actors in the play that gave you pain, rejection or fear. Move into a place of deep recognition, compassion, and love for yourself. As you breathe in starlight, star love, ask Venus to lift all the negative thought forms from you and open yourself to forgiveness, for it is in pardoning that you are pardoned. Breathe in starlight, feel your whole Being inside and out filled with love, light, healing, feel your body glow with vitality and health.

Allow the starlight to spiral out the top of your head and rejoin Venus, the Source, your own love star. As you breathe in and breathe out feel your eternal connection with your star. See yourself sitting on top of your star, like the Little Prince, on top of his. Feel the sparkling starlight. You are a star. You are love. Your heart is filled with starlight, with love, a double helix of healing spiraling eternally upwards and downwards connecting you to the Universe in an ever constant star dance. Thank you Venus. I love you. You are love.

When you are ready, open your eyes.

A BODY MAKEOVER

Marilyn found out that Sinatra was going out with Juliet Prowse, a stunning dancer from South Africa who was only in her early twenties . . . already becoming famous for her legs. They were supposed to be the most beautiful in Hollywood, Marilyn told me. Now Marilyn, who had never paid much attention to her legs couldn't stop looking at them. "They're too short and fat," she moaned with a look of disgust. "They're horrible." She was constantly on the phone, asking everyone she knew "how bad" her legs were. Of course, they weren't, but that didn't matter. Legs and age were the only things Juliet Prowse could ever have on her. "How could Frankie do this?" Marilyn despaired.

MMMM BOY, IS YOUR BODY BAD:
YOUR DAILY BODY RAP AND
BAD WORKOUT TAPE

Ready to beat up your body? Ready for your bad workout, some really bad abuse? Let's get down and go for it . . . and a five, six, seven, eight . . .

Hold your breath. Don't breathe. Look in the mirror, shake your head, make a face and say, "Mmmm boy do you look bad." Repeat it three times.

Now start with your hair, say, "Boy does it look bad." three times. You need a haircut. A perm. A better conditioner. Your hair is so mousey. Your roots are showing. You need everything. Why not give up and get a wig? Look at your face. Say, "Boy, are you ugly" three times. Your eyes are too small. Your nose is too big. Look at all those lines, those wrinkles. Your skin looks sallow. Watch out for that pimple sprouting, it's going to ruin your whole day, everyone's going to notice it. Now for the chin test. How many chins do you have? Count them. More than one? It's time for plastic surgery. You need everything done. The works. From an eye tuck to collagen injections for your lips. Better start saving.

Now move down into your upper body. Repeat three times, "Boy do you have terrible breasts." They're too small and men don't like women with small breasts. "Boy, could you use implants." They're too big. You look like a cow. "Boy, could you use a breast reduction."

Now move into the pièce de résistance, your stomach. Repeat three times, "Mmm, boy is your stomach fat." There's nothing you can do about it, you'll never lose it. Look how it sticks out even when you hold it in. You're gross. A blimp. No eating for the next three days for you! There's liposuction in your future, it only leaves a small scar.

Now let's talk about your legs. Say three times, "Boy, do I hate my legs." You're right, they're monsters. No amount of work can get you in shape to wear a short skirt with such thunder thighs, with such big calves, with such thick ankles, with such dimpled knees. Too bad for you but short is in.

Now let's talk about your hands and feet. Say three times, "Boy, do I hate my nails." Why can't I ever grow them long enough, why does one keep breaking? Why do I have such short, ugly fingers and such fat hands? To finish off your body say three times, "Boy, do I hate my big feet. Too wide. Too narrow. Fallen arches. Bunyons."

And-a-five, six, seven, eight . . . Get ready for the rap. Hold your breath. Don't breathe.

My eyes are too close
My nose is too big
My lips are too thin
I look like a pig
Everything's low that used to be high
The best I can do is cry, cry cry
My hips get wider day by day
Cellulite will never go away.

Be sure to abuse your body for the rest of the day. Make sure you don't do anything good for you, don't get enough rest, starve or overeat, forget vegetables and fruit, binge out on fried food, steaks and oil, pile up cholesterol, don't do any exercise, or overdo it, don't take a break from work, sit in the same position all day, worry, get sick over disappointments, keep piling up stress, drink at least five or six cups of coffee so you can get more anxious, more tense, pop pills, bathe your liver in alcohol, kill those brain cells with substances, let your body go to pot, keep feeling uptight, push yourself till you drop, ignore any warning signals, keep away from doctors, don't ever have a checkup. Breathe in, hold your breath and jump up and down three times, "You can't work it out, you can't work it off, you're stuck with it." Remember to say three times, every hour on the half hour without fail, "Boy do I hate my body. It's a nice place to visit but I wouldn't want to live there." Keep up the bad workout! When you abuse, you lose!

THE EYE OF THE BEHOLDER

You have a distorted body image that has nothing to do with reality, with how you really look. All you can see when you look in the mirror—if you can bear to look in the mirror—is what's wrong, your faults, imperfections, real or imagined. You play your tape over and over so that all you can think about is how ugly and overweight you are, how much better you'd be if you didn't look how you looked. Your life doesn't work because you're ugly and overweight. If you ever lose weight you gain it right back because all you see when you look at yourself in the mirror is the bad body image you're stuck with—a fat person. All you think about is how much better you'd be if you didn't look how you looked.

You live on the edge. Somehow or other you come down with a cold every year, the old if-anyone's-going-to-get-it-it's-going-to-be-me routine. You suffer from chronic backaches, allergies, migraines, asthma or other psychosomatic illnesses. And as we noted before, you probably suffer from illnesses of the reproductive system.

You let your body go, neglect it, punish it, abuse it, hate it and wonder why things have started to go wrong, why it never feels good, why you never feel good. You take care of your machines better than you take care of your body.

You have a lovesick relationship with your own body.

Every day you play your tapes, your raps, and every night feel sorry for yourself, your bad body image connected to your disappointments. He didn't like you because you were too fat/thin, your breasts were too little/big or your thighs were too skinny/big. Your body has become a cop-out, it's your body's fault if you don't get what you really want.

But it's the only body you have!

You're doing it to your body. You're the one who's abusing it, beating it up. No one else is doing it to you.

The bottom line is that your body is not bad, you're being bad to it. You are not your lovesick body rap.

Your body makeover is about changing the way you feel and think about your body, letting go of your self-destructive patterns, your negative body image. Your body makeover is about jamming, re-programming the negative tapes into positive ones, developing a positive body image and a healthy way of living in your body.

Yes, you can learn to love your body and make it a beautiful place for you to live in.

Yes, you can make your body your buddy.

Your body makeover starts with getting in shape, exercising, saying affirmations, doing visualizations and learning how to take care of it instead of abusing it.

Your body makeover is learning how to love every inch, every part, every cell.

The only way to do it is to break through your denial about how you're mistreating your body, so you can break the lovesick molds and reprogram your bad body tapes into healthy ones.

BREAKING-THROUGH-DENIAL EXERCISE:
A WEEK IN THE LIFE OF YOUR BODY

Keep track of your body for a week. That means everything you eat, drink, your daily habits. Make the following headings and fill them in day by day:

Eating: What did you eat today? That means everything including snacks. Did you overeat? Did you diet? Did you eat a normal portion? Did you eat fast? slow? normal?

Drinking: What did you drink today? Include glasses of water, coffee, diet soda, alcohol.

Exercise: When did you exercise? What did you do and for how long? Do you have a daily exercise schedule? Do you stick to it?

Sleep: What time did you go to bed? Were you tired? How did you sleep? What time did you get up in the morning? Did you feel rested? How many hours of sleep do you need? How many hours of sleep do you average?

Ailments: Did you have body aches and pains, colds, an upset stomach, a back problem, a toothache? How long did it last? What did you do about it?

Your responses to these questions will give you an overview of how you treat your body, what you do to it, how you take care of it, whether you abuse it. The bottom line is that if your body doesn't feel good it's because you're not taking care of it properly. No one else is living in your body. No one else is neglecting your body or abusing it. There's no one else and you only have one body. Your body makeover is about taking responsibility for your own body. Your body makeover is about learning how to be good to your own body, to appreciate it, admire it, take care of it—love it.

BREAKING-THROUGH-DENIAL EXERCISE:
YOUR BODY HISTORY, WHAT'S WHAT,
WHAT'S HAPPENED—WHAT REALLY HAPPENED

Make a list of all the illnesses, ailments, hospitalizations, allergies, surgery, since you were a child. Make six headings: Year, illness, description, duration, what was going on in your life when it happened, did it reoccur?

Whatever the answers to these questions is the lovesick pattern of your physical body life. Look at the illnesses you've had and see what the connection is between your life at the time and getting sick. What did you get sick over? What was the deep reason for your illness? Was it a him? A rejection? Were you run down and depressed? Was there an upset that triggered your illness? Probe until you find the connection . . . there is a connection. Your body has taken a terrible beating consciously through your abuse and unconsciously through your inability to love yourself. Your body has reacted to all these emotions. All those negative feelings, beliefs, attitudes and responses have had to go somewhere. They have—they've been stored in your body. Recurring psychosomatic syndromes are your body's message to you, a warning signal to you that your body's had enough, that you need to stop and reverse these illnesses with your growing awareness, with self-love.

VISUALIZATION: YOUR BODY, YOUR BUDDY

This visualization was created to help you change your negative body image into a positive one.

Light a candle and ask Spirit to bless this healing. Close your eyes, relax; take three long breaths, inhaling relaxation, exhaling the tensions of the day. As you put your attention on your breathing, glide through the columns into your Temple of Love and Healing. When you're ready, take the path down to the meadow.

It's a beautiful sunny day, you can smell the perfume of flowers in the air as you go down the path. From the distance you see a house. As you approach it, begin to notice every detail. When you arrive at the front door, open it. Walk in. Look around you. Notice the interior of the house, all the details, the curtains, the tables, the pictures on the wall. Walk from room to room until you see a closed door that says your name on an oval plaque.

Open the door. Enter. You're in a room full of mirrors. In the corner there is a year clock. Notice how you feel as you look at yourself in the mirror. Take a few seconds and become aware of your thoughts and feelings.

There is an enormous VCR with a comfortable place for you to sit in front of it. Load the VCR with the tape you find on top of it. Push the start button. Sit down and relax. The lights dim and onto the big screen comes the title, This is Your Life. The clock turns back to the year you were born. See yourself as a baby. Look at your perfect little body, your legs and hands and feet. Spend some time with this perfect little baby.

The clock turns to the time you were five. The tape fast-forwards. See yourself on the screen playing as a five-year-old. Spend some time with this little girl. How do you feel about your five-year-old body? What does it look like? How do you feel about yourself? Experience yourself as a five-year-old.

The clock turns to the time you were ten. The tape fast-forwards. See yourself on the screen as a ten-year-old. Spend some time observing yourself. How do you feel about your body? What does it look like? Experience yourself as a ten-year-old. What are your emotions?

The clock turns to the time you are fifteen. The video tape fast-forwards. See yourself as a teenager. Spend some time observing yourself. What does your body look like? What do you feel about it? Are you in good shape? What do you feel about your body? Experience yourself as a fifteen-year-old. What are your emotions?

The clock turns to the time you are twenty-two. The video fast-forwards. See yourself as a young woman. What does your body look like? What do you feel about it? Are you happy with it? Are you in good shape? Experience your self at twenty-two. What are your emotions?

The clock comes back to the present time. The video fast-forwards. See yourself in the mirror as you look right now. What does your body look like? What do you feel about it? Notice what comes up for you when you look at yourself in the mirror now. Watch yourself from every angle. What do you feel about yourself? Do you like your body?

Breathe in healing pink love light, breathe out black smoke and self-hate. Continue breathing.

Notice a pair of heart-shaped rose-colored glasses on the floor next to you. Put them on. They are truth glasses that will allow you to see yourself in the light of love. When you wear them, you can only see how you really look, how you really are.

Push the button on the panel and rewind the video of your body life.

Look at yourself as a baby. See how cute you are. Tell the baby, I love you. I'm proud of you. I love every part of you. You're perfect just the way you are. Breathe in pink light and out any negativity.

Fast-forward the video to when you were five. Look at yourself as a five-year-old. See what an adorable little girl you were. Remember how many things you could do with your body. See yourself playing, laughing, drawing a wonderful picture, dancing. Love this little child. Hold her. Kiss her. Hug her. Tell her "I love you." Breathe in pink lovelight and out black smoke, any negative thoughts.

Fast-forward the video to the time when you are ten. Look at yourself as a ten-year-old. See how tall you've grown. See how much you can do with your body. Picture yourself doing your favorite sports, running, swimming, skating, dancing, horseback riding. Think about all the wonderful things you've learned. Love this little girl. Tell her how proud you are of her. Tell her you love her. Hug her. Kiss her. Hold her in your arms. Breathe in pink lovelight and out black smoke, any negative thoughts and feelings.

Fast-forward to when you are fifteen. Look at yourself as a fifteen-year-old. See how you've developed, how your body has changed, how tall you've grown, how grown up you've become. Picture yourself doing your favorite sports. See how fast you can run, how gracefully you swim, how good a dancer you are, how high you can jump, how good your forehand is, how fast you ski, how well you skate. Admire your accomplishments, achievements. Love this teenager. Tell her how proud you are of her. Tell her you love her. Hug her. Give her a kiss. Breathe in pink lovelight and out black smoke, any negative thoughts.

Fast-forward to when you are twenty-two. Look at yourself at the age of twenty-two, a young woman. See how strong you are, how capable you are, how you can do anything with your body, how you can enjoy it. Picture yourself dancing, walking, doing your favorite exercise. Think about how much you can do; how beautiful you are. Love this young woman. Tell her how well she's grown up, what a terrific young woman she is. Tell her you love her; she can do no wrong. Give her a hug. Breathe in pink lovelight, out black smoke, any negative thoughts, feelings.

Fast-forward to the present time. Look at yourself as you are now through your rose-colored glasses. Breathe in pink lovelight, out black smoke, any negative thoughts. Allow yourself to see all the good things about your body. Congratulate yourself on having such a wonderful body. It's served you well, has always been there for you. See yourself walking through your life with your head held high, loving your body. Tell yourself you love you just the way you are. Tell yourself that you are capable, strong, attractive. Apologize to yourself for hating your body so much for so long. Tell yourself that your body is beautiful, that it is healthy, that it is a safe place for you to live, that you're going to take care of it, cherish and protect it. You know this for sure and no one can stop you from this sacred trust. Give yourself a hug. I love you. I love you. Breathe in pink lovelight, love, breathe out black smoke, any negative thoughts and feelings you've had toward your body.

When you are ready, turn off the screen, open your eyes.

BEEP-BEEP BAD BODY TALK

Notice everything you say to yourself about your body from the moment you wake up in the morning until you go to sleep at night. As you become conscious of your negative body thoughts, attitudes, opinions, your bad body rap and hear yourself beating yourself up or putting yourself down, stop it, interrupt it by saying BEEP-BEEP. BEEP-

BEEP. Give permission to your buddies to BEEP-BEEP you if they hear you saying something negative; get their permission to BEEP-BEEP them.

BREAKING OUT OF YOUR BODY CELL

Ninety-five percent of all models interviewed when asked about their body found something wrong with it.

Marianne Sagebrecht, the Rubenesque West German actress whose films include "Sugar Baby," "Bagdad Cafe" and "Rosalie Goes Shopping," has become a star in spite of being overweight by American standards. When interviewed by the New York *Times* about her success she replied, "I think people like the idea that I'm happy with who and what I am. What I am is round . . . people can see how happy I am as a round lady. This is what I am. This is the form I have: my body is a genetic gift. My ancestors were farmers and I'm very healthy and very strong and I'm liking my round form. . . . For me my weight is not a problem. It's my sign to the world. In America they say you have to be thin to be sexy but it's not true. Every era has its ideas about women . . . soon I think more and more you'll be allowed to be round."

There's no difference between Cher and Marianne Sagebrecht, both are able to look in the mirror and like what they see. They have a positive self-image. They like themselves, they like who they are.

The only thing standing between you and loving your body is your head. It doesn't matter how much you improve your body if you take along your negative body tape with you. You can do anything with your body with proper diet and exercise. Anything. You can slim down, firm up, tone up, limber up, stretch out, build up muscles, add bulk, anything.

But if you don't love your body you won't be able to see the change and you'll change back, blind to the "improvements," a skinny person with a great body who sees a fat person with a terrible body in the mirror. Who is the fat lady? No matter now fat or thin you are, unless you love your body it will always be you. Your body makeover is about loving your body. You can get it if you really want it as long as you love your body.

MIRROR, MIRROR ON THE WALL, WHO'S THE FAIREST OF THEM ALL?

I-Love-My-Body Affirmations

Stand in front of a full length mirror once a day and repeat these affirmations out loud:

I am a beautiful woman inside and out.
I am willing to take care of, accept and love my body.
I am at peace with my body.
It's safe to be in my body.
I am thankful for the gift of my health and I am committed to doing everything I can to keep my body healthy.
I love my body. It is perfect the way it is.
I have an abundance of energy to devote to getting and keeping my body, mind and spirit in perfect shape.

HALF AN HOUR A DAY KEEPS THE DOCTOR AWAY

There is increasing data to support that patients who are fit have fewer incidents of cardiovascular events. They have a lower incidence of heart attacks, high blood pressure, seem to suffer less anxiety, have an easier time controlling their weight, an improved cholesterol level. The additional benefits to being fit are lower risk of certain kinds of cancer. The converse is also true. People with a sedentary life style are at higher cardiovascular risk. What may be even more important is that the quality of one's life is better if one is fit.

To achieve fitness requires effort, persistence and planning. It requires a sense of priority.

Research data suggests that exercise duration and intensity should be 30–45 minutes, 3 or 4 times a week with an intensity so that a target heart rate is achieved in that time, 60%–85% of the maximum heart rate. This varies by age and weight and should be discussed with your own doctor.

Even achieving a minimal level of fitness will bestow many health benefits, you don't have to climb Mt. Everest to become fit, the lowest level of fitness is good enough to be of benefit. Exercise should not be taken lightly. If you have been sedentary, consult with your physician to set up an exercise program.

—DR. STEVEN LAMM

One of the best possible ways to learn how to love your body is by exercising. If you've let yourself go, gotten out of shape, never bothered with fitness or exercise, now's the time to change your outlook, how you look and your daily routine. The latest health reports published by the A.M.A. conclude that just taking a half-hour walk every day makes you live significantly longer. You don't have to be an Olympic jock to live longer, just walk. Amazing! That's right, a half hour a day keeps the doctor away. Exercise also does wonders for your sense of well-being, retards depression, inhibits stress, gives you a natural high.

LET'S GET PHYSICAL

It was so hot that day at the beach, that I took off my twenty-five-sizes-too-large T-shirt and went into the water. When I came out my brother, Mr. Suave, said, "You look terrible. Boy are you out of shape. Look at your legs, they're like jelly."

I waddled off the beach and cried. I stood in front of my full length mirror naked and cried some more. When I was finished feeling sorry for myself, I looked at myself, stood tall and said, "I'm going to get back in shape, d——it, I'm going to start exercising again, I'm not a wimp, I can do it. I promise you that a year from now I'm going to stand in front of this same mirror naked and smile."

The next day I made a plan. I needed to have an exercise program that I could afford, more important, one that I could stick with. I knew me, I'd joined four different health clubs over the years, got bored doing Nautilus and climbing stairs, the stairway to heaven as I used to call it because I never got there . . . stopped going. No, it had to be something I liked doing which meant not walking, running, jumping around in aerobics classes.

I got my bike out of the cellar, took it to the bike shop, filled the tires with air, bought a new fanny pack, basket and lock. I did a survey of swimming pools, the cleanest, closest, cheapest and longest. I joined the neighborhood Y for fifty dollars. They had a new seventy-five-foot pool, it was easy to bike there and the price was right, five dollars a half-hour swim. I decided to take a course in Tai Chi, a combination of yoga, ballet, martial arts and meditation. I had taken it once before, it burned up more calories than running and made me feel good. Then I started my exercise regime, swam laps four times a week for a half hour, took Tai Chi class twice a week for an hour, practiced it faithfully once a day, looking at myself in the mirror, began biking around town regardless of the weather, doing my errands for at least a half hour a day.

In the beginning it was a little iffy, exercise seemed to be getting in the way of everything else, like my life. Then I started to see changes in my body, in how I felt. Little by little my whole attitude about exercising, about my body, changed 180 degrees. I exercise now, otherwise I don't feel good. I understand why runners run, after a while those endorphins start kicking in and you get this fabulous feeling of being high on yourself, centered, strong.

I was walking down the street the other day and heard a wolf whistle, "What legs!" I looked around to see who the whistle was directed at. The construction worker was looking at me. I turned to him, smiled and said, "Thank you."

—S.I.

How do you start to exercise? Make yourself a deal that you'll try it for six weeks. Only do things you like to do or you won't make it. If you like to walk, concentrate on walking a half hour a day. If you hate to walk then do something else.

How to get physical:

Join a gym and get into a routine, learn how to work out on the Nautilus machines, run, use the stairmaster and climb Mt. Everest indoors.

Buy a bicycle (indoor or outdoor) and start biking a half hour a day. Bike for fun, bike to get places instead of driving, taking buses or taxis.

Join a health club with a pool and start swimming laps. Take water ballet or synchronized swimming, be Esther Williams.

Take Tai Chi, yoga or any of the martial arts. They burn up more calories than almost any other exercise and connect your body, mind and spirit. Play softball. Find a local team, get your mitt out of the mothballs and play ball.

Take ballet, dance and make your début at a recital.

Go horseback riding. Learn how to jump.

Rollerskate or iceskate. Buy yourself a new pair of rollerblades.

Run. Do it for fun, one mile, two miles, five or a marathon.

Tennis anyone? Get into a steady game. Play doubles, singles, squash, racketball.

Take an aerobics class. Buy a workout tape and go for it once a day. Ask your buddy to do it with you.

Work out with free weights. See your body get strong and beautiful.

Get into a daily routine. Make exercising your number one daily priority, build your day around it rather than trying to squeeze it into your day. Make a commitment to yourself, I am going to exercise once a day and mean it.

Write down a schedule for the next six weeks. You'll take a half-hour walk at twelve-thirty every day, you'll bike for half an hour on Mondays, Wednesdays and Fridays. You'll take Sunday off. Stick to your guns, keep to your schedule no matter how much rearranging of the rest of your life you have to do. After six weeks, review how you feel. Better! The probability is that just sticking with it for six weeks will get you hooked for the rest of your life.

You can learn to love living in your body because you love your body. You'll start to see results in your sense of well-being, in how your body looks in the mirror in broad daylight, in how you feel physically. You'll have more energy and self-confidence, begin to like you a whole lot better. Look what you're doing for you, you'll be able to see it.

UNITED YOU STAND, DIVIDED YOU FALL

"A Vitamin Be One Shot"

It's your mind, your spirit, your body and your life. You can take back your power, take charge, take control of your life and recover. You are not your mindspeak station, your negative belief system or your bad body tape. You are not your lovesickness.

Recovery is about being one. One you. Your body mind and spirit integrated. Whole. Centered. You are one. You can be one! United you stand, divided you fall.

VISUALIZATION: MARRYING YOU!

This visualization has been created to integrate, marry your body, mind and spirit.

You may want to make some special preparations for this ceremony, take a shower, a bath, put on clean white clothes. It's also a good idea to buy yourself a white flower or flowers and place them in a lovely vase.

Light a candle to invoke Venus, the Goddess of Love to bless this wedding ceremony. Close your eyes, relax, breathe deeply, inhaling peace, exhaling the tensions of the day. Breathe in white crystal light, breathe out white crystal light. When you are ready move through the columns into your Temple of Love and Healing. It's a perfect day, the brilliant blue sky silhouettes your temple. Notice that it is adorned with beautiful white flowers, crystals and candles. White orchids, tulips, baby's breath, cascade from graceful vases, while crystals dance with rainbow light.

See yourself in your wedding dress. Notice everything about it. Notice your wedding bouquet. Breathe in white crystal light. Place the fingers of your left hand over your brow, your eyes, and as you breathe in white crystal light feel the energy accumulate in your mind's eye, bathing, clarifying it. Bless your inner vision, your intuition. As you breathe in white crystal light move your right hand down to your heart. As you breathe in, feel the energy move down from your head and flood into your heart. Feel the glow of love and healing expand your heart.

As you breathe in white crystal light, keep your hand on your heart and move your left hand to your mound of Venus. As you breathe in bless and purify your sexuality, your female you. Feel the connection to your heart. Love and adore your female essence, your womb. As you breathe in and breathe out feel the white crystal light connect your mind's eye to your heart, your spirit to your femaleness in a circle, a wedding ring of white crystal light. Experience wholeness.

When you are ready ask a trusted one, ordained by love, to come to your Temple to perform your wedding ceremony. Notice what he or she is wearing. You may invite a wedding party, any friends or relations to stand by you as you take the vows. Notice what they are wearing. Feel their love. Breathe in and out white crystal light. When you are ready approach the flower laden altar, stand before it and tell the priestess you are ready to take your vows. She will read them to you.

"Do you _____ (your name) take yourself, body, mind and spirit to be your life partner, mentor, divine inspiration, creative muse, and best friend? Will you cherish and appreciate, honor and love yourself for better times, for a better life, for your wholeness, for your health as long as you shall live and love?"

When you're ready, answer out loud, "I do."

"Repeat after me, I love me, therefore I am. By the power you have vested in me, I now pronounce that you are one, body, mind and spirit. You are love. I bless your oneness, your wholeness, I bless you."

As you breathe in and out, repeat three times, we are one.

As you breathe in and breathe out feel the wedding ring of white crystal light that connects your mind's eye to your heart, your spirit to your femaleness in an eternal circle of love.

When you are ready, open your eyes.

CHAPTER 12

Loving You, On Your Own

THE MOMENT OF TRUTH!

A wise woman once said to me, "Guess what, there's no one else out there!" I puzzled over this and finally came to understand what it meant. I'm in charge of my own life. I take total responsibility for my life. Everything in it is a reflection of my inner being and every situation is an opportunity for growth.

—LILI

This is it. The moment of truth. To win or lose. To succeed or not. To change or not. No one else but you can make this decision. No one else can live your life. All there is is you. The choice is yours. You can choose to start a new life, to turn over a new leaf. You can choose winning, being a winner, to succeed, to stay open, to change, to recover. You can do it but you have to choose it day by day, do the work, follow the rules.

PLAYING IT SAFE

Recovery is about safe conduct, drawing boundary lines around you so that you don't let anything bad in, so that you're always safe. It's about playing safe, learning what's off limits, only choosing to have experiences that feel good, that are good for you.

How do you learn? Start by acknowledging that you don't know the difference between healthy and self-destructive behavior, that everything you've been doing, thinking, how you've been acting, reacting, your patterns, thoughts, responses, from the moment you wake up in the morning until you go to sleep at night have been lovesick, off 180 degrees, and you need to change them.

You can't do this alone. You need your buddy and your network. This is a learning process and you can't learn in a vacuum, without healthy role models and teachers.

Starting over is like going back to school. There are a lot of things to learn, courses to take, a lot of studying to do plus a lot of homework. There will be good days and bad. Some things will be more fun than others, some things easier than others. Learning new things is a mixed bag. Being on your own is a mixed bag. So is life. Some days you'll feel triumphant, everything worked, other days you'll wish you'd never heard of the word recovery, you'd like to throw it and your lovesickness out the window. As long as you choose you and your recovery, as long as you stay with it no matter what, as long as you take little baby steps day by day you'll get a gold star.

VISUALIZATION: THE BIRTH OF LOVE

Now that you are married, that you are one, body, mind and spirit, it's time to give birth to your new you. That's what this visualization is about.

Light a candle to invoke Venus, the Goddess of Love, to bless this birth. Close your eyes, relax, breathe deeply, inhaling peace, exhaling the tensions of the day. When you are ready go to your Temple of Love and Healing. Breathe in radiant golden sunlight, breathe out golden sunlight. It is a perfect day. Leave your Temple, follow the path and make your way down to the curving beach of a blue lagoon. There is a bridal veil waterfall on the edge of the lagoon. As you breathe in sunlight step under the waterfall. As you breathe out release every thought that is not love. The waterfall cleanses and purifies you. As you step out of it every part of your body feels refreshed, every organ.

Breathe in the sunlight. Allow the warmth of the sun to dry you off. Lie down at the edge of the lagoon on a green lily pad. As you bask in the sunlight imagine that you are pregnant with possibilities. As you breathe in sunlight feel love for yourself. Think about all the good things you can do. Breathe out white light. Breathe in lovely thoughts, how capable you are, how strong, how wise, how creative. Feel the presence of a baby within. As you breathe in golden sunlight fill the baby with love.

Imagine the child within your belly is growing. As you breathe in love and golden sunlight, imagine your belly is expanding. Breathe out any negativity that may come up, thank your mind, say good-bye and let it move on. Breathe out white light.

As you breathe in golden light imagine that it is nine months. Ask yourself if you are ready to have this baby. Ask Venus to bless the birth with love. When you are ready, take a giant breath, slip off your lily pad, ease to the edge of the lagoon into the sea of love. With one giant exhale, the baby is born. You feel exhilarated. As you float on your back, the baby swims over to you. You reach out, hug the baby, say "I love you" and give her her first kiss.

The baby opens her eyes, smiles, laughs. "I love you, too."

Notice what your child looks like. Tell her you wish to be her parent. Tell her you love her no matter what she does. She is perfect just the way she is. As you breathe in golden sunlight feel your love connection to your child.

It's time to cut the cord. When you're ready ask for the assistance of Iris, the Goddess of the Rainbow, who comes from the waterfall bearing a diamond scissors and two rainbow patches. As you breathe in golden sunlight cut the cord. Iris applies a healing rainbow patch to you and your child where the cord was cut. Both of you are free to follow the rainbow trail of life, of love and beauty.

As you breathe in see her swimming along with you in the sea of love. You will always be together. You will always love each other. She is born. You are reborn. Congratulations!

When you're ready, open your eyes.

SOMEONE'S HOME

As a new mother you're going to have to learn how to take care of yourself and your child, make sure nothing happens to you, that you're safe, no matter where you are, who you're with or what's happening so you can build your life around positives, begin to enjoy your life and yes, even have fun. This means not crossing enemy lines, going overboard, overdoing, letting anyone violate your safe space, steal home; it means being able to stand your ground.

The sheet of paper is blank. It's time to write a new script for your life, and you can, based on self-love, self-care and self-respect. What's good for you, what's going to make you feel good, what's going to make you feel happy. You've found your you, your home. It will always be there, within you, and you have the power to keep it safe.

ON-YOUR-OWN RULE NUMBER 1:
NO HIMS ALLOWED

Don't even *think* about being with, dating, chasing, having an affair with, marrying a him during this period. The most important thing you can do for yourself right now is to be with yourself, on your own.

THE TEN RECOVERY COMMANDMENTS

1. I will love myself for who I am, who I am not.
2. I will keep healthy, body, mind and spirit day by day by day.
3. I will allow myself to feel good, to feel love, to feel loved.
4. I will be my own person, my life defined by my goals, desires, needs.
5. I will take care of myself, nurture myself.
6. I will depend on myself, trust myself, listen to myself.
7. I will protect myself from harm, hurt, rejection, pain or negativity, from anyone or anything that's unsafe.
8. I will stay open to change, to new ways of doing things.
9. I will respect myself, my opinions, beliefs, ideas, values.
10. I will have fun, joy and laughter in my life.

SAFE CONDUCT RULES

1. If you're in a situation and you don't know what to do ask: What would a healthy person do? Does this feel right? Does this feel safe? Does this feel good? Is this good for me? Is just thinking about this putting me off balance? Am I abandoning myself by doing this and filling myself up with something wrong? Does this feel like an escape? Who's going to benefit from this?
2. Ask your body how you feel. Is my stomach rolling around? Do I feel queasy? Do I have butterflies? Do I feel shaky? Anxious?

Nervous? Panicky? Is my back tense? What is your body telling you? If you don't know the answer, call your buddy.

3. If you think you know the answer, but you're not quite sure, call your buddy. Ask her: "What would a healthy person do?" Discuss it with her.

4. If your buddy doesn't know ask your support group, ask another buddy. Keep asking until you figure it out.

5. If all else fails and you can't reach anyone, don't do it or put it off until you know what to do.

6. You have the right to say no to anything that doesn't feel right.

7. You have a right to stand your ground based on nothing else but trusting your gut feeling or not knowing the answer.

Recovery is about remembering that you come first.

Recovery is about saying no to anything that isn't safe.

Recovery is about saying no to anything that doesn't feel good.

Keep asking, "What would a healthy person do?" "Does it feel safe?"

"Does it feel good?" One of these days you won't have to ask any longer, you'll know.

EXERCISE: THE CHARMED CIRCLE

Draw a large circle on a piece of paper. It's a magic circle. In the circle write down all the things that you want to have, do, or experience in your life, things that add to, enhance your life, that bring joy, happiness, fun. This circle represents your new boundaries, what you will allow in your life. It defines your space. Anything within this charmed circle is safe for you to experience. Anything else is not safe, is not your choice, lies outside of your boundaries, invades your boundaries. You have a right to refuse anything outside of the circle.

HOME

Here's a short exercise to do when high anxiety strikes. You can do this anytime, anywhere.

Sit on a pillow with your legs crossed in front of you or in a chair, make yourself comfortable, loosen any constricting clothes.

Imagine that the sun is directly overhead. Breathe in white light from the sun through your nostrils. Inhale slowly and deeply allowing your belly to fill and expand with oxygen; allow your belly to collapse as you exhale through your nostrils. Imagine that you are sending roots down into the Earth each time you inhale. The roots travel down through the floor, deep into Mother Earth. Inhale the sunlight, expand your belly, exhale into the earth and collapse your belly.

Begin to feel how solidly you are connected to the Earth. Feel your heartbeat, imagine that you are aligning it with the heartbeat of the Earth. You are positively rooted in the Earth. Breathe in the white light and feel it move down your spine. Exhale, allowing the sun's energy to flow into the Earth. Feel the light relax you, filling your body, your mind, your spirit with deep peace, love. You are at home within your own body.

Affirm to yourself: I am one with the Earth. I'm grounded. I'm home. Feel how strong, calm and centered you are.

When you are ready, open your eyes.

FEELINGS

TO FEEL, *v*, to perceive in any other way than by sight, hearing, taste or smell, as to feel hunger; to be conscious of (oneself) as being in a specific condition of mind or body.

FEELING, *adj*, sensation received otherwise than through sight, hearing, taste or smell; power to experience sympathy, tenderness, love or the like.

I feel
You feel
He or she feels
We feel
You feel
They feel

This obviously is the conjugation of the verb to feel. Feeling a feeling isn't that obvious, especially a good feeling. Your feelings have been frozen, buried in the black hole for a long time and now as an essential part of your recovery it's time to dig them up, unthaw them. In the beginning it's going to be hard work to recognize a feeling. It will come. Do these exercises and visualizations on a daily basis to get in touch with your feelings. It's equally important to learn how to release negative feelings as it is to be able to recognize and feel positive ones.

MULTIPLE FEELINGS

You may feel a lot of different feelings, experience multiple feelings, positive and negative almost simultaneously. There's nothing wrong with that. On the contrary that's what you should expect. No one experience is just black or white. Life is about feeling shades of feelings, different feelings, a mixed bag. Recovery is about feeling all your feelings. The more the merrier, the more the better.

On her wedding day, the happiest day of her life, a bride feels love for her husband-to-be, exhilaration at the thought of getting married but right before the wedding ceremony she might also feel sadness for the end of a certain time of her life, fear or uncertainity for the new and unknown. Everyone cries at weddings, the happiest of life's occasions.

The more you dig up your feelings the more good feelings you'll be able to feel, the more the black hole will disappear.

FEELING-A-FEELING RULES

If a feeling comes up, no matter what it is, let it be and go with your feeling. If your mindspeak station starts to give you an opinion, shut it off.

If you feel a few different feelings don't edit them. Let them be.

If you can't find a feeling and you know it's there do one or two or all of these exercises until you find and release your feeling.

Listen to your body. Your body will tell you what it is feeling.

FEELING-A-FEELING EXERCISE:
THE GOOD, THE BAD AND THE UGLY

This exercise will help you distinguish between a good and a bad feeling.

Sit in a chair, or lie down. Make yourself comfortable, close your eyes. Breathe in energy and vitality, breathe out tension. Keep your consciousness on your breathing until your mindspeak station is still.

As you take a giant breath clench your fists, your toes, legs, arms, buttocks. Feel the tension everywhere in your body and hold it, hold it, hold it. Feel how your body feels in this tense state. Experience the feeling of tension. This is what tension feels like. Let it all go with a rush.

Now imagine a time when you were with a small child or an animal that you love. As you picture your interaction with this Being, allow the feeling of pure love to fill your heart. Breathe in a giant love breath. Feel how simple it is to let your heart open, to feel love. Feel how much you love this being. Hold that picture in your heart. Hold that feeling. Feel the feeling. Hold it. Hold it. This is the feeling of love. Let go a sigh of relief. You love. You know how that feels.

When you are ready, open your eyes.

VISUALIZATION: STAR BATH

The purpose of this visualization is to thaw your heart. As you can tell by the title, this visualization is going to take place in your bathtub. Set the stage, in this case your bathroom, for a special event. A star who deserves very special attention is going to take a bath. The star is you! Prepare your bathroom. Clean it, so that everything sparkles. Arrange some flowers in a pretty vase. Have a fresh towel or two ready for yourself after you've completed your bath. Turn off the phone. Be sure that you feel safe. Run your bath with bubbles, a fragrance that you like. Put on Mozart, Handel, Bach, the sound track from "Superman"—anything lofty, elegant and relaxing, that you love.

Light a candle and dedicate this healing to Venus, the Goddess of Love and Beauty. Turn the lights off so that your candle is the only light source. Get into your bath. Close your eyes. Relax.

Breathe in pink cloud light and breathe out emerald green light, the colors of the heart. Allow the water to anoint your body. Picture your heart frozen in ice, disconnected from your body, spirit, and mind. With every breath feel the ice begin to melt. Breathe in love, breathe out fear that began when you were very small, breathe in love, breathe out self-hate and resistance. With each breath the ice melts, more and more. It's cracking now, splintering away. Take an enormous breath, breathe in security, warmth and pink cloud love, feel the love swirling around your heart. There it all goes, all melted, as you exhale emerald light. Feel your heart free of the ice. Feel your beautiful heart now, strong and full of self-love. I love you. I love you, you're wonderful.

Submerge yourself, all the way under, and as you come up, picture yourself reborn, like the Birth of Botticelli's Venus, rising, naked and beautiful out of the water. You are Venus, the Goddess of Love, a star.

When you're ready, get out of the tub and dry off with a fresh towel. Look at yourself in the mirror, smile and say, "It's safe to feel, to express my emotions. I am beautiful. I love myself. I'm a star."

FEELING-A-FEELING EXERCISE: BEDTIME STORY

This exercise is designed to put you in touch with your feelings on a daily basis, the good and the bad. This will allow you to release upset feelings rather than store them, enjoy good feelings rather than ignore them.

Before you go to sleep, while lying in bed close your eyes and begin to breathe in deeply and slowly. Breathe in relaxation, breathe out tension until you have stilled your mindspeak station. Begin to journey through your body starting with your head and ask your body to tell you if it is holding onto any unhappy or upset feelings. Is there a place that feels tense? Is there something that aches? Are you aware of any soreness, pain? When you find a place that does not feel good, pause there. Let the feeling talk to you. Give it a voice. Let it tell you what it is. Listen to its bedtime story without judgment. Be sympathetic. Be supportive. You have a right to this feeling whatever it is. Own it. Embrace it. Ask yourself what you need to do to release it. Listen to your body, it will tell you what you need to do. If your mindspeak station starts to broadcast, thank it and shut it off: "Nice try, but a thought is not a feeling."

Now put your attention on your heart. As you breathe in relaxation and breathe out tension, put your hands over your heart. Ask your heart to tell you how it feels. Were there some good feelings today? As you take a giant breath recall a time during the day when you were feeling good, happy, when you smiled or laughed. Picture what you were doing. Recreate where you were, what you were doing, saying. Remember that feeling. Hold it. Hold it. Now with a sigh of relief, exhale. Thank your heart for helping you to feel.

When you feel complete, open your eyes.

ONLY YOU

I realized that Susan had made tremendous strides and was getting better when she came to group one day and related the following story.

—E.M.

I sat down in my back yard one Saturday afternoon. It was a beautiful, clear late August day, fall was in the air. I watched my next-door neighbor at work in her enchanted flower garden. Fiery reds, flaming oranges, sun yellows, shocking fuchsias cascaded in bushes, burst into mid air. Should I paint a picture of the flowers? Maybe I should take a bike ride. How about swimming some laps? I could call up and try and get a tennis game. Was there something I'd forgotten to worry about? For a while I began to worry that I'd forgotten something, what I wanted to worry about. Then I laughed. The joke was on me. There was nothing to worry about. Everything was just fine. I was enjoying being with myself for the first time in my life. I was so used to living on adrenalin rushes that the absence of anxiety, dead calm was enough to give me an anxiety attack. I was bored with peace. "Lie down and take it like a champion. Come on, you can do it." It was time, as Dr. Pangloss said, to cultivate my own garden.

—S.I.

You're on your own for the first time in your life by choice. There's no one to think about, do things for, fill your time with except you. You may feel strange, odd, uncomfortable, off balance, worried, frightened, anxious, scared at the absence of negative feelings, worry, fear and anxiety. You may even feel panicky. There are times when you're going to feel good but you won't recognize that that's what you're feeling, it will feel more like the absence of anxiety, of stress. You may even feel bored. Then there will be times when you see a rainbow, a patch of blue, when you feel happy for no reason at all. Chances are you'll be all over the place running the gamut of emotions in one day. Don't worry if you feel any of these feelings. It's natural to feel this way. This is practice.

SPENDING QUALITY TIME WITH YOURSELF

You're free! Liberated. At liberty. Miss Liberty. For the first time in your life *you* can do anything *you* want without worrying about him. Time to celebrate, indulge, pamper, treat yourself to anything you want. Time to enjoy yourself, to have fun with yourself. Time to put a hundred percent of your time and energy into discovering, getting to know yourself. **This is the opportunity of your life.** Make a date with yourself every day, Ask yourself where *you* want to go, what *you* want to do and when.

A movie date. Ask yourself out on a movie date. Have fun deciding which movie *you* want to see.

Dinner for one. Would *you* like to have dinner? What do *you* feel like eating? Would you like to try that new recipe for tuna you've been saving? What time would you like to eat? Set the table for your important guest, you! It's always polite to bring the hostess something, buy yourself flowers. Don't forget to compliment the chef.

Other dates to look forward to:

A book date. Go to a book store, browse as long as *you* want and buy yourself that new book.

A party date. Accept the invitation to the party, invite yourself, get all dressed up—for you, get your nails done for you, compliment yourself on how great you look and go.

Dinner for two. Ask your buddy for dinner. Pamper her. Ask her what she'd like to have and prepare it or surprise her with something special.

A spa date. Plan a health and beauty day for yourself. You're going to get a massage, work out at the health club and take a steam and a sauna, or you'll give yourself a clay and ginseng facial, followed by a chamomile face steam, a protein hair treatment, a manicure and pedicure. Pamper yourself.

THE BIG CHILL-OUT

And now it's time for the big chill-out. Why? Because the way you've been living is killing you. Since you're the one who's been doing it, you're the one who can undo it! The way to begin is to put yourself on a realistic daily schedule. **One you can meet.** One that gives you time to be early, get everything done, avoid stress, anxiety, worry, fear, upset and chaos. One that lets you go from 78 rpm to 33⅓. Day by day by day.

1. Discuss the whole day with your buddy the night before or in the morning before you leave the house. If you can't do it with your

buddy buy a Filofax, Daytimer, a legal pad or a day-to-day calendar. Your schedule for the day should include all your plans from the time you're going to set the alarm and get up till the time you go to bed at night.

2. Allow a half hour of extra time for contingencies, the old Murphy's Law routine. If something can go wrong it will go wrong. Avoid tight scheduling and you'll avoid gridlock and lateness.

3. Plan the day around your priorities: what time you're going to exercise, for how long and where. Are there any things that you absolutely must get done today? Bills? Cleaning? The doctor? What are they? Identify them and include them in your day.

4. Decide what time you should get up in the morning in order to do everything you want and need to do to get to work on time without panic, rush or lateness. Plan what time you should get to work. How much time do you need to get there, how are you going to get there, when should you leave the house in order to get there ten minutes early? Right, early!

5. Plan what you're going to do at lunch. Make sure you take your hour or whatever time you get off, *off.* Plan what you're going to do. Is it enough time to exercise? Is there anything you need to buy for your home? For you? Are you going to have lunch with a friend? Do you have enough time to do it, get there, eat lunch and come back without feeling the crunch? Do you want to go to a quiet place and just read for an hour?

6. Plan what time you're going to leave work. Don't accept any assignments that you can't do. If you haven't done everything you need to do by the end of the day leave anyway. If your boss insists you stay make sure you get overtime. If you're the boss there are no excuses—leave. You can do it tomorrow.

7. Plan what you're going to do after work. Is this the time you're going to do your half hour or hour of exercise? Are you going to meet someone for a drink or a dinner date? What time? Where? Do you have more than enough time to get there? Are you going to go home first or go straight from work? What do you plan to do after that? Is there enough time to go to a movie? Are you going to be tired by then and want to go home? Think it through.

8. How much sleep do you need? What time do you want to go to bed so that you get enough sleep?

Slow down, you'll live longer!

I HAVE A DREAM

When people used to ask me where I went to college I used to start mumbling, I'd say something like "Well I went to a few different ones . . ." and let the sentence hang in the air hoping that they'd assume that I'd graduated from one of them. I had a great job, was making a lot of money, but I had a secret, I'd never graduated college. No one at work cared. But I did. I felt like a cheat all the time. After I broke up with Ed I realized that I'd never done anything for myself, never dreamed my own dreams, that I'd cheated myself by not graduating. I decided to go back and get my degree. I took courses at night, kept my job by day. It took me three years, but I did it. Graduation day was the greatest day of my life!

—TERRY

In the movie "Working Girl," Melanie Griffith plays a secretary with a dream, a goal. She wants to be the boss with a corner office, her own secretary, a lot of responsibility and great clothes. She has a dream, a goal, but more importantly a positive spirit, a belief that she can do it. She dreams the dream, acts the dream, dresses the dream, talks like the dream never once editing, questioning, putting it down, sabotaging it, until it comes true.

You've been Millie Melodrama, soap opera queen acting in nightmares all your life, so now, put your great talent to use and act in, create some positive dreams and scenarios for your life. (We're not talking about having one of your hims leave his wife for you.)

Make a list of dreams, wishes, fantasies, goals, the things you'd like to do when you grow up, those crazy, off-the-wall things you always wanted to do, be, or accomplish but were afraid to, didn't dare dream about. Shut your eyes and see them, go all the way. You have that corner office, you can even see how you've decorated it; you win an Academy Award for best screenplay and see yourself on television accepting the Oscar: "I'd like to thank . . ."; you get your PhD in psychology and see yourself getting your diploma: "Congratulations Dr. _____ (fill in your name); you start your own company and a year later go public; you have your first art exhibition and sell out—you can see your opening night and all those beautiful little red dots next to your pictures.

Write down all your dreams no matter how crazy, strange, miraculous, bizarre, far out or off the wall they seem without editing. If your mindspeak station or negative belief system starts to talk to you BEEP it. Start to play Melanie Griffith and keep dreaming. They can come true!

MAÑANA

Procrastination is your middle name. Mañana. Tomorrow. I'll do it tomorrow. I'll get it done in the morning. Why get it done today when you can put it off until tomorrow? The trouble is tomorrow never comes and if it does it's too late. You don't get it done and you have another adrenalin rush trying to get done what even Superman can't get done in one afternoon.

Recovery is about getting it done today! Do it today! Do it!

EVERYTHING YOU ALWAYS WANTED TO DO BUT DIDN'T

Make a list of all the things you ever wanted to do but didn't in your life: play an instrument, paint, sew, sail, snorkel, collect posters, become an architect, decorator, learn French, take a course in art history, astronomy, have a rose garden.

The only way to do it is to do it! Start by doing one of them. Just one. You can get it done if you really want to.

EVERY PLACE YOU EVER WANTED TO SEE BUT DIDN'T

Make a list of all the places you wanted to see in your life but didn't: Go for a weekend to Paris in the spring; go punting on the Isis; go on a photographic safari in Kenya; go white-water rafting in Colorado; go for Indian Week to Santa Fe. Now plan a trip, start saving, go for it, do it!

EVERY BOOK YOU EVER WANTED
TO READ BUT DIDN'T

Make a list of books that you always wanted to read but never did or books that you said you read but never did. Go to the bookstore and buy one of those books. Start it.

EVERYTHING YOU EVER WANTED
TO LEARN BUT DIDN'T

Make a list of classes you wanted to take, things you always wanted to learn: how to type, speak Greek, Italian, cook, rollerblade, play tennis.

Sign up for a class. Take it! Do it!

THOROUGHLY MODERN MILLIE

In your past while playing Millie Melodrama you put all your attention into taking care of him while escaping from you. Everything in his life was perfect. He had everything he needed, you saw to that; after all it was your mission in life. You were his maid, valet, cook, executive shopper, home secretary, sometime nurse, travel agent. Meanwhile, back at the ranch, the only time your home ever saw a dust rag was when he was coming over for a visit, your dirty laundry was heaped to the sky, your bills unpaid, your fridge as empty as Old Mother Hubbard's, your papers in piles, your life in shreds around you. The same laissez-faire philosophy applied to your personal health, as you ignored taking care of your body as well.

"Oh, no, I can't do my laundry. Moi? Do laundry? For myself? Me do bills? Me, clean my apartment for no good reason? Me, cook a meal for myself—all that effort for nothing? Me, make a dentist appointment and show? I hate getting drilled. Me, go to the doctor and have a mammogram? You gotta be kidding. Are you off your rocker? Sure I'll do it. Sure. Next Sunday in the middle of the week."

Millie Melodrama has to go. It's time for Thoroughly Modern Millie, self-efficiency expert. Need anything done? Let Thoroughly Modern Millie do it. No one's going to tell you that you're going to enjoy doing your laundry, paying your bills, cleaning your apartment, cleaning out the closets, tossing old papers, getting your teeth cleaned, making sure your body is running well in the beginning. You're not going to enjoy it. Feel better? That's the key. You're going to feel better about yourself when you have a clean house, when your drawers are straightened, when you can open your closet and shut it without everything falling out, when you know that you've paid all your bills, seen the doctor, the lawyer, the indian chief and they've given you a clean bill of health. You can grumble all you want but there's no feeling in the world like knowing that your house is in order and so is your life.

CLEANING OUT YOUR CLOSETS AND CLEANING UP YOUR LIFE

Make a list of everything you need to get done:

Your laundry. Make piles and do it. The works. Everything from underwear to sheets. Go to a laundromat, take the rest to the cleaners.

Your bills. Pay them. Set up a schedule for the first of the month or the fifteenth. If you can't do it yourself hire an accountant. Get into the habit of balancing your checkbook as well.

Your closets. Clean them out. Be ruthless. You'll never be a size 4 again and you know it. Those bell bottoms from the sixties have had their day. Make piles. Label them. The Salvation Army and the homeless, your sister-in-law, your size 4 friend.

Your medicine cabinet. Clean it out and toss all those old prescriptions (you forget what they were for anyway), the rusty razor and the almost-used-up special hair conditioner for perms no matter how great it was. (You don't even have a perm anymore.)

Your home. Clean it. That includes everything. Neatness counts. The floors, the rugs, *under* the rugs, the windows; when was the last time you could see out of your windows? Do you need a new paint job? How about changing that light bulb that's been out for two years?

Your kitchen. Clean it including under the sink, your stove, the fridge, the oven and stock up. Buy things you like to eat so that you can actually make yourself breakfast: oat bran muffins, skimmed milk, coffee, juice.

Dentists, accountants, doctors, lawyers and indian chiefs. Whatever your greatest fear, whatever you've been putting off is what you need to do first. If you're worried that you have something wrong your worry is making it worse. It's the old ounce-of-prevention story. Make an appointment and do it, see them. If you're really frightened take your buddy with you.

THE LITTLE PRINCE HAD A THORN IN HIS ROSE, TOO

In *The Little Prince* by Antoine de Saint-Exupéry, the little prince left his planet to set out and seek his fortune because his rose, although very beautiful, had a thorn. She was very vain, to boot. After traveling around the universe the little prince returns to his planet because he realizes that even though his rose is not the only rose in the world (she told him that she was unique), vain, has a thorn and is not perfect, he loves her anyway, inspite of her imperfections . . . for her imperfections. He's become a very wise little prince able to enjoy what he has rather than worrying about its imperfections.

Nothing is perfect. Nothing. You've been basing your judgment on perfect ideals, illusions. The trouble is that since nothing is perfect, being a perfectionist is a no-win position. A trap. Recovery is about dropping the word perfect from your vocabulary, getting off the fantasyland express, exorcising the perfectionist demons from your life and accepting that every rose no matter how perfect has a thorn.

HOW TO AVOID PERFECTIONIST PITFALLS

Set a limit. Before you start a project give yourself a limit on how much time you're going to spend on it during the day. When you get to that moment no matter how close you are to perfecting whatever you're doing stop and let it be just the way it is. Get that? Stop.

Give yourself permission to make a mistake. Forgive yourself immediately. BEEP-BEEP any mindspeak insults. Counter them by saying, "I'm not perfect. I'm doing the best I can." "I forgive myself for not getting it right the first time, or I forgive myself for not getting it at all."

Try something you can't do well. Try something that you're not perfect at. Speak French with your fifteen-word vocabulary, brave a waiter in a French restaurant and dazzle him with your pronunciation. Ask someone to play tennis with you, explain that you're a beginner, with no backhand, and ask them if they'll give you a few pointers.

Limit your expectations. Don't expect people, places, or things to be perfect. As soon as you fantasize, dream, or have expectations about a person, place, thing or event you've already ruined the person, place, thing or event. There is no way on this Earth or any other place that the reality can measure up to your fantasy.

THE RED DRESS OR THE YELLOW?

Making a decision is not a life-threatening act. Furthermore, nothing terrible will happen to you if you make the wrong decision. No one up there is keeping score on your decision-making process such as it is, which isn't much. Since nothing is perfect and no one else is perfect, no one expects you to be perfect; you shouldn't either. You don't have to make a perfect decision because there is no such thing. Who says that choosing a red dress is a better decision than choosing the yellow? Who says that having a chocolate ice cream cone is better or worse than having a vanilla one? You might compare the calories (chocolate has more calories than vanilla), but then again chocolate tastes better than vanilla, so with one for chocolate and one for vanilla, where do you come out? Pick one. It doesn't matter. The decision is not life threatening, earth shattering, world changing.

If this is beginning to sound like philosophy 101 that's because it is. There is no such thing as a perfect decision because the things you're deciding between are two different things; therefore, either one has pluses and minuses, both are good and bad, positive and negative. The only thing that counts is picking one. The rest is philosophy.

DECISION-MAKING TACTICS

If you're choosing between two things that appear to be equal, ask. Is this one good for me? Consider both alternatives.

If the answer is Yes, they are both good for me, then toss a coin, pick one. If the answer is one is good for you and one isn't, then pick the one that's good for you. If neither one is good for you then don't choose either.

Don't go back on your decision after you've made it. If you find yourself saying, I should have had the chocolate, BEEP-BEEP yourself.

PEP TALKS

During the day remember to give yourself a little pep talk. Of course you can handle the situation, of course you can do it! Come on _____ (your name) you can do it! I know you can! Go for it!

I BELIEVE IN YOU

In the musical, "How to Succeed in Business Without Really Trying," Robert Morse played the hero who goes from the mailroom to being C.E.O. of a company because he learns from a book how to succeed in business without really trying. As a daily ritual, while he's shaving, he looks at himself in the mirror, smiles and sings to himself, "Oh, I believe in you . . . I believe in you."

As a daily ritual, look at yourself in the mirror and pick at least three of these affirmations to say to yourself while smiling:

I believe in myself.
I'm the greatest.
Watch out world, here I come!
Something wonderful is going to happen to me today and I deserve it.
Nothing can stop me now
Someone up there loves me.
I deserve to be happy.
I'm perfect the way I am.
I'm lovable the way I am.
I love myself just the way I am and I don't need to change a thing.
I have a right to be happy.
I'm a winner.

HOW TO ACCEPT A COMPLIMENT

Lovesick

Someone: Boy you look great! I love that dress.

The lovesick you: This old dress? I've had it for a million years. I didn't even buy it, it was a hand-me-down. See this spot? I could never get it out. I wouldn't have worn this dress today if I knew I was going to bump into anyone.

Healthy

Someone: Boy you look great! I love that dress.

The healthy you: Thank you. I love it, too.

HOW TO ACCEPT A CRITICISM

Lovesick

Someone: Boy, do you look bad. Where did you get that dress? It makes you look so heavy . . .

The lovesick you: You really think so? My night is ruined. I shouldn't have worn this dress, I must have gained five pounds and not realized it, maybe I should go home and change. I've always hated this dress.

Healthy

Someone: Boy do you look bad. Where did you get that dress? It makes you look so heavy . . .

The healthy you: Thank you. I appreciate your comment. I happen to love my dress.

HAPPY HOUR

Spend at least one hour a day devoted to enjoying yourself and having fun! You're only allowed to do things *you* want to do, that make *you* feel good, that make *you* happy. Say something nice to yourself and give yourself a compliment or two during the hour. Plan some fun. Have some fun. Extend it to two hours, then three and then, you guessed it, the whole day.

HOW AM I DOING? Q & A

Q. *How am I doing in recovery? How will I know if I'm doing it right? What should I look for? What are the signs?*

A. In the beginning you're going to feel overwhelmed by all that's new, by all the things you have to do, by all the things you have to redo, by all the things you don't know how to do. It's normal to feel that way. How are you doing? You're the one with the answers. Are you feeling better about yourself? Are you happier? Are you able to live in the moment from moment to moment, day by day? How are you doing? You'll know.

Q. *How long does it take to recover?*

A. You've been Miss Instant Gratification all your life so saying patience is a virtue will probably fall on deaf ears. Patience is a virtue. There's no right answer to how long recovery takes. Recovery is a process. It's definitely not going to happen overnight. As you do the work you'll begin to have moments, hours, then days strung together when you feel great, when you feel as if the sun's come out from behind the clouds and is streaming down on you. Little by little the sun comes out even on rainy days; that's when there are rainbows.

DEAR MISS LIBERTY

Dear Miss Liberty,

Now that you're at liberty, liberated from the yoke, the oppression of your lovesickness, it's time to remind you once again of your fundamental rights.

You're entitled as a human being, just by being born to life, liberty and the pursuit of happiness. You have a right to peace, pleasure and joy. You have a right to love and be loved.

It's your basic right as a human being to enjoy your life, to enjoy being you, because you love who you are.

Don't worry, be happy. Have fun. Enjoy yourself. Make your life a daily celebration.

Sincerely,
E.M. and S.I.

P.S. If it's not fun don't do it. If you must do it, make it fun!

—LILI

CHAPTER 13

Loving You, Loving Him, Loving You

(Mr. Right *Is* Mr. Right)

"Finders Keepers"

You've been on your own for awhile, you're used to it, feel good about yourself, like your life. But every so often the thought flickers through your mind, what about a new him? Am I ever going to have a relationship? Am I ever going to meet Mr. Right? How will I be able to know if he's Mr. Right? Am I going to be able to handle it, without losing it, without obsessing?

The answer is yes, you can have a love relationship with the right love partner as long as you keep what you've worked so hard to find, your you.

Finding a new man, a love partner, starts when you feel complete on your own, when you don't need someone to fill you up, when you're not looking for one.

Finding a new man, a love partner, someone who you love for who he is and who he is not happens when you love yourself for who you are and who you are not.

Finding a new man, a love partner, someone you love, whose love you can accept, starts with keeping you.

Finders keepers. Losers weepers.

EVERYTHING YOU'VE EVER KNOWN ABOUT LOVE AND SEX, FORGET IT!

Everything you've ever believed about relationships, men, sex, dating, marriage, love, is wrong. You need a new script and yes, you have

214

to toss all your old lovesick ones; those old responses, attitudes, expectations, behavioral patterns, everything. You've substituted control, makeovers and caretaking for love, anxiety, and obsession, and pain for being in love and now you have to learn the difference. You need to accept that in any situation that involves a love partner, your first response will be lovesick, you'll go on automatic lovesick pilot.

Remember that question? What would a healthy person do? In the beginning you're going to have to ask that question all the time, closely followed by two other equally important questions: Does this make me feel good? Is this good for me?

This is another big-time learning . . . unlearning experience. Bring in your buddy, your network, your support group, the marines, because you need all the help you can get.

The first thing you need to do is sign a prenuptial agreement to assure that *you* take full responsibility for having a love relationship not a lovesick one.

YOUR PRENUPTIAL AGREEMENT

I, _____ (your name), sound of body, mind and spirit do make the following agreements on my behalf, before I enter into any love relationship. This agreement is binding to me no matter who I shall be with, for however long the relationship lasts and whatever its terms: whether I am just dating, in a relationship, living with someone, engaged or married.

Terms of the Agreement

If someone makes me feel bad, upsets me in a consistent manner, I will acknowledge, accept that this is a threat to my well-being and I will terminate our relationship.

If anyone makes me feel off center, off base, off balance and I begin to obsess on a consistent basis so that it becomes threatening to my recovery, to my me, I will terminate our relationship.

If someone doesn't make me feel good about me, doesn't like who I am, doesn't let me be me on a consistent basis and I find that I am beginning to slip back into my old lovesick patterns, I will terminate our relationship.

If someone makes me feel jealous, is irresponsible, doesn't keep his commitments, is unpredictable, dishonest, unable to give, I will terminate our relationship.

If someone is using or abusing me on a consistent basis, sexually, financially, mentally or in any way and he refuses to deal with it, talk about it, go to therapy, I will terminate the relationship.

If I discover that someone I am seeing is unavailable, rejecting or unattainable, I will terminate our relationship.

Furthermore, I _____ (your name) agree that I will not be in a relationship no matter how much I am attracted to him, how hot he is, how many sparks fly if it makes me feel bad, threatens me, makes me lose my me, distracts me, brings back those good old bad feelings or in any way interferes with my recovery, with my loving me.

_____ (signed and dated)

WHAT IS A LOVE RELATIONSHIP?
THE LOVE EQUATION

RELATE, *v*, to connect, establish a relation between, to interact with others in a sympathetic relationship, to establish a sympathetic relationship with a person.

RELATION, *n*, state of being mutually or reciprocally connected, a significant association between people.

RELATIONSHIP, *n*, sympathetic connection or involvement.

A love relationship is a significant association between you and a love partner. It is a reciprocal connection, you both accept and give love. It means that you love him unconditionally for who he is, the way he is; he loves you unconditionally for who you are, the way you are.

> You love you unconditionally
> +available, attainable man who loves you
> +your acceptance of his unconditional love
> +you love him back unconditionally
> =a love relationship

IS HE MR. WRONG OR MR. RIGHT?

This may come as a shock, but the rule of thumb for telling if someone is Mr. Right or Mr. Wrong is the reverse of everything you've always believed:

If you're instantly attracted to him he is Mr. Wrong.

If sparks fly, hotter than the Fourth of July, he's Mr. Wrong.

If you hear wedding bells chime the second you meet him he's Mr. Wrong.

If you want to go to bed with him and start thinking about sex the minute you meet him he's Mr. Wrong.

If you get goose bumps just looking at him he's Mr. Wrong.

If you start to obsess over him, lose your you to him the first second you meet him (or even a half an hour afterwards) he is absolutely, positively, 100 percent Mr. Wrong.

If you have to chase him, start to plan the campaign to win him over, he is Mr. Wrong.

If you think he's nice but feel no big-time instant hot chemistry, he's a potential Mr. Right.

If you like him but don't care if you see him again because you don't feel hot, because you haven't felt goosebumps and you haven't lost your you, he's a potential Mr. Right.

If you feel that he could be a friend he's a potential Mr. Right.

If you feel that he likes you, is on your case, your trail, is starting to mount a campaign to get you and this gets you nervous, it's a sure shot that he's a potential Mr. Right.

Yes, it's true, sad but true, terrible but true, upsetting but true, horrible but true. You can throw a tantrum, jump up and down, yell, say it isn't so and it's still true. You've chosen a Mr. Wrong all your life, every time, because you believed in chemistry; if someone turned you on, *that* was love; you were attracted like a magnet to rejection, repelled by love. Accept that you've failed chemistry. If someone turns you on, he's definitely Mr. Wrong. If he doesn't turn you on, he may be Mr. Right.

PRACTICE MAKES PERFECT

In the beginning your instincts and judgment are going to be off. You're going to make mistakes. Don't beat yourself up if you do. This is a learning process. It will get easier with time. You don't have to marry everyone you meet. You're just practicing. You're working on you and not losing it by having a practice relationship with someone who can give you the space to be who you are and appreciates you for being you.

Nice guys are responsible, predictable, stable, reliable, attentive, caring, loving. You won't obsess over a nice guy because he'll be there for you and you'll know it, he'll call when he says he's going to call, will be reliable, supportive.

You have a homework assignment. Practice saying yes to Mr. Rights, dating only Mr. Rights, having relationships only with Mr. Rights. Practice keeping your you when you're with Mr. Right. Remember what it feels like to feel good about you and not lose it. Practice appreciating Mr. Right and enjoy having him appreciate you back. Practice liking Mr. Right and enjoy him liking you back. In other words practice relating positively, giving and receiving with someone who can relate back.

Practice saying no to Mr. Wrongs, not dating Mr. Wrongs, not having relationships with Mr. Wrongs. It's not safe for you to be with Mr. Wrong. You can't keep your you while being with Mr. Wrong. It's mutually exclusive.

Obsession is the first and best clue that someone is Mr. Wrong. If you find your self obsessing, in pain, waiting for that phone call, worrying, unable to function, feeling those good old bad feelings BEEP-BEEP yourself! Mr. Wrong is wrong for you. Terminate the relationship. Quit while you're still ahead. You can't afford him—you've worked too hard to find your you to lose it over a him.

SAMPLE PRACTICE SCENARIOS

Scenario #1. You meet a man and fireworks go off. Your body starts sending you warning signals: you have butterflies in your stomach, you get the shakes, adrenalin rushes, you feel off balance, nervous, panicky, anxious. Your mind starts to send you warning signals: you can't stop thinking about him, you can't get him out of your head or off your mind. Your spirit starts to send you signals: you lose your sense of well-being, of being centered, of being one, of being connected, of being there. All those bad old feelings come back, you lose feeling good, you lose your you.

Your body, mind and spirit are talking to you. Listen to the message: S.O.S. S.O.S. S.O.S. Mayday! Mayday! Mayday! Mr. Wrong! Mr. Wrong! Mr. Wrong! They're telling you that you can't handle him and you can't! If *you*, your body, mind and spirit, don't feel good, you can be totally, absolutely, positively sure that he's bad for you. If he upsets *you*, gets *you* off base, off center, there's something wrong with him, he's unavailable, unattainable or rejecting: too dangerous for *you*.

What should you do? No matter how fabulous, wonderful, handsome, attractive, seductive, rich, famous, talented, educated, athletic he is, you have to take a walk. Are you kidding? Right. Be good to your body, your mind, your spirit, yourself and walk away, leave. Just like that. As soon as possible. The more time you spend with a Mr. Wrong, the harder it is to leave, the more ground you lose, the more of you is lost to him. There are no exceptions. This is a must.

Scenario #2. You meet a man. He's nice. You have a good chat with him. He's interesting, seems to be interested in you. You may like him, you may even be attracted to him but no sparks fly. You don't obsess over him, you feel relaxed when you're with him, you're you, yourself. You keep it together. Your body feels good, your head's on straight. You're having a pleasant/good/alright/medium time. It could range from merely the absence of aggravation to neutral to terrific. What should you do? Give him a chance. If you start to list all the bad things about him, you know that he wears brown socks, etc., BEEP-BEEP yourself. If he asks, give him your card or your telephone number. If he asks you for a date, make one.

THE FIRST DATE:
HOLDING-YOUR-OWN-GROUND RULES

Don't start makeover procedures.

If you start to feel argumentative, want to push the reject button, notice that this is happening to you but don't act on it. Hang on, bite your tongue and hang in. The rule of thumb for you, as a charter member of the Groucho Marx Club, is that the more you want to reject him, the more available he probably is.

Don't do anything that doesn't make you feel good just because he asked you out. Don't go to bed with him.

Leave your expectations behind. Stay in the moment.

Interview him. Get to know who he is. Practice being nice to someone who is nice. Pay attention to how he makes *you* feel.

If he makes *you* feel good, you like what you've found out about him, who he is (not what he looks like), and he asks you out again, say yes.

HOW NOT TO JUDGE A BOOK BY ITS COVER

Seeing Straight

The best way to get to know him is by interviewing him rather than basing your judgment on exteriors, how he looks or what he's wearing. This is like breaking ground, before you can lay a foundation. But dig you must. There's no way you can find out everything in one hour or even one date, so relax. The point of the interview is to offset your clouded vision and get underneath what he looks like or what he's wearing to find out: what he's all about, what he's really like, what he really likes, if he's capable of having a relationship, if he can give, if it's worth it for *you* to spend any more time with him regardless of how much you like his green eyes, his Polo shirt or his adorable red Porsche. You've always given your heart right away to people who couldn't give back, so the purpose of the interview is to see if it's safe for you to give to him. These are the questions to ask, the things you should find out.

Availability

Is he available? (That means no wife, girlfriend(s), live-in relationship, you know what it means!)

Is he looking for a relationship or is he just getting out of a marriage or relationship and into dating as much as he can?

If he's not in a relationship what's his reason for not being in a relationship?

What is his relationship history? What does he say about his last or previous relationships? Did he enjoy being in a relationship?

Health

Does he have a history of addiction? Is he presently addicted to anything? (Come on, you can tell.) If he's been addicted is he in any program currently and for how long?

Does he have any sex-related health problems? Does he exercise? Does he have health problems?

Work and Economics

The important thing is not how much money he has or makes, the size of his portfolio, his D&B rating but whether he's a sport or cheap, whether he's self-supporting and can pay his own way or whether he expects you to pay yours.

What's his work history? Is it stable or does he switch jobs a lot? Is he currently employed? Can he pay for his own—not to mention your—drink? Does he want you to pay for yourself? Does he insist on splitting everything down to the last penny? Does he want you to pay for him?

Thoughts, Beliefs, Attitudes

Does he like himself? Is he happy with his life? Is he open to new ideas? Is he positive, optimistic?

Lifestyle

What are his interests? What are his hobbies? How does he like to spend his free time? Does he like to read? Travel?

The Spirit

Is he spiritual? Is he interested in things like visualizations? What or Who does he believe in, a higher power, God?

Interview Results

If he's only interested in himself and watching sports on television, is terminally cheap, not interested in being in a relationship, an active alcoholic, a womanizer, lovesick, this is a red light, a red flag, a stop sign, grounds for you to discontinue seeing him. The sooner the better, the sooner the easier.

If you share interests, find him to be stable, kind, generous, positive, happy with himself and his life, interested in being in a relationship, preferably with a positive history of past relationships, that's a green light, go ahead.

Whatever, whoever he is, he is. You're not going to change him, you're out of that business. If you like what you've learned about him and you still feel good about *you* after being with him, go out again.

JUST DATING, GETTING TO KNOW HIM

Just dating means just that. You're not getting married, you're just dating. You're going to find out if it's safe for *you* to like him. You're not going to have sex with him until *you* are ready. This is practice. It's not about worrying whether he likes you but whether *you* like him. Is he good enough for *you*? Is he a Mr. Right? Notice the following things about him.

Conversation

Does he talk about himself all the time? Is he attentive or does he ignore you? Does he remember what you said, does he come back to it? Does he ask you for anything? What? Is he interested in you? Does he get angry if you have an opinion? Is he argumentative? If you start to talk about you does he switch the conversation back to him?

Call Waiting

Is he predictable? Does he keep his promises—if he says he'll call you on Thursday at five does he call you on Thursday at five? Do you find yourself constantly waiting for his call and worrying if he's going to call, feeling that old bad way because he didn't call when he said he would? This is a danger sign. A red flag. A violation. A warning. He's being irresponsible, uncaring, unreliable, in a word, a him, possibly a Mr. Wrong. If he does this more than one time whatever his excuse and *you* start to feel bad, get rid of him, he's a Mr. Wrong for sure.

Sex

Did he try to go to bed with you? If you resisted, how did he react? Were there uncomfortable innuendoes and suggestions? Direct hits? Inappropriate behavior on his part? Did he threaten you that if you didn't do it with him he wouldn't see you again? Did you feel comfortable about saying no? Did he make you feel wrong for saying no? Did he criticize you for saying no?

If you felt big-time pressure to go to bed with him immediately and you resisted and he wasn't a gentleman about it, made you feel bad for resisting, this is a red light. A nice guy waits until you're ready. Mr. Wrong wants you when *he's* ready.

The End of the Date

How did he end the date? Did he make another plan? Did he say he'd call? Did he? How did you feel at the end of a date: complimented, understood, acknowledged? Did you feel good about you?

At this stage you're working on friendship. You're finding out if you can become friends, if you like him enough to be friends. Is he fun to be with, do things with, do you have a good time together, can you talk to him, be yourself, trust him? Do you like being with him?

WHAT SHOULD YOU TELL HIM ABOUT YOU?

If he asks you about your past, it's not necessary for you to confess right away, "I used to be a sexaholic and have gone to bed with more than a hundred guys." You also don't have to tell him that you discuss every move you make because you're not sure what to do and you're learning how. Not till you really know him better and only if you feel totally safe and he's proven to you that you can trust him.

If he asks you why you've never been married (if you've never been married) tell him that you've never found a man who you both liked and loved. That's true.

SAFE SEX

You like each other, a friendship is budding; when is it safe to have sex with him? After how many dates? Is sex going to ruin your friendship? Will having sex with him put a period at the end of your relationship? What are the guidelines?

It should be okay with him to allow *you* to make the decision. In your time frame, not his. Without pressure.

Safe-Sex Rules

Don't have sex with him unless you're sure that you like him, that he likes you and it's safe for you to be intimate with him.

Don't have sex with him until you're ready. It is not acceptable to have sex with him because he's putting on the pressure.

Accept that having sex is going to change your relationship, it will become closer.

Don't expect sex to be perfect the first time. You're not going to have the same fireworks you used to have when you were with a partner that was rejecting, unavailable or unattainable. Not in the beginning. A good sexual relationship takes time and practice. Intimacy takes practice.

Don't bring your old sexual bag of tricks along to this new relationship. If you were used to being taken, abused, battered by him, pleasing him at your expense in bed, remember that making love is about reciprocity, about loving each other.

MISTAKEN IDENTITY

He passed all the tests, said all the right things, was available, attentive, called you ahead of time, waited until you were ready, then you went to bed with him, and your greatest fear happened, he didn't call you back. What happened? What did you do wrong? What should you do? Don't call him. Don't beat yourself up. Don't obsess. He was another Mr. Wrong. That doesn't make you wrong. It just means that you misjudged who he was. You made a mistake. He only wanted sex, the chase, the game, the conquest, no matter what he said!

Go for the lesson. What did you learn? Why were you fooled? Was there a part of you that didn't buy his act? Could you have listened to yourself? Was their a way to recognize that he was a wolf dressed in sheep's clothing?

There's almost a 100 percent possibility that you're going to make a mistake. Your radar still has some bugs that you have to work out. The probability of having the perfect relationship first time around is like hitting a home run with the bases loaded first time up at bat.

Go back over the relationship and see if there were some clues scattered here and there that you didn't notice. Look for the lesson. If you're obsessing, then you know he was Mr. Wrong. If he didn't call you after you had sex he definitely was Mr. Wrong. Nice guys always call. Mr. Right will call. Let it go. Accept that you learned something, you're not mistake-proof yet, you had a great practice session.

If you have trouble letting him go, do the Sunflower Power visualization or The Head Balloon.

I'M HAVING A RELATIONSHIP, WHAT DO I DO NOW COACH?

You're seeing him on a regular basis and have been for quite a while, holy moly, you're having a relationship, what do you do now?

There are some everyday, common garden-variety type issues that are going to come up, ranging from how to tell the truth, how to keep your own space, how to let go of control, to how not to do too much for him, how to allow him to do things for you, and the big one, how to say, feel and accept the "L" word. We're going to discuss them all.

I'M HAVING A GREAT TIME, WHEN IS IT GOING TO GO WRONG?

You don't believe that he could be so nice, that he could like you, that he's for real. You have a live one going but every two seconds you have an anxiety attack and good old Millie Melodrama makes a housecall. You worry your way through the day in spite of the fact that there's no evidence, not one shred, to make you believe that something's going to go wrong. It's normal to be anxious in the beginning. If your mind-speak station starts broadcasting, "He's going to leave you, he's not going to call, he's going to find someone else on the way home, in the elevator, while he's working out; It's only a matter of time before he trades you in for a new model," get that it's only your mindspeak station.

If Millie comes to visit and you find yourself in the midst of a soap opera or melodrama, real or imagined, day or night, "I'm always going to be alone but I don't want to be alone, the telephone hasn't rung, he's forgotten that I exist," take three belly breaths, then do a reality check. What's really going on? He isn't going to call you until tomorrow morning unless he gets out of his meeting early because he's working late and you told him not to call after eleven-thirty.

Worry-Wart Rules

If you start to worry, BEEP-BEEP yourself. Don't let your mindspeak station or Millie get the best of you.

If he's a nice guy he'll continue to be nice. A nice guy is a nice guy is a nice guy.

You may have high anxiety attacks for a while but they'll start to disappear in time as long as you kill them before they multiply.

RICHOCHET ROMANCE

I didn't feel Fourth of July fireworks explode when I met Robert but I thought he was an attractive man. I waited until I was ready, more than five dates, before we became lovers. Impressive. Astonishing. I was calling the shots for once. The next two weeks, our honeymoon I suppose, went very smoothly. Trouble in paradise arrived when we decided to cook our first dinner together. It was the sequel to "Annie Hall," Woody Allen, Diane Keaton and the lobster in the kitchen. The menu was pasta and fresh corn.

"What are you using that boiling water for?"

"The corn, Robert."

"That's not enough water."

"Yes it is."

"No it isn't."

"I'm sorry, Robert, I thought you knew how to cook."

"Of course I do. I come from out here where they grow the corn, obviously I know how to cook it."

"Any dummy knows that you're not supposed to drown the corn. All you need when you have fresh corn is a few inches of water so you can steam it, not kill it."

A pall settled over the kitchen. We scrutinized each other's every move waiting for the other to make a mistake.

"Let me taste the pasta sauce."

"You don't have to taste it. It's Contadina. You don't have to do anything to it."

He added some cayenne pepper, anyway.

We sat down in stony silence. We'd argued about everything, the corn, the pasta sauce, the length of time you have to boil fresh pasta, how to slice a tomato. I hated him. He was stupid and critical. I tasted the pasta, my mouth was on fire. After downing two glasses of water I said, "You ruined it, it wasn't easy but you did. Any idiot knows that you don't dump cayenne pepper! Besides that, it was perfect the way it was." He got up from the table and left without a word. I was relieved. I didn't want to see him ever again.

After I cooled down from the hot pepper I called Elizabeth, "I can't stand Robert a second longer. Of all the guys to choose from, I had to pick an idiot."

"You had a fight with Robert? Do I sense that you're trying to get rid of him?"

"How can you possibly say that? I dare you to find one good reason I should continue to see him."

"He's a nice, sweet guy. You don't have to marry him. It's just a trial relationship. Practice. Try appreciating him for what he is rather than getting angry with him for what he isn't."

I called Robert up on the phone and apologized. I felt like the way the astronauts must have felt on the first moon walk. No experience. Nothing to fall back on. No role model. My emotions ricocheted like the balls on a pool table after the first break, all over the place. If I thought he liked me too much, I didn't like him, tried to sabotage the relationship. If he didn't call for a day . . . deal me back in. After three months of richocheting we called it a day. I wasn't ready. I had to do some more work before I could be with someone.

—S.I.

As a charter member of the Groucho Marx Club, the most difficult hurdle for you to overcome will be your desire to push the reject button. If he comes too close for comfort because he likes you, he's too nice, Mr. Right incarnate, you're going to feel uncomfortable. It's your old allergic reaction to love, a defense mechanism against having to cope with intimacy, loving, accepting love. Mr. Right is going to make you feel very wrong in the beginning. Nervous. Threatened. Frightened. You're going to want to hit the reject button, try to eject him from the driver's seat, eliminate him, blow him out of the water. The closer he gets, the more you're going to want to get rid of him. You may feel angry, irritable, argumentative, a nuclear reactor ready to explode, wired. It's fear of intimacy, fear of sharing your you.

His action: He wants to spend more time with you.

Your allergic reaction: He's invading your space, he's too demanding, suffocating. You want to push him away. You push the panic and reject button.

His action: He tells you how much he likes, loves you.

Your allergic reaction: Terror. Anxiety. You want to run away. You push the panic and reject button.

What should you do if you get that feeling? (It feels like a switch inside you gets turned off, suddenly you can't stand him a minute longer, you want to run away, get away, get rid of him.)

NO, NO, NO, NO, DON'T PUSH THE REJECT BUTTON

If you start to do it, here's what to do:

Admit that you're having an allergic reaction, then short-circuit the switch.

Talk to yourself, tell yourself that you're doing it again. BEEP-BEEP.

Catch yourself, count to one hundred. Look for the trigger. What did he say or do that's making you feel this way?

Excuse yourself, go to the bathroom and do belly breathing. (Breathe in through your nose and out through your nose. As you breathe in let your belly extend, fill up. As you breathe out let your belly collapse. Do this slowly five times.)

Call your buddy on the phone. Get some fresh air. Take a walk. Bite your tongue. Kill it before it multiplies. Stop it dead in its tracks and expose it for what it is, a panic attack. "Not so fast Groucho, you're not going to get me this time. Hit the road, Groucho! Adios, Groucho!"

Think of something you like about him, there has to be something, and every time you get the impulse to destroy the relationship, the evening the date, whatever you're doing, list the good things.

TO TELL THE TRUTH

I needed a date for my party. I started to obsess about Billy again. There didn't appear to be any other prospect in sight and I didn't want to be alone. What would people think? What people? My friends didn't care if I had a date or not. They'd like it better if I didn't, I'd be a better hostess. Why did I need a date with Mr. Wrong Incarnate? I pictured those deer eyes and called him anyway. I got an adrenalin rush as the phone rang, the signal that I was doing something bad. He was charming. He couldn't make it for my party but why didn't we see each other the night before? Why not?

Group, who had lived through my Billy obsession, was tough on me. "If you're going to see Billy you're going to have to level with him."

"What do you mean by that?"

"Tell him the truth."

"What's the truth?"

"You like him and are interested in having a relationship."

"Are you crazy? Tell him that? What for?"

Elizabeth said, "So he knows that you're serious. So that you don't sell yourself short as just another sexual conquest."

"I can't do it."

"You have to."

I was in a state of high anxiety the hour before he was supposed to pick me up. Was he going to stand me up? If he didn't, how was I going to tell him? When I saw him I felt even worse. He was so attractive, so wonderful. Adrenalin was pumping and rushing like crazy. If only he would propose. Instead he propositioned me. It was now or never. I managed to blurt out that I really liked him and wanted to have a relationship, not a one-night-stand. Awkward, uncool, and the second I said it the tension was cut, I felt better. Incidentally, it was never. He left, never called me again. He didn't want to have a relationship, he just wanted to have sex.

—S.I.

To tell the truth there's no way you can have a healthy relationship without learning how to tell the truth. Relating, connecting, a relationship, by definition means sharing your concerns, opinions, feelings, secrets, vulnerabilities, even your fears without fear.

You're going to have to make a commitment to stay honest, shoot straight, no matter what, no matter how hard. This may be one of your toughest recovery assignments. In the beginning it will feel as if you're jumping off the top of a mountain blindfolded, walking on a tightrope without a net, rollerblading for the first time without knee guards. Expect all your demons to come out, a lovesick mindspeak broadcast: "You're not going to tell him 'that,' he won't like you any more if you level, better let him speak first and get the sense of which direction he's going before you commit yourself to saying something he won't like." Don't be surprised if your body starts to talk back with stress signals from an upset stomach to hives to a back attack. Do belly breathing, a visualization, exercise.

Spitting it out, getting it out whatever way you do it, haltingly, awkwardly, weirdly, has a payoff. You'll feel absolutely triumphant, fantastic. You did it. You told the truth and the world did not end, a crack did not open up underneath you and you didn't fall in. On the contrary you had one of the most satisfying, greatest wins of your life.

If you lose someone by being honest then they shouldn't be in your life to begin with. If people in your life cannot deal with your honesty then you don't want them in your life.

Psychic deep freeze, emotional cover up were my grandmother's legacy. It was not "done" to bare the soul. Now I know that truth wins! My life is an open book and I am free to share what was formerly hidden. What a relief to be able to be up front all the time. "Tell the truth faster" has become my motto. It works.

—Lili

CONFLICTS OF INTEREST

If you were in a lovesick relationship and had a conflict of interests, a fight, argument, words, your lovesick response was either to bail out, pack your bags and shove off, or swallow it. You either overreacted or underreacted. There was no middle ground.

No two people can agree all the time; sometimes you may have a conflict of interests. Dealing with it does not mean swallowing it or leaving him. It means finding the middle ground. It means acknowledging that neither one of you is perfect, either one of you can make a mistake, disagree, even be wrong but that doesn't mean that the relationship is over, that you should leave; it just means that you're having an argument, disagreeing about something. The test of your relationship is the ability to resolve it.

HEART-TO-HEART TALKS

If you have a conflict of interests, have a heart-to-heart talk. Come from your heart, your feelings, from the truth. Do it as soon as possible so that you're not holding onto it.

He forgot to call you when he said he would. It's the first time he ever did it. Instead of gathering up ammo for the big battle, blowing up and throwing the book at him, resolve the issue as soon as possible. Tell him, "It made me feel bad when you didn't call me today. I felt abandoned, ignored." Ask him what happened. Listen to his side. "I was in a meeting under a lot of pressure and I simply forgot. I'm sorry. I love you. I didn't mean to cause you any pain." Accept his apology. If you're having trouble dropping it, take a walk, take a bike ride, take a swim, do the Pele Visualization. When you're calm again, finish the heart-to-heart talk. If you find that you're holding a grudge, bring up the topic again and work on what's underneath the grudge together, until it's worked out.

Work on working it out. Institute regular heart-to-heart talks to clear the air before you get fogged in. The more you can come from your heart, the more you tell the truth, the faster you'll clear up the differences.

THANK YOU, CENTRAL CASTING:
GOING WITH THE FLOW

In the old days, before recovery, you were a control tower, always in control, making sure that life happened your way, on your time schedule, on your terms.

Recovery is the ability to let go of control. You're not the Mistress of the Universe, in control of the whole planet, if not the galaxy, anymore. You're out of that business. Once you let go of your plan, of control, of your rigidity, once you go with the flow rather than trying to resist it, control it, or change it then you open yourself up to other possibilities. Instead of getting obsessed over what isn't going to happen, what isn't going your way, accept that it's for the best, that something better will happen, that it's part of a divine plan. Thank central casting.

Your best laid plans, no matter how perfect, how much time you've put into them, change. You have the perfect Saturday night evening with him planned. You're going out to dinner, later you're going to spend the night, have breakfast in bed the next morning. You plan your dress, shoes and jewelry, the perfect lingerie. You look forward to the big night all week. Then disaster strikes. He doesn't check in the way he usually does Saturday morning. You start to worry and by five o'clock when you still haven't heard from him you're a basket case. "He's going to stand me up. He forgot. I'm never going to see him again. Shall I call him and remind him? Why did I make a date in the first place?" Then the phone rings. It's him. You have to cope with your voice, your anger. It's hard for you not to hang up on him, get sarcastic. "Hi, I'm sorry I haven't called you but I have the worst migraine headache and I've been hoping against hope that I wouldn't have to cancel our date but I feel so terrible that I can't do anything except lie down in bed. I'm sorry. I promise I'll make it up to you, if I feel better we'll do something tomorrow."

He does have a migraine headache. He doesn't want to go out for dinner, see you, make love, he wants to be alone. Something's happened beyond your control and there's absolutely nothing you can do about it. Your best laid plans have gone down the drain along with your control of the situation. What should you do:

Take three deep breaths, let it go, then turn it around immediately, it was meant to be, it's perfect. "Thank you, central casting, for giving me a chance to visit my girlfriend whom I haven't seen in ages. It's totally perfect with me that I'm not going to see him tonight."

Have a reality check, what's the real situation? "The reality is if he doesn't call me that's all right, because if he's a good guy he'll call and if he's a bad guy he won't, if he's a bad guy he shouldn't be in my life anyway."

Don't take it personally. It's not your fault if something goes wrong.

GOING-WITH-THE-FLOW
APHORISMS AND PROVERBS

Let it go.

Let go.

Let it be.

It's easier to ride the horse in the direction it's going.

Qué sera, sera.

Thank central casting.

The best laid plans of mice and men often go asunder.

All's for the best in this best of all possible worlds.

There's always going to be another train, another bus, another chance, another man.

All losses are unrecognized gains.

The more I let go, the more I can get.

DON'T MAKE HIM OVER,
HE'S ALL RIGHT THE WAY HE IS

Don't make him over. Don't even think about it! If you find yourself taking charge of the relationship, trying to change or make him over, say this sentence out loud three times: He is all right the way he is.

Eight little words. Count them. He's been doing just fine all his life without you to take charge and change him.

If you hear yourself Cecil B. de Milling, "Don't you think you need a better secretary, a new job, a better file system, a haircut, a new suit . . ." closely followed by action central, you need to help him do it, BEEP-BEEP yourself. Sorry Cecil.

Share decisions with him. Share choosing. Make a deal. Compromise. What does he want to do? What do you want to do? Make a deal, you'll do what he wants one night and what you want the other. He's not wrong if he wants to do something you don't and you're not wrong if you don't want to do something he wants. It's not grounds for a fight or a blow up. You can't always get what you want. You can't control the relationship and get what you want. You can compromise and get what you both want.

TIME OFF FOR GOOD BEHAVIOR

You need time for you, your home, time off for good behavior to keep up with your needs. Caretaking for him at your expense is a slip. If you're beginning to fall behind in your life you have to make a schedule that works for you. He isn't going to want to see you less because you see him less, have less time for him; au contraire, he's going to want to see you more if there's more of you!

Being in a love relationship is a balancing act: Make a schedule once a week of all the things you need to do for you. Check off what you get done. If you start to get behind take time off for you. A day, two days, a night, whatever you need to catch up.

Being in a relationship does not mean giving up your life for him it; means having a full life that includes him.

SEX, TRUTH AND VIDEOTAPE

In your lovesick relationships sex had nothing to do with making love. Sex was a reflection of your lovesick needs. You needed sex to feel loved, to fill the black hole. You related to men as sex partners only, not as people. You didn't know the difference. Sex was about getting rejected because rejection equaled love. The "S" word equaled *sturm und drang*, upset, violence, abuse and rejection.

In a love relationship, having sexual relations, making love is a reflection of your ability to give and accept love. Love making is about loving . . . caring, tenderness, safety, happiness, fun. Having a love relationship is the ability to express and accept love, to be intimate, to have your feelings be reciprocated in bed, in the bedroom.

There's no difference between straight shooting outside the bedroom and in the bedroom. The fundamental rules apply. It starts and ends with intimacy, with being honest, staying open. You may have little or no experience telling him what pleases you, not just pleasing him. In the beginning it may be very difficult. You may feel scared, uncomfortable, nervous, anxious, shy, embarrassed, wish the bed would open up and you could disappear inside it, couldn't you do what you always did and just please him? Couldn't you get high, let those sparks fly, get down and dirty? No, you can't. Not that way, the "last days of Pompeii" way, the old one-night-stand way, the lovesick way.

Having sexual relations in a love relationship is about reciprocity, not "doing it" or "getting it over with." It's about getting closer, not putting up barriers between you. It's not about going overboard in the giving or taking department. It's a question of balance.

PILLOW TALK

Making love means the ability to both give and receive love. Talk to him in bed, pillow talk. Express your needs. This is the closest you can ever be, the most intimate you can ever get. If you're afraid in the beginning shut your eyes and practice telling him just one thing, what you want, what turns you on, what you feel, anything. Don't expect him to be a mindreader and if he's not, get hurt or angry. Talk to him.

Pillow talk means discovering what he likes and allowing him to discover what you like. Intimacy means getting to know him; means letting him get to know you.

TIMING

It takes time to develop intimacy. Don't expect miracles the first time, the first few times, the first few months. As you both relax, get to know each other, practice intimacy with each other, making love will become just that; making love. It's also important to remember not to go on automatic make-love pilot. Making love is part of a healthy relationship, not the whole thing. That means don't expect him to make love to you every night, every morning, all night, anytime you feel the need, needy. If he doesn't want to make love to you because the timing is bad or off, he's tired, it's too late or too early, that doesn't mean he's rejecting you. All it means is that the timing is bad. Talk to him. Discuss it.

Making love will get better. Give him a chance. You may be tired of hearing this, but practice makes perfect.

GROUCHO VISITS THE BEDROOM: MAKE LOVE NOT WAR

He loves you, wants to make love to you. Unaccustomed as you are to having sex with someone who cares about you, in the beginning you may feel turned off instead of being turned on. Don't be shocked if Groucho makes his début in the bedroom. Your feelings can range from apathy to anger. Instead of feeling excited, you may feel bored, indifferent, neutral. You may have trouble having an orgasm. You may feel disgusted and start fault finding—you don't like his skin, you don't like the way he touches you, you don't want to have sex with him. Your defenses against intimacy may multiply. You'll go to war, get hostile, angry. You'll think up reasons not to do it—Excedrin Headache #4: what can I do to avoid sex tonight? You may even feel like pushing the reject button, blowing him out of the bedroom. You'll start obsessing about how wonderful sex was with Mr. Wrong. You've got a bad case of Groucho in the bedroom. Groucho is the one who has to go, not him.

Make a deal with yourself that you're going to give him a chance. You'll practice sex with him for three months minimum. If you start to push the reject button you'll say, Good-bye Groucho, instead.

THE "L" WORD

You've spent three months with him and he's still there. Not only that so are you. You're working it out. You've kicked Groucho out, limited your makeover to just one pair of black socks to replace the brown ones. You like him. He's interesting. You're not afraid he's going to leave you. He doesn't make you jealous when you're with other women, on the contrary he's proud of you, he wants everyone to know that you're with him. The more time you spend with him the better it is. You feel warm feelings toward him. Is this it? If it is, does this mean you love him? How do you know?

BREAKING-THROUGH-DENIAL EXERCISE:
DO YOU LOVE HIM?

Do you feel safe with him?

Do you trust him?

Do you enjoy his company

Do you feel good around him?

Do you feel good after you see him?

Do you feel happy when you're with him?

Do you feel calm when you're with him and not afraid that he's going to leave you when you're not with him?

Do you like doing things with him?

Do you like who he is?

Is it all right with you that he's not perfect?

Can you be you when you're with him?

Would you miss him if you were not with him?

Does he add to your life?

Do you feel warmth toward him?

Do you enjoy hugging, touching, holding hands—being affectionate with him?

Do you feel close, loving, fulfilled when you make love?

Do you have a special time when you're with him?

If you've answered yes to most or all of these questions, the answer is yes, you love him.

WHAT A FEELING!

Love feels good. You feel safe. You feel happy. You feel joy. You feel up. You feel terrific. Your you feels good.

Love is a lush carpet of well-being for you to tread on. It makes your footsteps lighter.

HOW DO I LOVE THEE,
LET ME COUNT THE WAYS

Tell him that you love him.

I love you because you know all the baseball averages.

I love you because your smile lights up the whole room.

I love you because you sing off key but know all the lyrics.

I love you because you're funny and make me laugh.

I love you because you remembered that I love anemones.

I love you because you don't like Chinese food, either.

I love you because you threw out the garbage without complaining.

I love you in spite of your being a bathroom hog.

I love you because you're attached to your old clothes.

I love you because you give great bear hugs.

I love you just the way you are.

OOPS, A SLIP!

Everything with Roger was going fine. We'd been dating for six months. He was attentive, loving, successful. We traveled a lot together, had a great time. The moment he began to drop hints that he was ready to settle down, I began to obsess over my ex, Patrick. Patrick got the telepathy. He called and told me that he'd heard I was going to get married. He said that he was thinking of getting married, too. I lost it. I knew somewhere that Patrick hadn't changed, twelve years of fighting was twelve years of fighting, but I flew to California the next day anyway. I couldn't believe the look on his face as I appeared at his condo. Shock. Amazement! I begged him to stay with me, told him that he was the love of my life. He said that he'd never thought I was so crazy about him. He promised to think about our being together. He said he would call my hotel in the morning to let me know. After waiting by the phone until six o'clock that night, I finally understood that we were back playing an old game, that he wasn't going to call. The more I wanted him the more he rejected me. He would never be able to change, I had.

I returned to Roger and thanked my lucky stars that he was a nice guy. Once I let go of Patrick my relationship with Roger grew. We got married a year later.

—GAIL

At some point or other you may do it again, create an argument, a precarious situation and use that as an excuse to try and sabotage your relationship, test him, prove that you're a victim, get back into the good old bad space where nothing works, get comfortable by feeling uncomfortable. Slips usually happen when you're doing well, too well. You may begin to fantasize so much about an ex or a new man that you may slip. If you slip:

1. Get out your Anti-Slip Kit.
2. Look for the lesson, the trigger. Feel your physical reaction to the slip. Experience what it feels like to feel bad, upset, anxious. Feel the fear, the pain, the depression, the blackness. Feel what it's like to lose your power, have your lovesick you try and slip back in. Recognize the destructive power of your lovesickness. Understand that you can't afford to have a him in your life.
3. Get back on track.
4. Recognize that your loving you is stronger than your lovesick you.
5. Congratulate yourself for getting back on track.
6. Forgive yourself. Let it go.

TEN COMMON GARDEN-VARIETY QUESTIONS

Q. *Is it normal to be anxious, scared of rejection even though he's a nice guy?*

A. You'll experience high anxiety, be suspicious, expect the worst from him in the beginning. The only way to make it through this period while you adjust to a love relationship is to face your fear, keep having reality checks, keep staying honest with yourself, with him. There's a difference between anxiety and obssesion. You may worry but you won't obsess. (If you are obsessing then he isn't the right guy for you.)

Q. *How often should I see him?*

A. In the beginning you have to make sure that you keep enough time for yourself so that you have time enough to cultivate your own garden. Later you can see him more frequently but never at your expense.

Q. *What do I do if I have a jealousy attack?*

A. Mr. Rights don't make you feel jealous. They're considerate. If you feel jealous, talk to him about it. See if it's real or imaginary, if it's your problem or his.

Q. *What should I do if we have a fight?*

A. Set up rules for fair fighting before you do. You have both created it, you can fix it together.

Q. *How long does it take to get to know someone?*

A. Between three and six months minimum.

Q. *Does sex get better with time?*
A. Yes.

Q. *How long does it take to develop a great sex relationship?*
A. Between three and six months minimum.

Q. *Is it normal to fantasize about an ex?*
A. Yes. The last hurrah of lovesickness is to hold on to your fantasies. It's also your last defense against intimacy with your present partner.

Q. *Is it normal not to feel anything if he says "I love you"?*
A. Yes. It's going to take some time to adjust to his love. That's not because of him. It's because of you. In the beginning you may feel surprised. Don't be surprised if you have an allergic reaction, want to pull a Groucho or get anxious if once he says it he doesn't tell you constantly. It will get easier with time.

Q. *When do I tell him I love him?*
A. When you feel it.

CHAPTER 14

Happy Endings, New Beginnings

You've gone the distance. You've succeeded in transforming yourself, your life, how you think about, experience everything. You have a new love relationship with you, you may or may not have a love relationship with a new love partner. This is the time for reentry back into the rest of your life, time to spread the love and joy around. You bring your new you with you, your rose heart, the power of love, of discernment. You can choose who to have in your life and not to have and your instincts will be right.

EXES

For the first time in two years I felt strong enough to go to one of Gene's parties. As soon as I arrived I thought about all the times I'd been to parties there with Jonathan, my ex, constantly feeling anxious, upset, crazy and jealous . . . Jonathan was always flirting with another women. I'd gotten drunk and stoned every time.

A half hour later Gene came over to me with that excited smile that spelled trouble. Jonathan. It had to be Jonathan plus wife. It was.

Jonathan said hello, his wife didn't. (We'd met twice before.) A deep freeze. Would I disappear if she pretended I wasn't there? I eased myself out of the way of her rudeness, back into the party. Should I leave? Why? What did I care? I didn't. I staked out new territory, yielding my space to them. Jonathan found me. As soon as I let go, he became the pursuer, just the opposite from the old days when I dogged his steps, tracked his movements, waiting for him to flirt, watching for missteps.

She found us, interrupted, "Doesn't Jonathan look good? He works out almost every day. He runs, too. And he's eating properly." She pinched his cheek like a Mother hen. I excused myself from the conversation. I didn't want her to be jealous of me, the way I used to feel. I watched her lead him away, like a bull with a ring through his nose.

I sat down in a corner. Here was the man I'd been addicted to for four years with the wife I'd obsessed over for two. What did I feel? Calm. What did I really feel? Calm. Nothing. No more anger, revenge, jealousy. I didn't feel like making something happen again, capturing him from the enemy. He was not the man of my life, never had been. I'd manufactured it all, tried to spin gold out of straw, like Rumpelstilskin. I'd put him on a pedestal, made him into something he never was, never could be. It had been a perfect production. I'd controlled every aspect of it from day one . . . wardrobe, locations, cast, action. I was the director, he the raw talent. But he'd paid me back, tortured me. Jonathan was a mysogynist. We'd been the perfect couple, Echo and Narcissus, feeding off each other's illnesses, needs, mine to be rejected, his to reject. What a way to live. It was a way to die. Now he'd replaced me with another woman that he could reject. Suddenly something snapped. The spell was broken. There was no more bad news cosmic connection. I was free. I thanked God. It was time to leave.

I retrieved my coat, said good-bye to Jonathan, wished him well and meant it, was on my way to say farewell to the host when Gene grabbed me, "I can't get over how you look. I've been watching you. You look so different, like another person. You've changed so much. You look, I don't know, happy, younger. When you walked in I didn't recognize you. I said to myself who is this beautiful woman and it was you. What's happened?"

"Thank you, Gene. It's a long story. I'll tell you sometime."

                                                                —S.I.

Exes have a way of coming out of the woodwork. Be prepared. There are two possibilities, you have the distance or not. You'll know. If you can't handle an ex it doesn't mean that your recovery has gone down the drain or out the window, that you haven't recovered; it just means that you're not ready to handle him now.

Ex Scenario #1: You bump into him in the supermarket. Your body starts to send you signals, your stomach turns over, you feel shaky, have trouble breathing. You start obsessing. You feel off balance, uncomfortable, as if you're about to lose your you, to fall, "Watch out for the black hole . . ."

Listen to your body. Listen to your mind. Listen to your spirit. You have the tools to discern who's safe, who isn't. If your body, mind and spirit say no, watch out for him, he's trouble. He's always been trouble. He'll always be trouble, you're not ready, you're not! You haven't got the distance to be around him. He's not safe for you. He's a threat to your you. Take a walk! Take a hike. Run!

Ex Scenario #2: You bump into him on the street. You look at him in amazement, here's the man you obsessed over for years and you feel nothing. No anger. No anxiety. Nothing. What should you do?

What do you want to do? You have the distance to choose what you want. If there were some redeeming qualities then you can choose to renegotiate the terms of your relationship. You can choose to become friends. You can also choose not to be friends.

What shouldn't you do? Don't beat yourself up, I can't believe I wasted so much time on him, with him, obsessing over him.

Thank central casting for a big growth opportunity. Accept that your lovesick relationship with "him" gave you the opportunity to grow, change, learn and heal. Forgive yourself. Forgive him. Let it go.

COMING HOME

I reluctantly accepted the invitation to visit Mother for two weeks, dragging my friend Amy along as maximum security protection. Mother and I had not had an easy time of it. She hadn't understood at all when I'd separated, asked for time off, for time alone, not at all. She blamed group, this was their fault. I blamed her for my problems, it was her fault. We had a lifetime history of pitched bitch battles, guerilla warfare, heavy artillery, big guns, no precedent for peace. I warned Amy, watch your back, watch mine.

The beast in the jungle never roared. Instead we had two of the best weeks of my life. Amy kept saying to me, your mother's terrific, attractive, fun, vivacious, intelligent. I would say, "that's just because you're here." It wasn't. I kept waiting for something to go wrong, for one of those good old bad old battles, for her criticism, for her control. It didn't happen. I slowly began to realize that nothing was going to happen. I'd changed. I'd found me. She did the best she could, knew no other way. It had been our legacy, hers, mine. A light bulb when off in my head. I'd come back home. She is terrific, attractive, fun, vivacious, brilliant, stylish . . . more important, Mother has become my best friend. I love you, Fritzi.

—S.I.

Your relationship with your family has come full cycle. You've cut the lovesick cords from your family in order to come back home, to renegotiate the terms of your relationship, to become friends. This time it means loving you enough to be able to love, appreciate your parents for who they are and who they are not. You're able to love them unconditionally. It's time to tell them. Communicate this to them. Call them up, write them a letter, visit them.

If you've done the work it will be a joy. If it feels uncomfortable, they get to you, they still upset you, this means that you still don't have the distance, you have more work to do on you.

If your parents are alive, thank central casting for the opportunity they gave you to grow, learn, become. If your parents are no longer alive or unreachable you can have a ceremony with them where you tell them everything you need to say, share your love.

FRIENDS INDEED! WORKING RELATIONSHIPS

I was part of an era when women were in tremendous competition with each other. In the last decade, thank God, I've come to know and to trust myself and other women. I've come to celebrate the caring and intuitive friendships which have contributed so much to my healing.

—LILI

You've had a lot of practice working out your relationships with your buddy, your network, your support system, your support group. You've been through the wars and you've come through them together with flying colors. You feel safe with them. You love them for who they are and who they are not. You trust them with your life. They're on your side. They enhance your life. You can tell the truth to each other. You're having a healthy relationship with a friend or friends whether they are men or women.

Now it's time to decide if you want to reconnect with the ones you let go of. Do you have the distance? Do they represent positive or negative contributions to your life? You have the capacity to know, to feel whether you choose to have them be with you. Choose.

VISUALIZATION: EVERYTHING'S COMING UP ROSES

This last visualization is a rite of passage to celebrate your journey's end. It's time for your graduation with highest honors.

Make yourself comfortable in your space, lighting a candle to invoke Venus, the Goddess of Love and Athena, the Goddess of Wisdom to bless this ceremony. Close your eyes, relax, breathe deeply, inhaling peace, exhaling the tensions of the day. As you breathe in golden sunlight imagine that you follow the path to the turquoise Pool of Wisdom under the waterfall. You see a rainbow arcing over the water-fall. As you breathe in golden sunlight and breathe out black smoke, immerse yourself in the pool, at the end of the rainbow. Experience the water on your body, refreshing, purifying your being, cleansing any residual psychic debris. As you breathe in golden sunlight breathe out black smoke and release the last tendrils of pain and fear, all that is not love. Sigh out loud.

Now imagine that you stand under the waterfall. Breathe in rainbow mist. Breathe in the brilliant red of courage. Breathe in the luminous orange of the spirit. Breathe in the radiant sunlight yellow of joy. Breathe in the emerald green of growth. Breathe in the sea green of caring. Breathe in iridescent blue sparkling with possibilities. Breathe in the intense indigo of trust. Breathe in the vibrant violet of truth. Breathe in the diamond light of clarity that is all colors, the Oneness of the rainbow, breathe out diamond light.

Imagine that you step out from the rainbow and take the path to your Temple of Love. You pass through slender mother of pearl columns that glow with opalescent light. Pink roses from the palest pink to the most vibrant festoon your Temple, cascading from beautiful urns. Breathe in the fragrance of roses, the essence of love. Breathe in pink lovelight and out pink lovelight. Notice a bed of rose petals. Lie down on it. Feel velvety pink petals caress your skin. As you breathe in pink lovelight imagine that there is a pink rosebud in your heart. Breathe out pink lovelight. As you breathe in see that the rose bud has grown into a beautiful rose, ready to open. Breathe in pink lovelight, breathe in harmony and peace. As you exhale imagine that one beautiful petal opens in your heart, more petals unfurl with each breath. As you breathe in pink lovelight breathe in beauty. More petals open. As you breathe in caring and tenderness the last petals of your heart rose open. Feel the love. Feel your heart flower, your rose heart radiate love.

Imagine now that Venus, the Goddess of Love and Beauty, beckons you. You arise feeling refreshed, dressed as a Goddess in white. Hera, the Queen of the Goddesses, Athena, the Goddess of Wisdom, Iris of the Rainbow, Diana the Goddess of the Moon, the Muses and the Graces carry garlands of roses forming a pathway. There is Marilyn, in her pleated halter dress, smiling. You walk in between them. You ascend the pink marble stairs where Venus and Athena stand and kneel before them. Venus says, "You have bested the dragons of your life, the demons of your mind, cut the negative cords of your inheritance, proven that love conquers all." She crowns you with a garland and presents you with a bouquet of pink roses, "I give you the power of love. You are love. The more love you give the more love there is." Athena bestows upon you a diamond star wand. "With this wand I give you the power of discernment to protect you. You will always be able to see with crystal clarity. You'll always be in Love and Light. Arise, Goddess."

As you turn to the gathering below you notice that everyone you love is present. You smile at them and say, "It's been a long journey but I've finally found love. It's within me. Thank you for your help. I couldn't have done it without you. I love you." You descend the stairs. As you go by they congratulate you, shower you with rose petals. You feel radiant with joy and happiness, filled with love.

When you are ready, open your eyes.

YOU'VE COME A LONG WAY, BABY!

You've found your you, your loving feelings, the capacity to love and accept love, to love yourself. You understand that this is an ongoing life process and love. Love is all you need.

Congratulations are in order. We propose a toast to your new life: To health, happiness, joy and fun! To love! To you!

Help List

Unless you live in a large city, it may be difficult to find meetings of some of the groups listed below. In that case, call the largest city in your area for the regional chapter of A.A. for all information.

The organizations listed below will give you the information you need.

Adult Children of Alcoholics
Central Service Board
P.O. Box 3216
Torrance, CA 90505
(213) 534-1815

Alcoholics Anonymous
Box 459 Grand Central Station
New York, NY 10163
(212) 686-1100

Al-Anon Family Groups
P.O. Box 862 Midtown Station
New York, NY 10118
(212) 302-7240

Codependents Anonymous
P.O. Box 496A Hudson Street
New York, NY 10014
(212) 727-1432

Debtors Anonymous
National Organization
P.O. Box 20322
New York, NY 10025–9992

Gamblers Anonymous
National Service Office
P.O. Box 17173
Los Angeles, CA 90017
(213) 386-8789

Narcotics Anonymous
World Services Office
P.O. Box 9999
Van Nuys, CA 91409
(818) 780-3951

Overeaters Anonymous
4025 Spencer #203
Torrance, CA 90503
(213) 542-8363

Sex and Love Addicts Anonymous (SLAA)
P.O. Box 119 Newton Branch
Boston, MA 02258
(617) 332-1845

Sexual Addicts Anonymous (SAA)
Twin Cities Sexual Addicts Anonymous
P.O. Box 3038
Minneapolis, MN 55403
(612) 339-0217

Sexaholics Anonymous (SA)
International Central Office
P.O. Box 300
Simi Valley, CA 93062
(818) 704-9854

Afterward, Two Years Later

Last Dec. 3, on my way to my favorite thing in life... a party, I had a hemorrhage. A bad one. Bad enough for a night trip downtown to the emergency room from hell, a D&C the next afternoon.

Somehow I was more upset about missing the party than about the ramifications... ramifications which were very serious indeed.... I was going to be anemic, again. I'd have to be a "good girl," remember to take my iron pills, eat liver, broccoli and asparagus. I'd have to accept being weak, being unable to climb stairs 'with a single bound' or play tennis without gasping for breath. I was used to the drill *and* I was in denial.

I'd had fibroids (benign fibroid tumors) in my uterus for ages. They'd started when I met 'him,' 10 years ago... more accurately when he'd stopped making love to *me*, three months later. They'd grown wild like weeds, strangling my uterus during these next four loveless years. Of course there was a connection.

Of course there was a solution: I could have a hysterectomy. This drastic possibility, the big H, had been hanging over my head these past six years, a heavy weight, indeed. I had prayed that recovery from 'The Marilyn Syndrome' would banish my fibroids forever. In the meantime I'd done everything I or anyone else could think of to hang on to my uterus, from modern Western science to early Eastern. Everything! This included taking a shot once a month of Lupron, a non FDA okayed drug that would temporarily fool my body—the pituitary gland in particular, into thinking I was in menopause: I'd stop having a period, and gain twenty pounds while the fibroids shrank down to an acceptable twelve weeks. (They measured growing tumors as if they were going to be born as children.)

The war of the worlds was going on inside me—my biological clock had become a detonator. One day I'd have horrible cramps, the next hot flashes. If I'd stop the Lupron, the fibroids would grow back, I'd hemmorage again. It was a bloody saga. I was in between Scylla and Charybdis, menstruation/menopause; menstruation/menopause. I was trapped with no way out. Either way I couldn't have a baby.

What was weighing in the balance? My identity as a woman, my sexuality, my attractiveness to men, my need to be attractive to men in the first place. . . my need to be loved. In other words. . .everything. My recovery from the Marilyn Syndrome, from being lovesick, from not loving myself, all hinged on my being able to totally know/feel/see/get/believe that sexuality was part of me, not the whole package. Like Marilyn, I'd confused sex and love. I'd substituted having sex, being sexually attractive to men, having men as lovers. . .for self love. Like Marilyn I'd become a sexaholic, addicted to sex with champagne and pot (she'd done champagne and pills). Like Marilyn I'd used men to fill the tortured emptiness of 'the black hole'. . .for just a few moments. I have to say. . .vice versa . . .they'd used me, too.

Dr. Dena Harris, my extraordinary gynecologist, and I had a long talk. This time my fibroid had grown enormous, as big as a mountain, as if I were twenty five weeks—six months and one week to be exact—pregnant. I'd lost a lot of blood, it had been dangerous. . .they'd considered a transfusion. The scales were tipping towards a hysterectomy. I'd lost the race! I wasn't in menopause yet, my fibroids weren't going to shrink naturally. I could limp on with Lupron, I could keep having hemorrhages when I got off it, until I reached Mecca. . .menopause, but was it worth it?

What were the probabilities of my having a child now anyway? My fibroid was in the way, if they took it out, it would grow back. To make matters even worse, she advised taking out Everything, with a capital E, out. . .that way I'd never be a candidate for ovarian cancer. . .so horribly undetectable (Gilda Radner had died of it). She said I'd feel better physically once it happened. I'd be a candidate for Estrogen replacement, I'd never ever have to go through real menopause.

I went home and cried at the unfairness of the world. Why was this happening to me just when everything else was finally going so well? Why did I have to face this decision? Why could men have children forever? I stayed home alone, began to make collages from colored paper. . . indians. . .babies. . .kids art. . .art kids, meditated, did Tai Chi faithfully, biked, watched a lot of movies on television. Color it black. I moaned, I mused, I meditated, I slept, I cried. This was the big one. The Big H. I had to give up all my baby dreams. I was never going to have a baby.

I went into mourning for the babies I was never going to have, for the babies I couldn't have when I'd been pregnant those three times (the last time the 'he' who'd empregnated me had already left), because I was never going to be a mother, for having to give up younger men who now wouldn't like me because I couldn't have a baby. . . for the end of the trail.

I considered having my uterus taken out and leaving my ovaries in for Dream Scenario, Fantasy #6. . . at some later date a handsome doctor . . . Sam Shepard in BABY BOOM, with a God-like gesture would take an egg out of my ovary, mate it with the sperm of an as yet undetermined man on a white horse, implant it in the ovary of a mystery woman who would turn out to be my long lost twin sister and then she'd give birth. . . .

No baby in the middle of a baby boom. No daughter. No son. I hadn't recovered in time. I'd never had a baby because I hadn't loved myself enough, wasn't healthy enough to be a mother, didn't want to propagate my illness. I'd had no clue about how to love unconditionally, which as everyone now knows is the only way to love a healthy baby. My life had never really been about making babies, anyway. My ability to have a child, be a mother, part of a myth, a myth about being happy ever after, only the dream of a we, an us, a family—a husband and I on the beach playing with our two children. I grieved about my nemesis, being too late. There was not going to be a deus ex machina, no stork was going to come and save me.

Was I also going to lose my sexuality? Would I stop being, feeling, acting or being seen as sexy? Attractive? F---able? I stood on my record . . . three years clean of sexaholicism, my lovers for the past year down to the fingers of one hand, sex had moved to the rear of the bus, so to speak. The aging sex queen had retired her crown, abdicated her throne. I was over my addiction so why was I hanging on to uterus? Sex had absolutely nothing to do with whether or not I had baby making equipment. Either did love. If someone was going to love me they would have to accept that I was unable to have a child. My friends kept telling me I could always adopt.

I feared. I grieved. I worried and faded in and out of denial that I was actually facing a major life change and the only one who could make it was me.

The family gathered for Christmas in the country. I played with my niece, Ally the artist. . . the next Matisse, whom I love unconditionally, then slept all the rest of the time from some none specific malaise. . . 'decisionitis'. Just before New Year's my brother, the voice of reason, (he'd been the one to take me down to the emergency room) confronted me in the kitchen, "Are you going to keep scaring the family? Do you want to die over this? You're going to get to menopause sooner or later, anyway. We insist that you get a second opinion."

I stormed out of the house. Did I want to die waiting for a miracle? Waiting to have a baby which I couldn't have anyway? Did I want to die from love sickness? Marilyn had died from it. After countless abortions, a miscarriage, longing to have a child from one of her unavailable lovers, she'd fallen head over heels in love with the most unattainable man of all, a man who'd just been named father of the year for his wonderful relationship with his ten children...Bobby Kennedy. Whether she'd killed herself that day or was killed, Marilyn died from being lovesick ...from being addicted to men who couldn't love her...from being involved with the wrong men, from needing a man to obsess over to fill up her 'black hole,' from her addiction to pain, to rejection, to sex...from not ever having loved herself or let anyone love her.

Something snapped. I broke through denial. No. Of course not! Die? Me? Not this kid. Not yet. No way. I was not, nor did I have to be Marilyn. I'd written the book. This had been a slip. I couldn't afford to play Russian Roulette once a month anymore. That was that! I wasn't going to die from an operation but I would die if I didn't have one. It was that simple. The new math. All right, I'd get a second opinion. (I knew he would say I had to do it.)

I trusted my doctor, Steven Lamm, to recommend a surgeon who I'd like at University Hospital (the only hospital my family trusts). After the examination, he told me, yes, I had to do it, as soon as possible. I should take it all out, go on estrogen replacement therapy. I put Dr. Robert Morris, male doctor, on the witness stand, interrogated him with one thousand and one of the most important questions I could think of and got informed answers. I began to trust him. As if disembodied, I heard myself make the decision to do it.

I got his handshake (it counts with men) that I was going to wake up with a bikini scar, that I'd be able to make love again six weeks after surgery, that I wouldn't get old, dry out, that I'd really feel better than ever, that I'd lose weight, that I'd still be able to have an orgasm, that I'd have the chance to beat him in tennis within a few months, that I'd be back to my old self, that estrogen was safe. Not necessarily in that order. I had an escape clause. I could always cancel.

As if on cue, in flew Lili Townsend, my former metaphysical fitness trainer. She was aware of my emotional anguish and had come to help me cope. She came over to do a healing ceremony on my poor, beat up uterus. In one sentence she changed what had started to feel like my death sentence.

She said, "Why, Susan, your hysterectomy is an AFGO."

"A what?"

"Another F-----Growth Opportunity. This is a golden opportunity to trade in your old self for a new self. What a great chance to clean out all the psychic debris that's gathered in your uterus from all the men who've come...and gone inside you all these years. You can cut out all the poisons...the disappointments, the unhappiness, the tears, the depressions that have build up inside you rock solid. Lighten up! Get rid of all the dead weight in one fell swoop. Not everyone is this lucky. It's a God given opportunity...."

I laughed. She was right. How many men had been in my life, then gone...leaving me feeling more empty than before? Too many, for too long.

"Suze, I think you've forgotten your spirit and your spiritual side. This is the other part of the AFGO."

Right again.

We decided that I'd pick one of the Medicine Cards. (Lili had given me a book, MEDICINE CARDS, The Discovery of Power Through the Ways of Animals by Jamie Sams and David Carson.) You picked a card at random from 44 possible cards. I pulled #6, whoops, my lucky number ...my birth date, the Snake Medicine Card...Transmutation.

It seemed like an omen. Was I never going to get rid of my own snakes, my fears, my insecurities about my own femininity? I looked up transmutation. It had two meanings: change from one nature, substance, form, or condition into another, as in metamorphose, convert, alter; #6. Alchemy, the conversion of base metals into gold. I read the card... excited. It had never occurred to me, at least lately anyway, that I could change so radically. If I shed my snake skin...I could be reborn... transmutation by fire, your basic life-death-rebirth cycle. According to my card all I had to do was to die to be reborn *whole*...then I'd transmute all the poisons into divine energy. The book continued, "Magic is no more than a change in consciousness. Become the enchantress: transmute the energy and accept the power of the fire."

Was I ready or not to accept the "Snake challenge"? Might as well bring on the snakes. We did a ritual/visualization/healing ceremony where I symbolically got rid of all the men in my life. I became Cleopatra, killed myself with an asp, died, burned in flames, then was reborn in turquoise water as The Little Mermaid.

The last weekend before the "Big H," I went out to Milo and Catherine's spa, safe haven in any storm, in Greenlawn for T (training) and sympathy. I worked out hard for three straight days...swam laps, walked miles on the treadmill. Catherine, a former nurse, told me that the most important thing for any operation was attitude. If I had a positive attitude I'd do well. Advice for living, for life. I listened to her; great advice is great advice.

The night before going into the hospital for the operation (I still couldn't pronounce the word hysterectomy...it sounded so hysterical), I had what I viewed as my last supper at Elaines' with friends to celebrate Ann's birthday two days early. She said, "Now Susan, don't you ever go and have a hysterectomy again on my birthday." (No, Ann I won't.) By phone I gave Jessica any painting she wanted in my apartment, and my taxicab yellow jacket. The next night, I talked to my anesthesiologist from my hospital bed. He told me not to worry, I was in the top one percent of the healthiest people who'd ever had an operation. That was how they rated people at the hospital—on their chances of surviving an operation. He assured me that, medically, the "Big H" was the easiest thing in the whole world. All you had to do was take things out; you didn't have to put new things in. A snap, a zap, and poof: my ovaries, uterus and fibroids would be gone. Just like that.

My last morning, I took a shower and did Tai Chi alone in the ladies room. I kept telling myself to let go of control and trust...in God, the surgeon I'd chosen, and my decision. The last thing I remember telling the doctor before I went under was to remind him to be the one on the cutting edge, so to speak, to go horizontal...I let go. Now I lay me down to sleep...

The anesthesiologist killed me. That's how I saw it. He took over my breathing for me; put my lungs and my heart on automatic pilot. When I woke up from the dead, it was with three tubes coming out of me, a sort of Catch-22 situation. One was down my throat, one in my arm, one came from my bladder. A hell of a way to be reborn. I tried to scream, like a newborn baby, but no sounds came out of my mouth. Boy, did my throat hurt. Thank God you can't remember pain! I thanked God I was alive. I'd made it.

PART TWO

I got up and walked the day after. A friend explained to me that the only way to go was to keep on walking...that way I'd get better sooner, the more I walked...the faster. (Incidentally, you're talking about a person who'd never walked anywehre in her life. Swam. yes, biked, yes, subwayed, bused, cabbed, skated...anything except walk.) I was definitely in Part Two, which was what I'd started to call my new life. Two weeks after surgery, I flew down to Florida with mother, for warm weather, the beach, the ocean and recovery. According to the doc, it was a six-week deal. Six weeks before, I could bend, swim, play tennis, make love, lift. I took a half hour Jay Walk (I decided to name my walks after their sponsor) on the beach every day, no matter how much it hurt, no matter what the weather. I began to look forward to this private time.

One day, during my walk, I found a piece of driftwood that reminded me of a snake. I brought it home, painted it with my niece into a beautiful, bright, Indian-looking snake, a diamond head. (I put a diamond in its head…diamonds are a girl's best friend! Right, Marilyn?)

Joan sent me The Sedona Method® on tapes. If I took the course, I could work on a Sedona public relations project with her. There were about eight tapes to be taken over a two-week period. I decided to do it with my friend Vivian…she had a VCR. We watched, listened, talked, answered questions, asked each other questions. First we learned how to actually identify a feeling…then let it go. Amazin'! In one megabite, think-a-second, noony nonny or whatever Mork from Ork called it, I could let go of anything, ranging from the most depressing thought, to feeling tired…to feeling good. Once you let go, you felt even better. I walked around letting things go all day for days. Next we learned that every feeling is either the need for approval or the need for control and in most instances the need for both. You had to let go of your need for approval or control every minute, every time, and the more you let go the better you'd feel. Laughter was the greatest release…you could let go of anything with a good belly laugh!

Six weeks to the day after the operation, I began to swim laps, started to play tennis, bend, do Tai Chi, get back into shape. I looked in the mirror one morning and boy, did I look good. A beautiful woman was looking back at me. It was more than that…I felt good! I was happy, relaxed, proud of all the work I'd done, proud that I'd listened to everybody's good advice and taken it, proud that I'd come back…ecstatic that I could let go of anything. I went to the beach in my new strapless black and white print bathing suit, my brand new body, a new me. All of a sudden I spied a seven-foot-long piece of bleached white driftwood in the shape of a serpent. I had to have it. I saw the piece of sculpture it could be, painted, but it was too heavy to lift. (I hadn't been allowed to lift on pain of death from mother—my nurse, Fritzi, to her friends. Incidentally she was the greatest nurse and help anyone could ever have. Thanks, Mom, I couldn't have done it without you.) I looked up and saw two hunks in tight black bathing suits. One of them, blond, gorgeous, green Tartar eyes, high cheek bones…model looks, a 10.

I said, "Could you help me move this?" Alix and his friend did. Then we took a walk. Alix and Andre and I laughed and talked about snakes, my Polish karma (he was Polish, too). In the water I told him that I'd just had an operation, couldn't have a baby, that I probably couldn't even "do it." I wanted to get the bad news over with. He was about thirty-two and I didn't want to misrepresent myself. I turned down his invitation to go out that night. I was still doing the Sedona Method and had a date with Vivian. Something was different this time. I was different. Totally. When I asked my sculptor friend what she thought of the driftwood (she'd been on the beach), she said, "Forget that. . .you don't see anyone looking like that gorgeous man walking on the beach, ever." And I had turned down a date. Was I crazy? No, I knew he'd call again; he was interested, so was I. We'd had a good time. I *was* in Part Two.

Two weeks later, I'd spent a lot more time with Alix. Beach walks, talks, swimming, dates. I called up my doctor, told him that it was eight weeks since, asked him if I could make love. He interviewed me about my new friend.

"How long have you known him? Is he nice, is he safe, will he be gentle?" I said yes to everything. He gave me his okay. It was as if I was a born again virgin and he was my father. I didn't have to talk him into anything. . .Alix had already passed my most rigorous tests. He was nice, he liked older women, he was smart, he didn't want to have children, he really liked me, he made me laugh, if he said he'd do something he did it, he'd already kissed my scar, I really liked him, he'd become a friend.

We made love. He was gentle and cool and it was hot, hot, hot. I cried, I laughed and laughed. So beautiful. So happy. I felt whole. Funny, I was more of a woman without my parts than I'd ever been with them. After, I did not obsess. Alix called me right away, made another date.

My time was up in Florida. I was better, ready to go home, in shape for Part Two, a new, improved me. I came back to New York. Mimi was the first one to notice, "Susan you're on a roll! I gave a great comeback party at Tatou. All my friends came. We danced and sweated to Denny LeRoux while he sang and played our kind of music, rock and roll. He said, "Fabu at Tatou, eh Susan?" It was.

Alix sent me the driftwood from Florida. We'll see each other again. We're friends. That's how it's been with everything. I've been on a roll!

It was five months ago today that I did it. In some ways it was the most amazing decision I'll ever have to make in my life. I had to do it, I did it and I'm glad. I've never felt better, looked better or been in better shape. I have a bikini scar that's going to fade into nothing, I'm taking the smallest possible dose of estrogen, twenty-five days a month. The only side effect I have is that I'm nauseous once in a while. I've been having great days and nights, great times and fun no matter what I'm doing or with whom. I laugh all the time. Life is a dream. Funny, I never dared dream that I could be sooo happy, feel sooo good, have everything go sooo right... I never dared dream, period. Obsess yes, dream no. Now all I have to do is dream up something and it happens. Just like that. Really. I cherish my time with myself alone. A friend says... alone is al(l) one. I am all one.

I have an absolutely remarkable circle of friends who've come through the wars, the fire with me, victorious, into Part Two. They've been my invisible shield, my net. They are my mighty fortress: Marjie, Jessica, Ann, Cliffeton, Joan, Sandra, Mary, Lisa, Susan R. Mimi, Catherine, Milo, Sissy, Jay, Lili, Steiger, Dan G., Robo, Mark, Denny, Lenny (in any order). We spend hours and hours talking about all the recovery issues. We learn from each other. We practice telling the truth, giving and taking, trusting, taking chances... loving unconditionally and accepting unconditional love back. That's what friends are for! Of everyone, my mother is my best friend. Really. Cross my heart and hope to live!

I used to define my life by men. The rhetorical question, "How am I doing?" depended on how many dates I'd lined up, with how many hunks, what were the possibiltiies of going to bed with them, marrying them, walking down the aisle. I've totally let that go. I didn't give up but I did. I gave up on men. Seducing them. Using them. Needing them to fill me up. Being needy. I don't need anyone anymore. I have myself. Now that's happened; I keep meeting men. They're attracted to me... for all the right reasons. My energy... power, how much fun I am, I have, how smart I am. I meet a new man on a project. We've played tennis together, walked, talked and worked together. We're becoming friends. On our first date, he said, "I'm through with dumb bunnies... right now all I want is friendship, laughter and having some fun with someone who's smart. Sex can wait."

Right on brother. Deal me in. The answer to the question raised by Sally in Nora Ephron's "When Harry Met Sally": can a woman and man be friends and lovers? is yes, yes, yes!

I looked at all my baby pictures and saw a beautiful little girl who never knew how beautiful she was. It was me. Marilyn died almost exactly thirty years ago today. I'm so sorry. She didn't have to die. I didn't. I had what a friend calls, "A resurrectomy!" I have a second chance to live *happily* ever after.

Susan Israelson
August 1992